My Name is Daphne Fairfax

My Name is Daphne Fairfax

Arthur Smith

HUTCHINSON
LONDON

Published by Hutchinson 2009

2 4 6 8 10 9 7 5 3 1

Copyright © Arthur Smith 2009

Arthur Smith has asserted his right under the Copyright, Designs
and Patents Act 1988 to be identified as the author of this work

First published in Great Britain in 2009 by
Hutchinson
Random House, 20 Vauxhall Bridge Road,
London SW1V 2SA

www.rbooks.co.uk

Addresses for companies within The Random House Group Limited can be found at:
www.randomhouse.co.uk/offices.htm

The Random House Group Limited Reg. No. 954009

A CIP catalogue record for this book
is available from the British Library

ISBN 9780091921033

The Random House Group Limited supports The Forest Stewardship Council (FSC), the
leading international forest certification organisation. All our titles that are printed on
Greenpeace approved FSC certified paper carry the FSC logo. Our paper
procurement policy can be found at www.rbooks.co.uk/environment

Mixed Sources
Product group from well-managed
forests and other controlled sources
www.fsc.org Cert no. TT-COC-2139
© 1996 Forest Stewardship Council

Typeset in Garamond by Palimpsest Book Production Ltd,
Grangemouth, Stirlingshire

Printed and bound in the UK by
Clays Ltd, St Ives plc

For Paddy Moxom and her parents,
Mrs Logan and Clare Creasey

CONTENTS

Prefatory notes   1

1.   Facts about myself   3
     I am born   7
     My name. What is it?   9
     Nearly dead   12
2.   A bomb-site in Bermondsey   15
3.   Running through the suburbs   25
4.   Young Arfur   37
5.   Senior boy   49
6.   The early Afro   60
7.   Monsieur Smeez   80
     'Paris Poem'   94
8.   Bachelor of arts   97
9.   First Edinburgh   110
10.   Rock 'n roll hovel   117
11.   Song and dance man   133
12.   Stand-up   141
13.   Pantomime Dane   163
14.   Rooms above pubs   174
15.   Me and Phil go off   191
16.   When I was thirty-five it was a very good year . . .   201
17.   BBC man   215
18.   Had to go into play writin'   229

19. Syd's return to Colditz   245
20. I dallied and I dillied   258
21. Gone travelling   276
22. Deep down in the dumps   289
23. Yes, I am Prince Hamlet   298
24. My summer with Des   311
25. Leonard Cohen, the Leith Police and Bill Clinton   319
26. Sprinting at a brick wall   333
27. Hospital days   341
28. *Come what come may*   352
29. Two deaths, a proposal and a birthday   366
30. Last facts about myself   377

Epilogue. And you?   381
All the people   383
Index   389

PREFATORY NOTES

1. When I mentioned to my friend Grub that I was thinking of writing a memoir he encouraged me grandly: 'You must, Arthur. It is time to erect your monument.' My nephew James's comment was, 'Oh God, that's just what the world needs – another celebrity autobiography.' I have tried to bear in mind both these reactions.

2. There are numerous bouts of heavy-duty name-dropping throughout the book and for those readers with a low tolerance for this activity I have signalled their approach with the letters *NdA* (Name-dropping ahead).

3. I have noticed in other books of this ilk that there is a lot of talk about 'setting the record straight'. Such record as exists of my own activities I do not consider to be especially wonky so there will be none of that here.

4. Having sent the relevant sections to some of those I have written about, I have learned that people can be *extremely* touchy. A few names have, accordingly, been changed and a couple of characters excised completely.

5. There are four chapter ones and here is the first . . .

CHAPTER 1. FACTS ABOUT MYSELF

My full name is Brian Arthur John Smith. I am 4ft 11¾ins tall and weigh about six stone. I have curly hair, glasses but nothing else unusual. I have dark brown hair and hazel eyes. I have scars on both my kneecaps. I am slightly above average height. I am skinny and wiry.

There is an agreeable solidity about the procession of biographical details, the 'facts about myself' which march by in my first autobiography, a school project undertaken at the age of twelve. It is the literary equivalent of an establishing shot.

Let me then record all this now, forty-two years on. My full name is Brian Arthur John Smith but, as you will learn if you continue reading, and as the title of this book suggests, I have other names too. I am six feet and a quarter of an inch tall, although you wouldn't think so as I am a lifelong sloucher, noted in print for my 'simian gait'. I weigh about eleven stone. I am above average height. I am skinny and might be called 'wiry' by someone trying to avoid using the word 'skinny'. The little hair I have is grey and, in my own mind at least, has a provocative hint of the curly mass it once was.

Following an operation for cataracts in my eyes, I am now long- rather than short-sighted, so I use reading glasses. I have hazel eyes, although, as I write this, I realise I have never been entirely sure what colour hazel is – is it the same as a hazelnut? I cannot recall the last time I was asked the colour of my eyes but, if ever I am, I will surely say hazel, because now, as then, it makes me think of Hazel, my mother. Beth says I have green eyes, 'like two big olives'.

One of those scars on my kneecap is still visible and has been supplemented by another permanent triangular blemish on my elbow, sustained in a misguided attempt to carry a large woman across a gravel car park while drunk.

I live with my two brothers and two parents. The younger, Nicholas (7), goes to Kidbrooke Park School. The oldest, Richard (14), goes to this school (Roan). My father is a policeman. My mother is training to be a teacher, at Avery Hill. My house is semi-detached and has a garden. It is about the right size. I take size four in shoes.

The age difference between my brothers and myself remains the same. The younger, Nick (49), works for the Charity Commission as a civil servant. Richard (56) was the editor of the *British Medical Journal* and now works part-time for an American medical company. Both are married with three children. My father, known to all, including his sons and grandchildren, as Syd, is dead, and my mother lives alone in Tonbridge. My house, now *our* house, known technically as a maisonette, is on the ground floor of a huge block of 1930s flats and has a tiny garden. It is about the right size, although Beth would like an additional toilet, especially since the one we have is in the bathroom. I take size nine on my left foot and ten on my right. Or possibly it's the other way round.

I do not share a bedroom but I did until two weeks ago when I swapped with my elder brother. My father has an ancient black crock of a car. I have between 2s 6d and 3s 6d.

I had not shared a bed on a full-time basis for fifteen years until five years ago when Beth moved in with me. I remember that 'black crock', and if I were the type of man who had any interest in cars I would no doubt remember the make. It broke down less often than previous models but, despite vigorous scrubbing, stank of petrol and had a back seat that was wet the day Syd bought it and, inexplicably, never dried. I became accustomed to the sensation of arriving in places with a damp patch on the back of my shorts. I have about forty thousand pounds – more if we sold the house.* When I hit sixty my pension will provide me with about ten pounds a week.

I live about one and a quarter miles from school and walk there and back every day. The journey takes me about thirty minutes. It takes me about an hour from getting up to setting off. I have a medium-sized breakfast but often a big one. Overall I like school but I don't like getting up at the ridiculous hour of 7.15.

I am currently writing this at home, so the journey to work is a few seconds, but it still seems to take me about an hour and a half from getting up to starting work. I have a medium-sized breakfast but often a big one. Since I now have diabetes I try to go easy on the sugar. I still don't like getting up at the ridiculous hour of 7.15. Avoiding early starts was one of my big early ambitions, one that I have, by and large, fulfilled.

I am left half for the school football team and I also like running, swimming, cricket and putting. I am a big head. My favourite hobbies are stamp collecting, reading, writing and many other things.

I continued to play football until I got into my forties, when ninety minutes became longer and longer until, one knackered evening, I deposited my football boots in a plastic bag outside a charity shop on the way to the pub. I hike in the country, run a little

---

* Everyone who has read this manuscript has suggested that I remove this sentence but I find it annoying when people are coy about their income.

and go swimming in the sea or Tooting Lido if it's hot. In my capacity as captain of the Dusty Fleming International Hair Stylists XI, I still play the odd game of cricket in summer but I no longer putt and, if asked, quote Barry Cryer: 'I don't play golf – I *like* women.' Sometimes I am a stand-up comic and you don't get much more big-headed than that. My stamp album is lost but my favourite hobbies are reading, writing and many other things.

My father is a big man with a big nose. He is a policeman. At work, I think he is considered 'a bit of a laugh'. He's practically held together by cups of tea.

The end of this opening chapter of my first memoir returns to Syd, as shall I throughout this sequel. Since I mention twice that he is a policeman I must have been proud of his standing, although not for a second did I ever consider joining the police myself. I remember walking with him, one afternoon when he was off duty, along Borough High Street, his regular beat, when suddenly I was alarmed to see two drunks shouting and running at us. But they ran to my dad and slapped him on the back, crying 'Good to see you, Syd! Is this your nipper?' Their affection spoke of the kindness he must have shown them at Kennington nick. If ever there was a 'nice bobby', then he was it. When people who knew him have said to me that I am like Syd, I am pleased and flattered. Big nose, a bit of a laugh, a love of tea – I am, as best I can be, my father's son.

CHAPTER 1. I AM BORN

Once upon a time in a land far away,* in an era only dimly recalled, a child was born. It was me.

My father recorded the occasion in the memoir he wrote forty years later:

> On the 27th November Hazel gave birth to our second son at 4 a.m. Fortunately, Hazel's sister Stella had arrived to look after Richard the night before as I was on night duty. It was a night of extreme weather. The South Goodwin lightship went aground. An ambulance was called at 2 a.m. to take her to King's College hospital. All went very well and Brian Arthur John Smith was born quickly and trouble free and weighing in at six and three quarter pounds. I wasn't aware of this until I came home after night duty. I visited that evening and it was a very moving sight to see Hazel sitting up in bed with Brian sucking lustily at her breast. We were both delighted to have a second healthy son. There was one hitch I forgot to mention; we could have had a girl instead of a boy. The nurse gave Hazel the baby for feeding and quick as a flash she noticed it had black hair and was female, whereas Brian was bald as a coot and definitely male. Apparently

* Depending, obviously, on where you are when you read this.

there were two babies tagged Smith. I'm glad we got the right one.

I am too. And so, like everyone else, I was born.

Baby – not me

CHAPTER 1. MY NAME. WHAT IS IT?

'My name is Arthur Smith – unless there's anybody here from Streatham tax office, in which case I'm Daphne Fairfax.' This is the first joke I have done at a thousand stand-up comedy gigs (and to anyone reading this from the Inland Revenue, may I repeat that it is a joke). I tried to give it up for a while but people kept asking for it; these days I follow up with, 'and that line has now gone into sheltered accommodation.' I have a well-earned reputation among comics for beating material to death over many years.

But I am neither Arthur nor Daphne. My name among members of my family, old friends and quite a few colleagues, is Brian. Since the death of Brian Boru, king of Ireland, in 1014, there has been a paucity of great Brians but, apart from a camping holiday with the Scouts when, for two weeks, I became Rufus, I have never fretted about the naffness of my given first name. Sometimes Brian and Arthur confuse people. I have compèred shows where the comic on stage has said, 'As Brian was just saying . . .' and the audience have been baffled. Did they miss an act called Brian while they were in the toilet? Friends studying amateur psychology have theorised that the dichotomy between private Brian and public Arthur is the key to my character but I think of Arthur merely as the Brian who gets paid.

When I meet someone for the first time now I am Arthur, since introducing myself as Brian will likely prompt the question

'Why do you have two names?', thus obliging me to go through the explanation that I have delivered more times even than the Daphne Fairfax gag. Here is why Arthur is the name on the front of this book, and yet it is Brian who is sucking lustily at his mother's breast.

I was Brian Smith until the age of twenty-eight when, after several years of trying, I was accepted as a provisional member of Equity, the Actors' Union, a prerequisite then for working professionally. The Union has a ruling that there cannot be two members with the same name, presumably to prevent unscrupulous young actors from exploiting the public by changing their names by deed poll to Judi Dench or Ewan McGregor before sending in their applications. ('Have you seen, dear, Tom Cruise is in *Mother Goose* at the Arts Centre?'). There already was a Brian Smith in Equity – although I am not familiar with his work. Because of him, I sat down one afternoon in the South London hovel where I lived and looked at the space on the form reserved for my new name. Whatever I chose would be my professional moniker, the name by which I would be known by the public and by my peers.

I wrote down 'Captain Wanker'.

It was, I reasoned, noticeable, subversive and funny. The downright stupidity of the name would surely make it leap out from the roster of other comedians featured in the listings magazines: Paul Merton, Jeremy Hardy, Mark Steel, Clive Anderson, Dave Cohen – dull names indeed – nearly as dull as Brian Smith. One could be certain that, whatever his act was like, Captain Wanker was committed to his comedy. The instant I posted the form I had doubts. What about my aspirations beyond stand-up? How seriously would an audience take an anti-war play written by the

Captain? What if I ever played King Lear? How would my billing affect ticket sales? Fortunately the Equity person processing my application had similar reservations, or perhaps there already *was* a Captain Wanker. My new membership card, at any rate, bore my second-choice name.

Arthur was an easy and obvious alternative to Brian. It has the central position among my Christian names and had been my nickname during my first three years at secondary school – although rendered in South London mouths as 'Arfur'. In the class newspaper I wrote a column entitled 'The Arfur Corner'. Then, as now, Arthur had an old-fashioned, comical quality (though I note a recent spate of young middle-class Arthurs), which was why my schoolmates had chosen it over the limp 'Brian'. Fellow Arthurs included the three old comics Askey, Mullard and English; the great American playwright Miller; 1960s one-hit wonder Brown (The Crazy World of), all-round intellectual Koestler, and the mythical King. Yes – Arthur, that would do. I became Arthur Smith.

Unless, of course, there is anybody reading this from Streatham tax office, in which case I became Daphne Fairfax.

CHAPTER 1. NEARLY DEAD

One Wednesday night, about half an hour after going to bed, I am woken by a stomach-ache. Downstairs I sit on the settee next to my friend Gary, who is staying with me and idly watching television. He sympathises and agrees with me that it's probably the pâté – I take two paracetamol and return to bed.

But I can't sleep because the pain is getting worse with every minute. I come down again and this time Gary asks, 'Do you need professional help?'

'Yes, yes – I think I do.'

He calls a taxi and, by the time it arrives five minutes later, I am doubled up in agony. The driver looks at me and says to Gary, 'You should have called an ambulance.'

At A and E my gasping and sweating see me promoted rapidly from the waiting room into a holding area. Gary helps me onto a bed and waits, as the pain continues to worsen. Suddenly I have to stagger to a toilet, where I vomit what looks like a large, black, glistening turd. Still there is no relief. Finally a doctor appears, the first of many I will see over the next thirty-six hours, and the first of them to ask the question: 'How much do you drink?'

Dispatched for an X-ray, I am shouting the pain now. It feels exactly like a mad rodent is trying to burrow its way out of my abdomen. I think, 'I would rather die than endure this much longer.'

'How much do you drink?'

It seems I may have an ulcer, which would mean an emergency operation. I am given pethidine, a painkiller something like morphine and, at last, although the agony is still intense, it is shocking me a beat less. No, I do not have an ulcer; it is something else that does not require surgery. Can I have some morphine? Not yet.

'How much do you drink?'

Now I am on a drip and connected to several machines. It is four a.m. Poor Gary is spent. I tell him to go home, make a couple of calls on my behalf and go to sleep. After he leaves I am wheeled on my bed into a corridor. I prefer it here; it seems a little calmer, airier, or maybe it's the pethidine. I still have not been able to consider this experience; it has been so violent it has blocked out any thought that is not of immediate use in dealing with it.

Ceilings start to roll across my eyes. Then a lift and more ceiling before I come to rest in a room bathed in hush. I am attached to more machines, administered more – but not enough – pethidine . . . is that Richard here? It is. I tell him that I've had the baby now, by which I mean that the super-pain has subsided, but must have sounded to my older brother like raving, and probably was. This is the first night I have spent in hospital since my birth but I have started at the top. I have joined the sad congregation in the Intensive Care Unit of Saint George's Hospital, Tooting.

Late the next morning, after some hours of confused, skithery dreaming, I come round enough to see that a large semicircle of people has formed around my bed: my mother and father, both my brothers and several of my closest friends. My father, Syd, is trying not to cry, but failing. 'This, then,' I think, 'is my deathbed scene.' Blimey, how did it come to this?

CHAPTER 2. A BOMB-SITE IN BERMONDSEY

It ended nine years before I was born but the War pervaded my childhood. Even before I knew what a war was I realised that this had been the Big Thing in the lives of the tall people who looked after me. They divided time into three: before, after and during the War. It was in stories, films, the news, everywhere. 'What did your dad do in the War?' was the question that little boys, whose own dads had done well, asked other little boys almost as soon as they could speak. Some poor kids' dads hadn't been in the War at all. They were to be pitied. I soon understood that my own answer to the question was a winner; my father had fought in North Africa and had been captured at El Alamein, ending the War as a prisoner in Colditz Castle, a place so glamorous that in the year of my birth they had made a feature film about it. Whenever I told people that my father had been a prisoner in Colditz they always asked me, 'Did he escape?' They still do.

Me and my mates might occasionally get involved with Martians or pirates but our most persistent enemy was the German Army. We had seen pictures in comics of these block-jawed, humourless Nazis; they were baddies whom our dads had beaten so we wanted to beat them too. When I was, at last, allowed to go out without mum or dad, I joined the other boys in ferocious military campaigns, shooting scores of Jerries and Japs with machine guns made of fingers and mortars wrenched from our vocal chords. We had the perfect arena for these battles. London was still Luftwaffe-pock-marked and a big, beautiful bomb-site sat conveniently within the confines of Landale House, the small block of flats where I lived with my mum, dad and another boy called Richard, who turned out to be my older brother. It was a patch of tussocky wasteland, grubby with rubbish, but I have never since found a more exciting place. Adults rarely ventured onto the bomb-site – they called us in from open windows – so it belonged gloriously to us alone. Some days I would arrive there to find that the ever–changing detritus smeared across the encrusted mud contained half a rusty old pram or a sliver of shrapnel. Raymond, the toughest of the boys, told me that he had dug up a hand grenade and was keeping it in a secret place at home, which he could not yet reveal. I begged him, but he was as resolute as an English spy tortured by the Gestapo. At the centre of the bomb-site, this repository of martial dreams, stood a lonely, withered grey tree which it cost me two trips to Casualty to finally climb.

As the youngest, and therefore smallest, of the Landale House boys I was obliged to participate in adventures which could turn out to be beyond my physical capabilities. One afternoon Raymond had acquired a ladder and dictated that we must all climb up onto the roof of the dustbin shed and jump off, or face excommunication from the gang. Ollie was too scared and was duly bashed with a stick, made to cry and sent home in disgrace. We others walked gingerly across the roof and lined up to take our turn. Raymond led the way, sustaining only a small cut and a hurt wrist. Bobby escaped with a twisted ankle. Blimey, it was a really long way down, especially for a five-year-old. Richard was next and if he was going to do it then so was I. Five minutes later my mother opened the door to an image that she has never forgotten: my limp and bloodied body draped over the outstretched arms of

Mrs Lightwing from the flat below. 'Hello again, Brian,' said the nurse at Casualty.

Raymond's dad was a copper – all our dads were; Landale House was built to house policemen with children. My mum and dad and various other families had all moved in to the brand new block on the same day, not long before I was born. It was a big occasion for my mother who was thrilled by the freshly painted walls, the white modconnery of the kitchen and, above all, the fantastic luxury of unlimited hot water. We even had a tiny balcony, out of bounds to me and Richard but the fatal precipice over which our neighbours' hamster plunged while under my parents' care.

One of my friends in Landale House differed from all the others in three respects: Paddy Moxom was younger than me, smaller than me and female to boot. Being the oldest kid was a new experience but one whose benefits I soon saw. I ordered Paddy around as we made our frequent sweeps of the patch of grass by the flats in search of insects and worms to imprison in a jam jar. 'Bring me that earwig, Paddy.' 'Paddy, get me a glass of water.' One day I instructed her to eat a worm and she shrank back in fright. Poor Paddy, she was small and a bit sickly. I felt the new sentiment of tenderness and, by way of apology, held the worm up myself and bit off the bottom end although I, unlike Raymond who had introduced me to this stunt, spat it out. I met a second creature younger than myself when Richard and I were called in from downstairs one day to be introduced to another brother who had appeared while we were out. I was delighted to meet Nicholas but he seemed a bit of a cry-baby bunting and didn't have much to say so I returned to my important military duties.

On one side of Landale House stood an imposing fence, so high that it was insurmountable – even by Raymond. Behind this imposing barrier lay Surrey Docks, although it would be hard to imagine anywhere that looked less like Surrey. From our kitchen on the third floor we could see across to the tops of great ships being loaded and unloaded by towering cranes. It was the deep midwinter of the Cold War yet many of these boats flew the hammer and sickle and at night the streets of Bermondsey might reverberate with the singing of drunken Russian sailors. On Saturday afternoons, a few Russians were among the burly dockers marching along the Lower Road to watch Millwall play at the Den. The River Thames brought these men here. The city's river, its oily smell, its surging tides, its bed lined with history, forms a part of the mental topography of every Londoner. Aged five, I was taken to Cherry Garden pier where I gazed up the river to Tower Bridge. What lay beyond there? Whatever it might be, I knew it was not yet time to find out; there was plenty still to discover about my own little universe.

Southwark Park, up the road from the flats, could not compete with the independent terrain of the bomb-site but it did offer the excellent possibility of a skirmish with one of the 'Parkies' – blue-uniformed men who patrolled the park holding pointy sticks designed to impale bits of litter and small boys. My greatest victory over their superior forces came when I evaded a Parkie by hiding inside a large pile of dead leaves, a trick inspired by the celebrated (failed) escape attempt made by one of my dad's colleagues in Colditz. The park had an open-air swimming pool, the Lido, in whose silver cold waters I learnt not to sink. On starting at Southwark Park Primary School* I traversed the park

* 'I say Primary School – it's a University now, of course' is a line from my stand-up routine.

every morning and afternoon with Richard and my mother pushing Nick in a pram. Rich had not enjoyed his first day in full-time education, but was consoled by the thought that at least he had now been to school. On learning that he had to go the next day too, and the day after that, he demanded that our mother write to the headmaster saying thank you very much but he wouldn't be showing up again. I was pleased with myself that I didn't cry on my first day at school although I felt pretty choked up when my mother abandoned me and I made the long walk across the unforgiving asphalt playground towards the classes. After a day or two I fought against my shyness and soon found a social circle when I became a founder member of the 'mischief gang'. I did well in class at Southwark Park and by the age of six and a half had a reading age of seven. Reading was a marvellous trick to learn, far more interesting than tying my shoe laces. It became a regular part of my life such that I would plead every night at bedtime, 'One more chapter, please!'*

* * *

* Among the books and comics I consumed (*Captain Pugwash, Boy's Own, The Victor, Biggles, Jennings,* and so on) I especially recall a book called *The Man who Never did the Washing-Up*. At the end of the story the man had no clean crockery left and a pile of intimidating dirty plates taller than himself. What to do? At that moment it started raining heavily and the man had the bright idea of shoving all the dirty washing-up outside. After the rain had washed the plates clean he resolved never again to postpone the washing up. Do it now or it won't get done at all. I, however, chose to interpret the story as an invitation to *always* leave the washing-up because somehow it would get done, and anyway, my hero was only of interest as the man who never did the washing-up. If he did it his claim to fame was gone. And this is by way of an apology to all the people I've ever shared a house with.

Six. That was the best. On my sixth birthday I ate a fruit sundae that gave me an enduring taste for the golden flesh of tinned pineapple chunks. At six, I scored centuries and took hat-tricks on our patch of grass and rampaged around the bomb-site wearing my sheriff's badge, slicing Nazis with my wooden sword fashioned by my father. Aged six, I was commended by Raymond for my heroic rôle in the big battle against the ginger kids from the estate and won a knobbly-knees competition at a party at which I also picked up the award for dirtiest hands (a bar of soap). At school that year I planted the stone from my plum in the thin stripe of garden in the playground, expecting a plum tree to grow by the next morning, played David to critical acclaim in the school nativity play and discovered the infinite possibilities of marbles. In Southwark Park the mischief gang was a thriving concern, having shoved a dead weed up the exhaust pipe of a Parkie's car. That summer our family went on holiday to Devon where for the first time I swam in the breathtaking seas of England. Every day of being six seems now to have been full of incident and emotion and intriguing possibilities. There were unpredictabilities but the world was essentially benign, constant, eternal and organised around me. The War, whatever it was, was over and I was here, God was in his heaven, all was right with the world. And I want to be six for ever and ever.

On our return from Devon, an interminable journey that, as usual, entailed a long spell by the side of the road waiting for an AA man, I rejoined the gang on the bomb-site for some late-summer adventures. The next day I wondered why Paddy was not around; she had been ill when we set off but that was ages ago. I found out later when my mum called me in and told me, in an unfamiliar, serious tone, that Paddy had died.

This was a shock, the biggest of all my life. Poor Paddy. She was only five. Such a little life she had.

That night I lay in bed next to my sleeping brother and looked up at where the street lamp outside shone a pattern on the ceiling, a pattern that danced to the headlights of every passing car. I would not see Paddy Moxom again. Ever. (And what did 'ever' mean then?) And I was like Paddy, so I would die too. My mum and dad would die and so would Richard and Nick and Raymond and Mrs Gomm at school – yes, even 'Gomm Gomm, the atom bomb' – even she would die. And when it came it would be . . . be what? It would be black, dark, an absence. I wouldn't be there any more and the world would not care. It would continue as it had continued long before me. This could happen at any moment – unexpectedly, like it did with Paddy. And the gang would still play on the bomb-site without me, just as I had been playing without Paddy.

I think it is these elementary revelations and the questions they throw up that signal the end of the first stage of life; any subsequent happiness becomes compromised in a way it is not when you are thrillingly poised on the top of the dustbin shed waiting to jump. Back at school one morning after my seventh birthday, I fell into conflict with Lyn Blewer and, as an act of aggression, told her to think about death before she went to sleep that night. I forgot about this but the next day she came up to me, her face drained and drawn like an old lady's. Mournfully, she informed me that she had indeed contemplated death, and I realised from her expression that her infancy too, like mine, was now over.

Perhaps it was these intimations of mortality that launched me into my pre-pubescent showbiz career. My form teacher was now Miss Marshall, a young Canadian on an exchange scheme. What she made of bashed-up post-war Bermondsey I cannot know but I flourished under her tutelage; she excited my imagination with tales of the great St Lawrence River and she comforted me when I arrived self-consciously in class one morning wearing a pair of round, pink-framed National Health glasses (later made iconic by the Milky Bar Kid). She read us the story of Johnny Apple-seed, a mythical figure in American children's literature, who toured the United States planting apple trees and singing. The Johnny Apple-seed song became my first party piece – sung indiscriminately for my parents, their friends, my uncles and aunts, in front of the school in assembly and at any gig where I could get a booking.

> The Lord is good to me
> And so I thank the Lord
> For giving me the birds and bees
> The sun and rain and the apple trees
> The Lord is good to me

It was the jaunty tune and the opportunity it gave me to show off that attracted me to the song, not its religious content. I did not consider that the Lord had been good to, for example, Paddy Moxom. Well, if he had, it was a funny sort of 'good'. We were told a lot about God and I loved the biblical parables narrated each morning at assembly by Mr Hughs, the headmaster. God, he said, was everywhere, in everyone, and not only knew everything but had created it all as well. Although God was presented in books as an old white man with a beard, we were told he was not a person, not like Lyn Blewer or Richard or Mrs Atom Bomb. You could imagine him, it seemed, in any guise and I chose to think of him as a kind of Captain Pugwash (who now had his own show on our new television set). Like the Captain he was well-meaning, vain but incompetent. And fictional. Syd and Hazel paid lip service to the Church of England but we never attended church. God may have been everywhere but I never saw him round much after school.

Johnny Apple-seed had been a useful vehicle for my performing début but my greatest theatrical moment at Southwark Park Primary came in December when Miss Marshall announced that our class was to do a production of *Peter Pan* in front of the pupils and parents at Christmas. Inspired, I went home that evening and wrote the show. Next morning I presented the script proudly to Miss Marshall who proclaimed its brilliance. God knows what I wrote (of course He does – He knows everything) but it was certainly unperformable. Miss Marshall told me this gently but deflected any disappointment by offering me whichever part I wished. Rejecting the eponymous hero on the grounds that he was too effete, I chose the rôle of macho baddy Captain Hook. My big entrance, snarling and brandishing my coat-hanger hook, frightened the fairy girls and squaws on stage but produced big laughs in the audience. As the girls cowered and the boys looked confused, the laughter grew louder. On a roll now, I left the stage and began to terrorise individual spectators. More laughs. Now I was laughing and so were the squaws, the fairies, Peter, the Lost Boys and Miss Marshall – everyone was laughing, and it felt very fine indeed. No doubt I had distracted from the thrust of the narrative with my self-indulgent antics but the people gathered in that hall were happy, however briefly, because of something *I* had done. I observed how the sound of shared laughter united people in a loud, visceral moment. I have sought it out ever since.

But maybe, like God and Captain Pugwash, I delude myself; maybe my real showbiz epiphany was not the grand Hook exploit at centre stage in the school hall, but rather the week after, when I was sitting at the back of the classroom during playtime and accepted a threepenny bit to show my willy to two girls. It was certainly my first professional engagement.

I had just turned nine when my mum told us boys that we were moving to a place called Kidbrooke, just a few miles away, near Greenwich and Blackheath; it might as well have been in Scotland since it meant changing schools and friends. As we pulled out of the flats, my father's decrepit old crock of a car sputtering and groaning with bags and children, I looked forlornly at Landale House. Raymond, Olly, Bobbie Lightwing and the lads, whose faces I no longer recall, came to say goodbye. We had fought our last battle. Our war, like the grown-up one, was now over. Behind the waving boys stood the new fence that had been erected to keep us kids off the bomb-site while it awaited its transition to building site and then to what it is today, Rotherhithe Police Station. I knew this was the end of an episode and wept softly when the car lurched left along the Lower Road. I looked back but the gang had turned to resume their play.

I never did find out where Raymond kept his hand grenade.

CHAPTER 3. RUNNING THROUGH THE SUBURBS

Kidbrooke is in London, just about, though even Londoners have hardly heard of it. Scattered shapelessly along the A2 between Deptford and Shooters Hill, near Blackheath, it had a station, an enormous pub called the Dover Patrol, a parade of shops and no bomb-sites. There was, however, the 'donkey field' which accommodated the animals who gave rides on Blackheath. Once my dad caught me prodding one with a stick and upbraided me in, for him, unusually stern tones. I felt ashamed that I had hurt the poor beast and have ever since felt an affection for the humble donkey (though please do not write in, you donkey people – I am not going to do a benefit for a donkey sanctuary in Devon). Our new home, the first my parents had owned, was a semi with, thrillingly, a small garden, in which I spent many hours over the next few years playing football and cricket with Richard, or more usually with Nick, who also became my new assistant when I resumed my important insect-torturing work. We shot bluebottles with my ball-bearing gun and, when the sun shone, fried ants in a tobacco tin.*

* Perhaps I was influenced by Syd who may have been a defender of donkeys but loved to insert stunned flies into spider's webs so that he could watch the spider going about its murderous business. I retired from assassinating bugs at the age of twelve and would now literally no longer hurt a fly, unless instructed to by Beth. In fact, I should like to apologise to the insect world for my small-boy brutality.

The neighbours on one side were a cadaverous woman called Lily and her husband Arthur who was big in shirts but simpered obediently under Lily law. He may have been the main man on the shop floor but in the evenings he was less important than his wife's cats. I got off on the wrong foot with Lily when she caught me in her garden retrieving our football but my stock improved when she realised that I was available at all times to go round to the shop to buy her fags, a service whose principal client was Syd. I genuinely enjoyed my role as errand boy and didn't even need bribing. I ran to the shops, bought a half-ounce of Old Holborn for Syd, twenty Number 6 for Lily, and ran home again. I could see no point in walking if you didn't have to; running was my most comfortable mode of transport. I didn't like sitting in trains, hated cars even more and found walking just too slooow. I ran errands for Syd, Hazel, Lily, Mr Cumbers on the other side, and any visitors who asked. I ran to school and home too. I ran with Richard through Oxleas Woods and up Shooters Hill. Eventually I ran cross-country for London Schools and once raced against future Olympic Gold medallist Steve Ovett (he came second, I was 264th).

Lily and her idiosyncrasies were a source of shared amusement to our family. She became noticeably more amiable as the day wore on and one night was *so* amiable that she fell into the tiny, and aptly named, lily pond which Arthur had been forced to dig in their back garden. On Tuesdays, after she went shopping in Blackheath and had a couple at the Railway Tavern before getting the train home, she would knock on our back door, her bony hand proffering a plate of the leftovers from her and Arthur's Sunday joint. Hazel accepted warmly but disposed of the meaty scraps later. There was much laughter when Syd learned that Lily had become so excited at her favourite cat's imminent birthday that my mother had gone out and bought it a birthday card.

It was only later that I understood the source, or rather sauce, of Lily's evening good humours. Alcohol, like God and girls, was not much present when I was ten. My mother had a taste for cider which she restricted to weekends while Syd was a hopeless boozer – hopeless in the sense that he found it hard to finish an alcoholic drink. He did not like liquor; he would ask for a pint of bitter in the pub, not because he wanted one but because a lemonade, which he would much have preferred, seemed to him *unmanly.* For the same reason he never ordered a gin and tonic unless it was clear to the barman that it was for a lady. He told me that he had not drunk a glass of wine until he was forty, which was not so unusual then. *NdA* When, years later, I interviewed Denis Healey in Naples, where he had been stationed during the War, he recalled that he had never tasted wine until he arrived in Italy and had assumed that, if he survived the War, he would not drink it again back in England. He was wildly incorrect in his own case but his generation was obliged by scarcity to take the grape up late. Wine was no more of a success for Syd than beer; he could just about tolerate a glass of sweet sparkling rosé because it tasted a bit like Tizer, but he took no pleasure in it.

We paid Sunday visits to my grandparents, anticipated with a heavy heart since it meant that instead of playing football I was trussed up into shirt and tie and told to *behave.* Syd's mum had a distant air and a careworn look, as though broken by life. Ethel Adeline had spent time in a 'mental hospital' and I can only speculate that the worry of raising five children and seeing four of them go off to war must have been an intolerable burden to her. Ethel's husband, my Grandad Bill, was a daunting figure with his stiff bearing, clipped moustache and disapproval of even the mildest facets of 1960s culture. He hated long hair, pop groups, television, long hair some more, modern clothes and the 'permissive society'. Fortunately for Bill, given his profound aversion to the *look* of the Rolling Stones, his deafness meant that he never had to listen to them. If treated with respect, however, he was warm and generous. It was Bill, I discovered later, who had lent the money to my parents that had enabled them to buy the house in Kidbrooke.

I have tried to imagine the mutual wariness when Bill met Jim, my mother's father, at their children's marriage on 23 December 1950. The two men, the ex-copper and the ex-prisoner (cooking the books, I think), could hardly have been more different. I am looking at a wedding photo now (see photo page two). There is Bill, smiling discreetly, hands behind his back, a military man, sober-suited, upright and solid. Looking past Ethel and the happy couple to the family flanking Hazel, I see Kitty, my grandmother – 'Nana' as I became embarrassed to call her – a vague and kindly lady. Standing obediently next to her, is Grandad Jim, bald and seemingly Jewish,* grinning carefully through his ill-fitting dentures and his thick horn-rimmed glasses in expensive spivvy get-up, looking every inch the wide boy that he undoubtedly was. On my mother and her sister Stella's birth certificates his profession is listed as 'poulterer', on Uncle John's he is a 'a music hall artiste', while on

* He was not Jewish as far as I know and neither am I, although some people think I am. Several websites list me as a Jew for some reason. Sometimes I feel Jewish. And other times Irish, like Kitty's mum.

Aunty Catherine's his job is 'turf accountant' – a truly classical CV for a professional ducker-'n-diver.

Kitty met Jim when she was a member of a concert-party dance troupe called The Seven Little Rays of Sunshine which perhaps accounted for her bunions. According to my mother, Jim had not been a model husband and in her teens Hazel had clashed furiously with him. To Jim, his daughter was an uppity grammar-school girl with pretensions; to Hazel, Jim was a controlling, feckless, womanising wastrel who mistreated her mother. Jim showed little interest in his grandchildren and made no effort to distinguish between us – we were all known to him as 'mate'. But, despite his indifference to me, I was captivated by him because of his roguish air and because he was so *funny*. The jokes and stories he told and anecdotes he related, which earned tuts from Hazel and repressed sniggers – giving way to guffaws – from Syd, were irresistible to me, even when I did not understand them. He told them with brio and no detail that was not milked for a laugh. There was something fascinatingly *adult* about these brief sessions with Grandad Jim.*

He rose stupefyingly early throughout his life and when Syd asked him once what he *did* at five-thirty in the morning, he replied, 'Oh you know, you have a cup of tea, a piece of toast

* Many years later at a memorial/benefit for the comedian Linda Smith at the Victoria Palace Theatre in London I started my set by saying, 'About sixty years ago a comedian did a spot in this theatre. He had never played such a big venue before and I suppose he can't have made much of an impression because he never played here again. He was 'Jimmy Kirk, the singing comedian' and he was my grandad . . . here's to you, Jim.' A big 'aaaah' escaped the audience.

and before you know it, it's quarter past six.' These days I get a laugh on stage from this story. Later in his life he redeemed himself somewhat in my mother's eyes when he doted on the young Catherine and proved to be a tender and loving carer to Kit as she descended into the sad oblivion of Alzheimer's. And when she died, he put his dressing gown on, took his teeth out for the last time, switched on the racing on TV and cheerfully introduced me to a new phrase, 'I'm just waiting for the grim reaper now, mate.'

On my first day at my new school, Kidbrooke Park Junior, I met the boy who was to become my oldest friend, recording the occasion two years later.

> My first friend was Mary Grimer (a boy with his name changed around).

It must have been some love of secret names and spies that caused me to create this crude anagram, but it would not take the code-breakers of Bletchley, whom I came to admire, too long to work out that 'Mary Grimer' was Gary Rimmer.

He was the only one who regarded me as anything. Girls acted as though I was a two-year-old. I have been grateful to him ever since. He is an individual-looking character with slits as eyes. He has a long face and brown eyes and long eyebrows. He walks like a duck.

How charming I was. Apart from a brief spell when I set up 'the Anti-Rimmer Club' he has remained my friend ever since. Gary did not like sport but, like myself, had intellectual and martial interests. Indeed, he told me he had sent off for information on joining the Parachute Regiment. The army had followed up his request a couple of months later with a letter asking why he had not pursued his application, whereupon* he had to write back to tell them that his mother wouldn't let him join the military yet as he was only ten.

Kidbrooke was no Kensington but it was more suburban than Rotherhithe and in this new environment, despite my glasses, which grew thicker, dirtier, more crooked and more scratched with every passing year, I was quite a tough nut – which might account for my brutal description of Gary. On my third day I told Peter Green that if he flapped his big ears he would surely be able to fly. For this cruelty I was taken aside by Miss Blane and told, 'I don't know what your old school was like but that's not how we do things here.' Nevertheless I was placed in the A stream where I became Richard Woolham's new challenger for the rôle of 'best fighter in the class'. In a public confrontation in the playground I got the better of him but, unable to accept his demotion, Woolham obliged me to bash him up every Thursday for a whole term. My weekends in the back garden with Nick paid off when I was selected for the under-elevens school football team – largely made up of boys from the B class. Several of these lads were real bruisers and I paid obeisance to their patently superior scrapping qualities. When one of them asked me to name the best fighter in the A class, I informed them it was Richard Woolham, whereupon one or other of them took to 'doing him over' on Friday

* One of Gary's idiosyncrasies – famous among his friends – is his use of 'whereupon' when he means 'whereas'. For his twenty-seventh birthday Babs, who will appear in three chapters' time, bought him a T-shirt emblazoned with the word 'whereupon'. Gary did not find this funny, whereas I did. He never wore it and continues splendidly in his (mis)use of 'whereupon' to this day.

dinner times. Weekends must have been a big relief to Woolie, who is the last person I ever hit.

Playing football for the school team in Charlton Park on Saturdays was the highlight of my week, anticipated so intensely that I could hardly sleep on Fridays. At this stage of my life all activities divided into two: playing football and doing stuff that prevented me playing football. I recorded every school game in an exercise book and the day that I wrote down 'Kidbrooke Park 2 Charlton Manor 0' (B. Smith scored both goals) was one of the proudest of my life. The balls then were leather and gained weight in the mud, as a million boring old men have reported ever since. Heading one of these leaden orbs towards the end of a game required real foolhardiness. I was obliged to wear my glasses to play, which made heading doubly hazardous, but on the occasion of my two-goal triumph I shut my eyes and thrust my head at the incoming missile. It broke my glasses and knocked me out briefly but when I came round I was ecstatic to learn that the ball had ballooned off my nut, over the fingertips of their goalie and into the net. B. Smith scores!

One Thursday after the traditional duffing-up of Woolie, we were informed that our forthcoming game, a local derby (although they were *all* local derbies) against Eltham Primary under-elevens, had been cancelled, not because of weather but as a mark of respect to the newly deceased Winston Churchill. Eh? What did Winston Churchill have to do with my football game?* I had never been the Churchill devotee one was supposed to be because of Grandad Bill who had been sunk and consequently gone deaf

* This, I think, was the catalyst for my subsequent years as a student revolutionary.

off Gallipoli, a military cock-up presided over by Churchill.* Having missed football because of the dead hero, I then had to write an essay about him. We dipped our pens in our inkwells and began. As we sat scratching away Gary put his hand up and asked Mrs Banfield if it was acceptable to put 'Winston Churchill was very, *very* brave'? Mrs Banfield said it was, whereupon I instinctively thought, 'No, it isn't. If you want him to be more than very brave then you should surely think of a new word – like *incredibly* brave.' But teachers couldn't be wrong, could they? My own grudging panegyric to the great statesman, containing the phrase 'he was a fat old man who did V-signs and liked to smoke', did not meet with Mrs Banfield's approval. She was very, *very* annoyed.

I was at Kidbrooke Park School for five terms, doing well enough at the eleven-plus to earn an interview at Roan Grammar School for boys where Richard was already a pupil. Richard had overcome his first-day aversion to school to become the straight-As student he continued to be throughout his education; failure to get into Roan would mean I had not kept up with Richard and I would have to go to a secondary modern school which was the low-status flip side of the grammar school coin. I was nervous as I was ushered into the august confines of the headmaster's study, where he sat magisterially in his gown. Our short chat culminated in the question that I had been briefed about. 'I know

---

* When Syd had been captured at El Alamein and was being sent back through enemy lines a friendly Italian soldier had shown him a picture of his wife and child, saying, 'Mussolini – no good.' Syd had replied, 'Churchill – no good.' I have always been moved by the thought of this solidarity among young soldiers, supposed enemies united in contempt for the politicians who had put them into this dreadful situation. Churchill, no good.

you're still very young, but I wonder if you have given any thought yet to what you might, eventually, want to do for a living?' 'Yes, sir', I said. 'I thought I might like to become a quantity surveyor.' In the absence of any suggestions of my own, this was the aspiration my mother had chosen for me, although I'm not sure that she had any clearer notion than I had about what a quantity surveyor actually *did.*

'What does a quantity surveyor actually do?' asked the head-master. We blinked at each other.

Despite this, three days later a letter of acceptance arrived and so when summer was over and England had won the World Cup I walked the first of a thousand times across Blackheath to school with Gary, who had also joined the ranks of 'John Roan's men'. We carried our new brown cardboard briefcases and wore our smart green blazers which, in my case, anticipated the size I would be in a year's time and remained smart only until I ate my first break-time marmalade sandwich. My new white shirt, meanwhile, had already defied my mother's tucking-in and begun its tireless attempts to escape from my shorts. Another new school, but this one contained some pupils who were nearer to young men than boys. My grandad had joined the army at fifteen – and the older boys here were seventeen or even eighteen. There it stood, right up ahead, alluring and foreboding, like Tower Bridge, the condition in which I would spend nearly all of the rest of my life, the world of the tall people, from whose bourn no child returns – adulthood.

But there was still time for the giggling joy of boyhood. In my final term at Kidbrooke Park I enjoyed the most entertaining and instructive lesson in all of my schooldays, inspired by Mrs Logan who took PE in the school hall on the first floor.

We didn't have any special kit, but for some reason we boys were required to remove our shorts, with their stains and comforting marbles, in order to do the exercises in our underpants. By the age of eleven this had become extremely embarrassing. We felt sheepish and vulnerable in front of the girls, who had no such humiliating requirement. As we gingerly stripped off one day Tom Simpson got his shorts caught on the end of his foot and kicked them free with such alacrity that they sailed through the air, straight out of an open window and down to the playground below.

There was a moment while everyone took in this stupendous occurrence. Then, of course, came shrieks of laughter. Tom Simpson, stricken with shame, began to cry as all the embarrassment we other boys felt suddenly rushed from us to him. The girls were laughing hard too. Everyone, except Mrs Logan and Simpson, was shrieking with the fun of it. Poor old Tom. Eventually Mrs Logan re-established an uneasy silence but not control. The lesson was in disarray until, in a moment of inspiration she surely never surpassed in her teaching career, Mrs Logan shouted, 'RIGHT! ALL YOU BOYS, THROW YOUR SHORTS OUT THE WINDOW!'

What a fantastic invitation! Tom's emasculation was forgotten; he stopped sobbing as we queued up to launch our shorts through the window. The occasion had become funny in a good way such that even Mrs Logan and Tom were enjoying themselves. In fact Tom now looked like a trail-blazing hero. The children in the class below must also surely have relished the strange sight of the sky raining boys' shorts. As we trooped down to retrieve them, chortling and tittering, our new-found solidarity meant that the giggling girls now seemed admiring rather than threatening and I learnt the truth that one man in public in his pants is pitiable but ten is a posse of fun.

I wonder if anyone else who was there that day remembers this incident? Tom Simpson may and possibly Mrs Logan too if she is still alive, but I doubt anyone else does (Gary, who was present, doesn't). The images of youth that stay with us into adulthood often seem to others arbitrary and without apparent significance. Or maybe it was for others in the class the astounding event that lives in my mind. At any rate, ever since that PE lesson the phrase has periodically returned to me, acting as a call to arms, a bold plan in a tricky situation, an invitation to creative mayhem. Boys, throw your shorts out the window.

CHAPTER 4. YOUNG ARFUR

Roan Grammar School for Boys, founded in the seventeenth century by a rich businessman called John Roan for 'clothing and educating poor children', was situated in a handsome building next to Greenwich Park, the oldest of the royal parks. Every raucous lunchtime, we boys, around six hundred of us, flooded into this glorious hilly green ground to play football, climb trees or, in the case of the older, harder lads, to lounge, smoke, fight, flirt with girls from Saint Ursula's and if nothing else was doing to torture the deer. I got to know the park and its crannies intimately (as a cross-country runner I must have run round it hundreds, if not thousands, of times). Long before the 3b crew threw sticks at the wildlife, aristocrats used to shoot them. In a hollow in the middle of the park there is an old dead oak tree with a plaque stating 'Queen Elizabeth took refreshment in this spot', which I interpreted as 'Queen Elizabeth had a piss here.'

At the top of a hill in the centre of the Park stands a marble statue of the eighteenth-century General Wolfe, who achieved the perfect imperial dream of dying young while overseeing a great victory, a lesser-known Lord Nelson. Here is one of London's grandest views. The eye glides easily over the masts of the old *Cutty Sark* boat, Queen Anne House, the Maritime Museum (best exhibit – Nelson's jacket bearing the bloodied hole left by the bullet that killed him at Trafalgar) to Wren's Royal Naval College and across the river to the Isle of Dogs where the horizon is now punctured by the looming towers of Canary Wharf. Next to the Wolfe statue, sharing this spectacular vista, stands the old Royal Observatory whose wall is adorned by the big brass clock that officially registers Greenwich Mean Time. This is, in a longitudinal cartographical sense, the centre of the world and there were always tourists having their photo taken standing astride the line marking the meridian, so that they might record the moment when they had one foot in both hemispheres.

Proximity to all the grand old monuments of Greenwich was reflected in various ways in the life of the school, most memorably in the stirring and bombastic school song which started:

'Here's to old John Roan who lived and worked and died,
In the mighty days of England, of Milton and of Blake.'

There was a clear suggestion here that Milton, Blake and John Roan hung out together – which seemed unlikely even to a humble first-year like myself who didn't really know who Milton and Blake were. The song continued rousingly, name-dropping astronomers, writers and admirals, none of whom had attended Roan but who, despite this evident handicap, 'gave the seas to England with continents beside'.

The last verse started portentously, sotto voce:

'Here's to those that come here after, the lads we shall not see,
The men of generations who will have new foes to fight.'

It rapidly advanced to the roared crescendo of the last line:

'Our Greenwich men are lighting new beacons in the night,
John ROAN's men the ROAN boys are building up the light!
Then to old JOHN ROAN, sing him loud, sing him clear,
SING HIM ROUND THE CONTINENTS, SING HIM
THROUGH THE YEAR!'

It was a much more dramatic tune than, say, the National
Anthem and I have continued to sing it ever since when the
moment is right; only last spring I met another Roan alumnus
and we boomed it together with more relish than his wife could
tolerate. We had to learn the song by heart in order to sing it at
the end of term and at Founder's Day. This event, which always
preceded an afternoon off, took place once a year at Saint Alfeges
church,* one of Hawksmoor's London masterpieces, though we
were less interested in the architectural features than in the girls
from our sister school across the aisle who were becoming ever
more interesting with every passing month.

I wonder if John Roan himself actually wished to be sung around
the continents and through the year? Is that the motive for philan-
thropy? I had similar reservations about God, who was one up
even from Mister Roan. I thought then, as I think now, that if
God, Jesus, the Holy Father, the Holy Spirit, the Almighty, the
Trinity, etc., etc. was the font of all wisdom and virtue, surely He
should not be such a big *show-off*. In assembly every song banged
on about how great He was, every prayer demanded several name
checks for the big guy. Can't the ceaseless praise at least be toned
down for weddings and funerals which celebrate specific people?

* More than thirty years after I left school, St Alfeges was the venue for the
best gig I have ever taken part in or attended (see Chapter 29).

My form master in the first year was the charismatic Alf Knott, an English teacher who was unconstrained by the material on the syllabus. We would read something Alf had selected (which was likely to be from whatever novel he was reading at the time) and discuss it for a few minutes until Alf was left ruminating alone – a situation that suited everyone. His musings would segue into a lengthy anecdote, rich with colourful detail, which meandered entertainingly but always came to a perfect ending moments before the bell went at the end of the lesson. He was proudly urbane, rubbishing country-dwellers with a scathing wit that set the form tables on a roar.

Most masters, I wrote in 'Facts about Myself', *are reasonable but most of them seem very slightly eccentric. Young ones wear gaudy ties and green shirts. Old ones walk around with cigarettes and pipes.*

Everyone's memory of school contains eccentric teachers; perhaps the profession breeds them, or maybe even the most ordinary person looks peculiar under the kind of prolonged scrutiny that teachers undergo in classrooms. Mister Witten, another English teacher, was the most prominent pipe-smoker and was duly nicknamed 'Shag'. Shag, who had taught at the school since the fall of the Roman Empire, was enthusiastic about poetry and read out chunks of Wordsworth. You knew when he was beginning to lose himself in the poem because he would unselfconsciously begin to pick his nose, first one nostril then the other, rolling the combined mass of snot into a ball as he continued his recital. When he arrived at the end he would examine his nasal excavation intently, gulp it down like a canapé and look up to return his attention to the class. He would decide halfway through a sentence that, since he was a teacher, he should be asking his pupils some questions. I recall the following exchange:

Shag: And you could find the answer to that in the *Encyclopedia Britannic . . . Britannic . . .* anyone?
Me: *Britannic . . .* 'a', sir.
Shag: Very good, Smith.

The economics teacher, 'Granny' Wood, may or may not have been a fantasist but he certainly had some tales to tell. Having been the reserve in the British hundred-metre squad in the 1936 Olympics, he became a member of the tank regiment during the War and displayed at home, so he said, a large jar of pickled fingers sliced off by the heavy lid on his tank. He had a showbiz dimension too; he had written the original script for the film *Zulu* (although, conveniently, he wasn't credited) and the BBC pronunciation unit often rang him to check on how to say words in Welsh.

Monsieur Briquet (translation: Mister Cigarette Lighter) was a French master who pleasingly fulfilled all the stereotypical requirements of a stage Frenchman; he had a heavy accent, wore eau de Cologne, chain-smoked cigarettes that smelled of dung and scandalised the school by arriving one morning in pink socks! Though I had never been to France (or any country outside England) it was clear from Mister Cigarette Lighter that they did things differently there.

Academically, I was good in the arts and in maths, competent in the other sciences, completely useless at carpentry and even worse at metalwork. I am not proud to say that I had no practical abilities at all and was frequently sent out of both woodwork and metalwork classes, not because I was badly behaved but because

I was a menace to myself and others. After two tears of toil in these disciplines I produced a small lopsided box decorated by unintentional smears of my own blood, and a candleholder that could hold no candle of any existing shape and which I deposited in a bin on the way home. In future I would need a strategy for the occasions on which I was confronted by needy inanimate objects. The best plan, I decided, was to persuade someone else to do this stuff for me – which aim I would achieve through charm, flattery, lovable displays of vulnerability and, these days, hard cash.

Richard was a little, but not much, better with his hands while Nicholas, if this is possible, was even *more* incompetent than I was. We might have inherited this ineptitude from our father, who happily described himself as a 'bodger'. When things went bump in the night in our house it usually turned out to be the sound of the shelves that Syd had put up during the day crashing to the floor. Once, when he was investigating the source of a faint gas smell around the house, he asked me how I thought we could confirm his theory that the leak came from the pipe to the fire. My studies in chemistry led me to suggest that we should light a match under the suspect area, an idea which seemed sensible to Syd. A small flame duly appeared and Syd successfully tightened the offending valve. We were both pretty pleased by this outcome but when my mother found out she blew her top at how close we had come to blowing the top of the house off.

Apart from the hours which revolved around the manipulation of wood or metal, I enjoyed school. The other pupils in my class, who now called me 'Arfur', numbered a handful of boys from ethnic minorities and all of us were from similar working-class backgrounds. The two tough guys in our year were Jim Roast, the school high-pissing champion, and Simon Church whose preferred hobby was kicking in bus shelters in his 'cherry reds', huge bulbous scarlet boots with steel toecaps from which he had removed the leather covering. One morning after assembly, the headmaster unexpectedly summoned Church onto the stage and enumerated his latest crimes, presumably with a view to shaming him into improved behaviour. It was a miscalculation; as Church stood at the front staring impassively out at us, his chest swollen with pride at the account of his assault on a bus shelter, he became an instant hero to every boy in the school. To complement their cherry reds, Roast and Church, as was fashionable among the emergent breed of skinhead, wore smart Crombic coats, Ben Sherman button-down shirts with braces, and a look that said, 'Do you want some?' I lived outside their circles and continued to go to school in my shorts. By the end of the first year there were only five of us still wearing them, a fact of which I was strangely proud. However, after a cold-kneed winter, I cast off another vestige of childhood and awkwardly pulled on my first long trousers.

In my second year at Roan I met the teacher who inspired me most. Nigel Ballantyne was a young English master, fresh from Cardiff University, who was full of enthusiasm for books, plays and cross-country running. He outlined to us a history of English poetry – revealing finally who Milton and Blake were – introduced us to the works of T. S. Eliot and encouraged me to indulge the pleasure that I found in writing and performing. Further literary and dramatic stimulation came from visits to the West End with my mother where we saw plays by Pinter, Stoppard and Beckett performed by famous actors like Ralph Richardson,

43

Peggy Ashcroft, Paul Schofield, John Gielgud and Maggie Smith. These grown-up evenings, when we got the train from Kidbrooke to Charing Cross and I walked for the first time up the Strand with my cap in my hand, or along Shaftesbury Avenue, left me giddy with big-city glamour. We went to plays at the new Greenwich Theatre where I saw Max Wall's one-man show. I felt an instinctive affinity with the pulse of live performance. In the diary I have kept sporadically throughout my life, the only schoolboy reference to a public death comes in April 1973 when I note that 'Noel Coward has gone and died. I didn't know much about him but he was obviously talented and always good for a bon mot.'

My desire, need even, to make a public spectacle of myself was given an outlet in school plays and revues. Junior boys played the female roles, and were sometimes alarmingly sexy – I still recall young David Scarbridge in high heels as a 'dolly bird' in some Pinter play. I was a flapper in the Christmas Revue but, despite being tall and slim, nay skinny, I made a hopeless female. I just did not *move* right. Striding onto the stage in my 1920s dress, cobbled up no doubt by my mother from some old curtains, I looked less like a dainty dancing girl than a gangling fourteen-year-old boy walking out to open the batting. However, I must have had some feminine allure because Alf Knott cast me as a French maid and former showgirl in the House Plays (the division of all boys into four different 'houses' was one of many homages that the grammar paid to the public school). Alf told me that, in order to walk like a woman, you need only remember to place one foot *directly* in front of the other. The review I got in the school magazine suggests this instruction had no effect:

B. Smith, although not having the undulating walk one would expect from an ex-member of the Folies Bergères, fainted well and was truly histrionic.

Fortunately, not long after this my voice broke and I did not play a woman again until fifteen years later, when I gave my Dame in pantomime at the Tivoli Gardens in Copenhagen.

Nigel Ballantyne helped direct the school plays and he also cheered me on in my attempts at writing. At the end of my childhood autobiography he had written:

Always interesting and intelligent, Smith. You are very observant and perceptive, not to mention honest. You can see into other people and yourself quite a bit – motives, feelings, thoughts. Cultivate this and allow it to become ever more developed; continue your writing. It's very interesting and well done, and should get even better in these and other respects as you grow older if you work at it and 'keep up the good work'.

Writing came naturally to me – like running or laughing. I tackled English composition with relish, entered and won essay competitions and, much later, helped Nigel edit the school magazine, taking the opportunity to publish my own poems, several of which I believe to have contained the word 'russet'. At the same time I followed once again in Richard's footsteps by editing the underground sixth-form magazine. But the publication which brought me most attention appeared when I was fourteen during my first spell as Arthur (or rather Arfur). *The Pirate* was a class magazine edited by myself and my mate Pud (also known, if his elder brother, the original Pud, was present, as Mini-Pud). My copy was never questioned except when Hazel, who typed it up onto the stencils, corrected the spelling or couldn't read my handwriting.

One copy of *The Pirate* has made its way into my archive. The cover, showing an impressive lack of interest in design, comprises the name of the publication above a skull and crossbones, both so pitifully rendered that I suspect I must have done them myself. Two typed sentences at the foot of the page concede defeat: 'Can you suggest a cover for *The Pirate*? YOU CAN WIN A PRIZE IF YOU DO', although it is not made clear anywhere what this prize might be. Inside are factual articles about stamps, sport, the War, chemistry and an account of how to make a barometer. Incongruously, since our readership was drawn exclusively from within the all-male school, there is a personal ad from an anonymous chap looking for a girlfriend, 'about 13–17, 5'2"–5'4", mousy hair, fairly good-looking.'

My own contributions were some breezy doggerel written under the name of Brian and, on the back page, 'the Arfur Corner' in which a schoolboy love of the pun rampaged across the paper:

'Good day . . . this is Arfur saying Hello, I'm first going to ask a question which you must answer. Why do you read this load of rubbish? Perhaps in pity of the fact that I'm to have a heart transplant. You see my heart keeps getting lost. Sometimes it's in my boots and once I found it in my mouth. But I'm not a heartless villain at least.'

'The Arfur club is blooming. Blooming useless . . .'

'My readers are invited to look up the word "oleo" in a Latin dictionary: "It will probably describe you." Even at this distance I remember that "oleo" means 'I smell'.'

The second half of the Arfur Corner is a more formal, humorous, and I suspect plagiarised, account of a football match, the end of which has been lopped off by an unappreciative paper guillotine.

These journalistic endeavours certainly gave me status in class and my celebrity was soon augmented when I wrote to the *Daily Mirror* about *The Pirate*, asking them to help out with our 'paper shortage'. I think I realised that they might pick up on the mag and that self-glory, rather than stationery, was the real motive behind my letter. Nevertheless, I was surprised when Pud and I were called out of a lesson and into the school office one day to take a phone call from a *Mirror* journalist telling us they wanted to write an article about *The Pirate*. The next day after school a perky reporter and a grizzled photographer turned up to meet us at Pud's house. We had our first experience of grown-up journalistic ways when the snapper asked me to stand on a couple of telephone directories to emphasise the difference in height between Pud and me. A couple of days later the piece appeared – a whole page, featuring a generous excerpt from the Arfur Corner and a big picture of me towering over a dwarfish-looking Pud, both of us beaming out from behind our thick black-rimmed National Health spectacles. A more sensible snap showed us posing pensively on a wall (see photo page four).

Although I had invited the attention, I found the ensuing brouhaha disconcerting and stressful. We got fan letters, requests for copies of *The Pirate*, two invitations to appear on the radio, a phone call from the *Times Educational Supplement* asking why we had not contacted *them* rather than the *Mirror*, and I even received an enquiry from a publisher. I did not feel ready for all this; the prospect of going in a car to central London to sit in a studio (or whatever happened) was especially terrifying, so Pud did it with another, less senior member of the editorial team. We sent the copies off, answered the letters and I batted the publisher back politely until he gave up. My schoolmates were surprised by my new-found modesty, but I knew that my boastfulness and apparent self-confidence were the carapace protecting an inner self-doubt, a conviction that I was essentially a lowly figure – like Syd, a lance corporal who doffed his cap to the officers, to the posh people who did not have a cockney accent. I would be intimidated in a radio interview with a grown-up. I could not be the laughing boy I was among my friends. Not long after the *Mirror* episode I abandoned the Arfur Corner while I was still at the top of my game and eventually Arfur, and Arthur, fell out of usage until my late twenties.

CHAPTER 5. SENIOR BOY

My father was eager to come and watch my début in the school under-fourteen cricket team but I was so fearful about how I might play that I forbade him. Syd was an excellent cricketer whom I had proudly watched hit fifties for the police; I did not want him to see his son fail – especially since I was using the bat he had given me, a slice of plump willow to which I had tenderly, and messily, applied coats of linseed oil all winter. But what relief! I batted well and made some runs. As I watched the ball running over the boundary from a leg-glance, I suddenly wished that my father *was* there after all. And then I noticed that the man emerging from behind a bush, sheepishly returning the ball, wore a familiar grin. It was Syd! We waved at each other, delighted. 'Great shot!' he shouted.

Syd was bemused by the academic aptitude of his boys and attributed it to Hazel's genes. In contrast, as regards sporting matters he was confident to the point of boastfulness. He would display the medals he had won for football, cricket and boxing, knowing, and pleased, that we would take the piss out of him for it. Every social function was improved by the presence of my father, who made people laugh and brought out their sunny side. He told jokes, anecdotes and war stories, but he was always interested in finding out about other people. In later years new guests had to be warned that Syd would likely interrogate them on arrival but they soon learned that he was not judgemental,

49

just curious. The phrase I associate most with him is the soft exclamation 'Good Gracious!'

Hazel, less socially confident, took a back seat to Syd on these occasions, harumphing indulgently at his forthright questions and fruity jokes while supplying the endless cups of tea that sustained him. My mother and I had frequent verbal clashes as I reached acned teenage stroppiness, and she once got in a mighty blow with a tin bowl, leaving it with a dent that can still be seen if you investigate the back of her cupboards. One of my beefs, now that I had declared myself a communist, was that we, with our new expensive table, had become incorrigibly bourgeois. Unsurprisingly, Hazel was irritated by my adolescent posing, going to extreme lengths to extract her revenge, as I noted in my diary: 'Mum gets very upset and does things like refusing to make me a cup of tea.'

My arrogance at this time, unsullied by any real experience, was boundless. I looked at the disastrous mess of the world and thought that these adults were dolts; if *I* ruled the world, instead of Harold Wilson, President Johnson or Harry Secombe, it was clear to me that everything would improve because *I* would treat everyone fairly and equally. In the sixth form my selfless idealism led to my volunteering to be a member of Task Force, an organisation that encouraged young people to help needy pensioners in practical ways. I spent weekends bodging away as an assistant decorator, although I was really more of an impediment than a helper After school, twice a week, I took an old man in a wheelchair round Greenwich Park. We didn't say much to each other, in my case because I could hardly breathe from the effort of pushing him up the hills.

Richard had done Task Force before me, as he did cross-country running, editing the sixth-form magazine, walking the Pennine Way and getting dumped by a female French pen friend.* To compete with him required that I do a lot, read a lot, engage with ideas and run round Greenwich Park ever faster. His braininess trumped mine but I had it over him on affability and knockabout humour, while my cover drive was far sweeter than his. It was Richard's determination, originality and evident ambition that helped me to envisage a life untroubled by the Institute of Quantity Surveyors, to imagine that I could go higher than a lance corporal. Richard was a remarkable person even then: academically gifted; a communist; a lover of art, music and experimental jazz; a painter, a novelist and a free thinker. He was also a member of the Scouts.

Except that Richard and his intellectual friends transformed the school Scout hut into a sort of Left Bank salon, which they decorated with a large mural of a pregnant man. It is a tribute to Derek ('Taff') Evans, Latin teacher and Scoutmaster that this was permitted. I too was a Scout, with Gary, but it became apparent that my military background and my long service in the bomb-site wars had not equipped me to be an obedient squaddie. I had little talent for knot-tying, bridge-building, or any of the practical aspects of scouting and I took no pride in my uniform — my woggle remained resolutely adrift. It was the running around, the hiking, the camping, the larking, the *boysiness* of Scouting that suited my nature.

Among my schoolboy friends I was at ease, extrovert — *flamboyant* even, but in the evenings I was a social zero. Vehemently

* Our exchanges were lively and promising until I sent her a photo of myself winning a cross-country race, after which she never wrote again.

opposed to the Vietnam War, I was too shy to go on the demonstrations with Richard and just too self-conscious to attend the youth club where Gary cut a swathe through the girls over the table-tennis bats. At fifteen, having lived with two brothers and attended an all-boys school, I had hardly spoken to a female who wasn't my mother for four years. It was the summer of love for my elders – for me it was the summer of staying in to wank and study cricket averages.

By now, of course, I was regularly 'polishing the bishop' or 'having one off the wrist', although on first discovering this brief but sensational pleasure I was confused. Hazel had already instructed Richard and myself on the peculiar mechanics of sexual intercourse but I wasn't sure if what *I* was doing was definitely related to it. Sometimes I would scribble down sexy scenarios and get turned on by my own writing before tearing it up and flushing it down the toilet, an activity which now strikes me as somewhat weird. Is this a metaphor for something? I certainly seemed to have learnt that Victorian suspicion of lust but, at the same time, I had also witnessed the glorious dawning of the miniskirt on the streets of London and found it to my taste. I have always been a leg man – my favourite sexy actress was not Brigitte Bardot or Sophia Loren but Una Stubbs and her fabulous pins as exhibited in the TV comedy *Till Death Us Do Part.* *

At junior school I had been chairman of the 'anti-girl club', distributing prizes to boys who had successfully skirmished with the enemy, but had otherwise cultivated a fine indifference to

* When I met Una years later I did not mention this, though she would not, I think, have minded if I had. Una is a doll.

everything feminine. As a hormonal teenager this position became untenable; these strange creatures called girls were mysterious, unfathomable and alien but absolutely desirable. They were unpredictable, seemed to be interested in hair and had high voices. Did they know what I wanted to do with them? Did *I* know?

Gary was neither a sportsman nor an eager participant in school life but he *had* been seen talking to a girl; indeed, he did not deny having *slept* with one. A question made its home in my brain and has never entirely disappeared: how can I persuade a female person to let me touch her? How can I manipulate her into willing intimacy? It was a trick I was keen to learn but when I found myself in places where girls too were gathered my traditional pose of pompous misogyny seemed not to impress. Further hindrances included my thick glasses, fuzzy white-boy Afro and beard of pimples. I have always appeared older than my age and never looked young, even when I was. In photos of myself as a child I already seem to have the wrinkles and sallow complexion of a twenty-a-day man.

Freud said that men go on stage for the love of beautiful women; I think that I would not have cultivated the skills that I did had I been good-looking and easy with the girls. Sexual repression fuelled me like it did the British Empire. Humiliating and frustrating at the time, rejection became a muse twenty years later, in my first play *Live Bed Show*, when I remembered being fifteen:

At the time I thought *Pride and Prejudice* was dead sexy. It was all foreplay, about *not* having sex – just like I wasn't. Well, I was, I suppose – with myself. Jane Austen supplemented by the underwear section of the Green Shield stamp catalogue. Mind you, I was so randy at the time that I could have got a hard-on reading train timetables. I didn't kiss a girl till I was seventeen. Hilary Graves. I finally persuaded Hilary Graves to let me kiss her. She had a harelip. It was fabulous.

Richard had entered the sexual fray with similar handicaps to me and although he impressed me mightily with the revelation that he had been thrown out of the Villiers Pub at Charing Cross for kissing a girl too vigorously, I don't think he was as adept with females as he was with theoretical physics. He could come over as unworldly. Rich, as I called him then, was my class prefect when I was in the fifth form and was renowned for having failed to notice Jim Roast beating up a boy at one end of the class because he was so engrossed in reading *The Mayor of Casterbridge* at the other end. Richard's determined intellectualism was a source of amusement to his more jocular friends, and the opening line of his diary which must, by now, run to several million words, runs, 'Will and Teef continue to persecute me . . .' This is not to say he had no sense of humour, merely that he lacked a talent for the frivolous. His high-mindedness was lampooned by his friends who gave him the ironic nickname of 'Happy', soon abbreviated to 'Hap'. In the school magazine I dug up for this book I see an article about IPHDIG – 'the Informal Philosophical Discussion Group'. The author is anonymous but even forty years on I can spot my brother's tone:

IPHDIG

After several disastrous setbacks the group has finally struggled to its feet and now has some ambitious plans. The first fiercely divided discussions were on 'The Ideal State', 'The

Value of Philosophy', 'Whether Man Has a Future' (with some going so far as to predict the end within thirty years), 'The Value of Emotions' and 'The Value of the Family'. Over the last issue the group crashed down as most of them had inbuilt beliefs on the subject which were shattered; and after furious argument, they all resigned, leaving only two members. These managed to re-establish the club, however, and now regular meetings are held to discuss such subjects as 'Are Ideologies Possible?' and 'The Analysis of Prejudice'.

In 1971 when Richard left school to go up to Edinburgh University, Nick arrived in the first year and I transformed from chippy younger brother into protective older brother, although Nick didn't need much protecting. My competitiveness with Richard was suspended but not forgotten. Me, Pud and fellow literato Dennis relaunched IPHDIG with a lighter touch, sending out a raft of speaking invitations to anyone we liked the look of, irrespective of their interest in philosophy. *NdA* We managed to attract to the Sixth Form Common Room local film star Glenda Jackson (whose dustbins I was destined to empty two year later), Terry Jones and Graham Chapman of the revered *Monty Python* team, and Doctor Martin Cole, a controversial sex educationalist who showed a film of a couple having sex, causing one blushing schoolboy to fall to the floor in a faint.

In the sixth form I tiptoed and then, finding the waters warm, plunged into a new social pool of parties and pubs, soon graduating from timid wallflower to winner of the Idiot Dancing Award at the school disco. I even began to feel (almost) relaxed in the company of (some) girls. Ah, those lengthy evenings canoodling with Mandy Lynch who kissed me with a no-tongues policy that made me feel as though my mouth was clamped to a toilet roll. Still hopelessly inexperienced, I complimented a girl who seemed to like me on her resemblance to Barbra Streisand, not realising that this, to her, sounded like 'You *have* got a big nose, haven't you?' It was an elementary error. I now know there is only one safe comparison in this situation: every woman, it seems, likes to be told she looks like Audrey Hepburn – even if she patently doesn't.

There was an opportunity to learn more about the other sex at the annual Sixth Form Conference whose theme that year was 'Will Women ever be Equal to Men?' Preparation for this entailed meeting girls from other schools and I got a terrible shock when I discovered that, incredible though it seemed, one of them – a redhead in her gran's old fur coat – seemed to be cleverer and more literate than me! Accordingly, I immediately fell in love with Barbara and contrived to sit next to her during the day of the Conference. One of the speakers was Rosie Boycott, then the editor of the new feminist magazine *Spare Rib*, who pointed out that all the most confident speakers from the floor were boys, implying that confidence did not equal wisdom. I expressed my own sexist views fluently, but, under Barbara's disapproving gaze, with an increasing lack of conviction. Equality by definition, I finally had to concede, means women being equal too.

My body, however, was not interested in feminist theory; it sought feminine flesh, although it could never find it in sufficient quantity. Barbara was elusive but I did not sit at home in a mope. Saturday nights would routinely find me in some South London backwater where, dispatched at a girl's garden gate with a thin kiss, I faced a five-mile walk home along the dull arteries of South London suburbia. It got worse; I was introduced to that miserable double act, Jealousy and Heartbreak, when Barbara ran off with a leather-clad biker in silver cowboy boots. Knocked off course by this unfamiliar wave of surging emotions, I recorded my eighteenth birthday in my diary with some sober reflections:

OH GOD I'M EIGHTEEN
OH GOD I CAN VOTE
OH GOD I CAN DRINK
OH GOD I CAN (a) LEAVE HOME
             (b) GET MARRIED
             (c) DO ANYTHING
             WITHOUT MY PARENTS' CONSENT
Oh ironic parody leave me to my Loneliness!

Nothingness!
Death!

Despite my moonings, I spoke vociferously in school debates and wrote a large chunk of the school revue in which I impersonated Mister Ballantyne so successfully that I have never since attempted to do another impression on stage. In the public-speaking competition I came second every year to Trevor Talbot, a boy who at fourteen already had the girth and figure of a country parson. Sporadically I receive a copy of the Roan Old Boys' magazine where, without fail, Talbot is to be seen, incrementally older and plumper, in a photo of the latest show from the Old Boys' Dramatic Society. Good on Trevor.

It was perhaps my oratorical skills that led to me being voted in (by the boys, not the teachers) as head boy in my last year, a job which required me to organise the different dinner-time sittings and not much else. I did, however, get to deliver my first public ad lib when the Chairman of the Governors introduced me on stage at Prize Day: 'And here is the head boy . . . er . . .' He consulted his notes and read out the first name he saw . . . 'Barry Weaver.' There were titters from the boys as I walked on. 'I should like to thank the Chairman of the Governors,' I responded, 'Mrs Doris Gladstone.' These days, on 31 December, I like to play a little game with myself, in which I nominate the best laugh I earned in the preceding year. In 1973 it was definitely Mrs Doris Gladstone.*

My last lesson at Roan Grammar School for Boys was an A-level history class with Mr White – inevitably known as 'Chalky' – an upright, magisterial figure who nevertheless had a twinkle in his patrician eye and an elegance unusual in a teacher. He made his concluding remarks about the nineteenth century while we took notes and then, with ten minutes to go to the bell, he stopped and said, 'Well, I've finished now. Good luck in your exams and I hope that after this you will still retain an interest in history. And now let us sit quietly for the last minutes of this lesson and of your school career and let us reflect . . .' And we did. Twelve teenage boys sat in silence on that June afternoon and wondered where we had been and where we were going. I never saw Chalky again but I have always, as he hoped, continued to read history books and I thank him now for that unexpected and beautiful lacuna at the end of my schoolboy days.

After my last A level paper I walked into the boating pond in Greenwich Park in a floppy hat and smoked a cigar. I was longing to cast aside my school uniform and take my place among the

---

* Doris, I expect, is an elderly friend of Daphne Fairfax.

great bohemians. And now I had my opportunity to enter a world of radical ideas, bright lights, outlandish clothes, dissolution and decadence . . .

I was going to live in Norfolk.

CHAPTER 6. THE EARLY AFRO

Every day during my time at Roan School I had walked past two large gilt-framed pictures which depicted the pretty old colleges of Oxford and Cambridge. It was not stated, but clearly understood, that to enter one of these famous old institutions was the highest aspiration a boy could have. Very few pupils from the school ever did (none in my year), and I had neither the desire nor, as it turned out, the A levels, to be an Oxbridge boy.

The University of East Anglia, founded in 1964 and given the marvellous resounding motto 'Do Different', is situated in green fields on the outskirts of Norwich, the city in Britain which is furthest from any other – and if that is not the case, well, it *feels* like it. It's an attractive older lady of a place with an above-average sublime cathedral, a square squat castle and a jolly, gregarious market. Norwich was once the second-largest city in Britain but that was a thousand years ago, and it has not moved on much since then. Syd drove me up and, although by now he owned a car that could make the journey without wheezing to a halt, as we left London we found ourselves at the back of a long procession of traction engines also trundling up the A11. There was a lot of time to talk but it didn't occur to me to ask how he and Hazel felt now that the second of their sons was leaving home. Perhaps it is hard-wired into eighteen-year-olds not to consider these things.* When Syd said goodbye we shook hands and, for once, I stood up straight and gripped his hand firmly as he had always told me to do.

The UEA campus looks like a series of variations on the National Theatre in London, which the architect Dennys Lasdun also designed – brutal, grey, angular. Having studied them in the brochure I had determined to love these buildings for their uncompromising modernity but seeing them now, in the concrete flesh, they looked austere and blank. I was to discover that when it is raining, as it mostly is in East Anglia, the breeze-block is eloquent in its sadness. Not that I cared much about the shape of the place; I was in a miniature city teeming with clever people of my own age. My room in Norfolk Terrace, one of the 'ziggurat' halls of residence which cut steps in the Norfolk skies, overlooked an expanse of grass, at the bottom of which flowed the river Yare. Across the water lay Bluebell Woods, as romantic as its name. But this was not a time for indulging the view – now was for birds, booze and books. On that first night of 'Freshers' Week', in a juvenile bid for the attention of female undergrads, I narrowly failed to kill myself on the bonnet of a speeding car as I took part in an unofficial attempt on the world record for the largest number of people in (and, in my case, on) a Mini.

New ideas were all around me. At the 'Societies Mart' I observed a woman hijacking a table and scrawling the words WOMEN'S

---

* It was only a few years ago I learnt that when Nick waved goodbye to our parents at St Alfred's College in Winchester, Hazel wept in the car all the way back to London.

LIBERATION on a large card. She was in her mid-twenties and blondely beautiful – an utterly terrifying combination. Of the various political parties touting for business – the International Marxists, the Socialist Workers, Fourth International, etc. – the most right-wing was the Communist Party. If there were any young Tories at UEA they certainly weren't going to admit it publicly.

Clubs acquiring my patronage included the Apathy Society (which refused to convene), the Film Club, the cross-country team and the Alan Whicker Soc, whose members got drunk and then impersonated the TV presenter. In that maiden term at university, wearing my new moustache, I met my first 'out' homosexual, my first feminist, my first Peruvian, my first public schoolboy and, most interestingly, my first public school*girl*. Annabelle, who had nearly killed me on my first night in her car, had an inflatable armchair in her room, owned her Mini, was two thousand pounds in debt and didn't seem to care. Two thousand pounds! That was half the amount that Syd and Hazel had paid for their house. A month after my arrival I made a prim diary entry:

Annabelle's friends from London are like nobody I've ever met. They all say 'darling', swear, wear mink coats, talk about 'going to Copenhagen for Christmas' and smoke huge amounts of dope. I was never really sure that people like this existed but they do, and it is repulsive their preoccupation with material affairs.

Oooo, get me. All the 'repulsive' posh girls I secretly fancied seemed to be in the School of Fine Arts and Music where it was once rumoured that Princess Anne was going to study. My degree was in Comparative Literature – a four-year course, the third year of which was to be spent in France. I was also doing a 'minor' in Linguistics, the hero of which subject was the American academic Noam Chomsky, whose name I had yet to associate with radical critiques of American politics. If I am asked now what Comparative Literature is, I reply that 'I spent the whole of my undergraduate days trying to work it out.' Then, if they persist, I cite the example of a seminar entitled 'Dante, Beckett and Eliot' in which we studied the different ways that Dante's apocalyptic poem *The Divine Comedy* had influenced and inspired the two modernists. 'Great art,' I explain, 'is not bound by time or place or culture – it is universal. Students who trawl chronologically through English Literature eat traditional fayre indeed . . .' and if I've got that far they've stopped listening. In my own less influential way I too have paid homage to Dante Alighieri; eighteen months after reading his lurid depictions of hell I co-wrote, and took part in, a show with friends I had yet to meet, called *SwingalongaDante*, and twenty-five years after this I performed a version of the *Inferno*, where Dante's escape from hell became my own account of giving up booze.

At all union discos I was first onto the dance floor, giving full rein to my Mick Jagger strut and my twitchy Gary Glitter look of startled excitement. And, finally, the long siege on my virginity reached a merciful end. It came not with a fellow student but with Barbara, my first crush, herself recently dumped by Silverboots. Barbara visited me for a weekend during my first term and was doubtless relieved to find that I was no longer infatuated with her and was therefore acting more like a normal human being. There was only a single bed, so drink and geography finally led to us to a not very satisfying encounter but at least, from my point of view, it took place. Now I could move on to those girls I *really* fancied. Poor Barbara. Looking at my diary entry for the two following days, I did not display much gratitude for her deliverance:

Sat Nov 24th

. . . in the evening went first to my trendy adviser's do. Barbara was not pleased when it took us an hour and a half to walk there. Anyhow I downed an impressive amount of wine, became very vociferous and started Arthur Horsefielding.* After this went to a party in the barn where I had lots of fun and danced with lots of girls + irritated Barbara who pissed off. Then I was in my kitchen making coffees that tasted of kippers and singing 'God Save the Queen' with lots of people whilst lying in a supermarket trolley.

Sun Nov 25th

I think Barbara's been quite impressed this weekend. I accompanied her to the A11 and left her to hitch.

I didn't see Barbara for a long time after this.

But a new Barbara, here-on-in known as Babs, entered my life soon after as a confidante and fellow entertainer. Babs, like me, had an appetite for the whole student experience and was present at the exhilarating high point of that autumn term. At an Extraordinary General Meeting of the Union a majority of those present resolved to occupy the university chaplaincy in order to

* Arthur Horsefield was a Charlton Athletic footballer and the chant went: 'A. R. T. . . . H. U. R. Arthur Horsefield Super Star!'

protest about our tiny grants and to overthrow the fascist regime in Chile. On the first night of the great occupation, having moved our bedding into the building (the chaplain, whoever he was, offered no resistance), we surged triumphantly into the square at the centre of the campus to find it snowing heavily. One of my fellow activists told me it was like the Russian proletarians running into the grounds of the Winter Palace in Saint Petersburg in 1917. Hurling snowballs at each other, we were intoxicated by our own youth and idealism. Although I knew in my heart of hearts that a strongly worded letter from the UEA Students Union was unlikely to topple General Pinochet, as we roared our slogans in the swirling blizzard I felt absolutely nineteen years old.

Not that I would have admitted it to any of my new friends, but I was also pathetically homesick at times. Theoretically opposed to the nuclear family, this conviction did not prevent me from missing my mum, dad, Nick, my school friends and even Richard. Some days I felt utterly dejected, a misery exacerbated by my falling in love with an unattainable posh girl from up the corridor. My outpourings of bad poetry filled up more and more pages and that nebulous existential angst that had come and gone since Paddy Moxom died did not abate; I stuck a quote from T. S. Eliot on the ceiling above my bed: 'Despair and disillusion are essential moments in the progress of the intellectual soul.'

At university, the sensible straight Brian who had never had a detention – the head boy, the chaser after street thieves, the 'Victor Ludorum' at school sports day, that Brian was in permanent dialogue with the unconventional unshaven Brian, who dressed like a hippie clown, sought to embrace all that was radical, occupied the chaplaincy and, despite failing to find any female adherents, advocated free love. I may have condemned the decadence of

Annabelle and her friends but I too experimented with hash and explored further my interest in public-school-educated women, 'a nice bit of posh from Burnham-on-Crouch', as Ian Dury sang. It was a penchant whose practice proved valuable in later years at the BBC where I like to bill myself as 'Radio 4's bit of rough'. Lowchurch Brian was not eclipsed – my essays went in on time, I wrote to my parents once a week while prudence and holiday jobs meant I did not get into debt during my first two years in higher education. *NdA** I turned up diligently for all my seminars and lectures plus any extra ones going (attending talks by, among others, Stephen Spender, Yevgeni Yevtushenko, Angus Wilson, A. J. Ayer and the World Frisbee Champion whose name I have forgotten).

There was much talk in the seminar rooms about literary theory, Marxist analysis, structuralism, Roland Barthes, sociolinguistics, formalism, semiology, transformational-generative grammar, syntagms and paradigms. Feeling as yet unqualified to form my own views on the best way to approach literature, I lapped up these ideas and regurgitated them in dull prose that got me decent but not brilliant marks. At the bottom of one of them a lecturer wrote 'always on the point of being something really good, this never quite made it', a remark that has nagged at me ever since.

The lecturers were often only a few years older than we students but their knowledge and worldliness seemed hugely greater than my own. The 1960s had carried on into the late 1970s in Norwich and one or two of my teachers were the kind of radical bohemian fictionalised as philandering Marxist Howard Kirk in Malcolm

* I am already tired of the *NdA* joke and now pronounce it dead.

Bradbury's novel *The History Man*. To me, these guys seemed effortlessly cool. Bradbury* was the big star at UEA. Famous for his novels, he was also an eminent academic and an inspiring teacher who had bravely imported the American idea of teaching creative writing into Britain. There had only been one student in the first year of the course but the principle behind it drew a great deal of criticism, criticism that abated somewhat when the student in question wrote his first novel and turned out to be Ian McEwan.**

My Wikipedia entry is wrong to state that I took the creative writing course at UEA – it was for postgraduates – but the system was arranged such that even as an undergraduate you could sometimes submit a piece of creative work in lieu of an essay. So instead of writing about futurism I wrote a parody of a futurist manifesto, while my essay on the form of the sonnet took the form of a sonnet. There was a student doing the writing course on my block who sat up all night trying to find words to describe

---

* Some twenty years after I left UEA I did a radio programme with Malcolm Bradbury in which I took him to Indiana University where he had been a young lecturer teaching freshmen and women (fresh women?) not very fine points of grammar. He was returning to see all his papers being archived, which I think he found a rather disturbing experience. Who wouldn't? He was charming, raffish, articulate and great company, reminiscing about the founder of the Kinsey Institute (of sexual studies) lecturing with his flies undone and the unimaginable luxury that America represented to a threadbare lecturer from austere post-war Britain.

** I interviewed Ian McEwan too, walking in the hills near Hay-on-Wye for a Radio 4 programme. I wanted to say, 'There's a lot of writing about walking in your books.' However, the question sounded rather lame as I spoke it and I faltered 'There's a lot of writing . . . in your books.' Oh dear.

the changing light. I heard later that he had become the editor of *Motorcycle News.*

Throughout my first year I continued to try things out, like crème de menthe, Acapulco Gold and contemporary dance classes, where I was intimidated to find I was the only dancer who owned a penis and had no leggings. Babs could not persuade me to return. I tried basketball but was barged off the pitch for ever by big American exchange students. I took part as a Roundhead in a recreation of a Civil War battle but, following several whacks on the head from over-zealous Cavaliers and with the bomb-site and the Scouts behind me, I discharged myself for ever from the military. The Poetry Society, of which I eventually became the president, was a more cerebral affair. Members would gather nervously in someone's room and take it in turns to recite poems by Blake, the Beat Poets, the Liverpool Poets, Sylvia Plath or a 'MacSpaunday' (MacNeice, Spender, Auden) until someone plucked up the courage to read out 'one of my own'.

Once the first brave poet had tested the waters, it wasn't long before previously meek girls started elbowing each other aside to deliver their own earnest doggerel and there was one Poetry Soc member whose readings would cast us all into despair, not because his poems were incomprehensible – a perfectly accept-able defect – but because they were so grindingly *long*. I was not alone in spending most of his monotone recitals staring at the pages he was reading from, trying to estimate how many remained. The evenings could drag; I began to modify my style to suit an audience and organised a public reading in the square pond in the centre of the campus (see photo page seven). One of the students in the Poetry Society was Marion – enigmatic Marion with the puzzled eyes, the little-girl voice, the bobbed hair and the slim frame that supported unexpectedly large breasts. Mysterious Marion, who kissed me momentarily, but with real passion, after a poetry evening in the Adam and Eve pub by Norwich Cathedral.

On 24 January my diary records getting pissed with her in a student bar:

What a gal! Lesbianism, troilism, prostitution, she seems to have indulged in them all – but not tonight.

On 1 February she is finally alone in my room:

I leapt on her and assumed that this was going to be it. But she suddenly said, 'Actually I'm a virgin.' In the light of all her previous statements I was flabbergasted.

O gormless young man.

After spending my first student summer as a dustman and on an inter-railing trip round Europe, I returned to Norwich in October tanned and homeless. Finding a room seemed impossible. Why did the city landlords discriminate against students? The phrase 'no-brainer' had yet to be coined. We worked ourselves into an indignant lather over this at yet another Extraordinary General Meeting which ended with a rousing resolution that a Union-backed squat should take possession of the Pineapple Hotel, a large disused pub out on the ring road on the other side of Norwich.

Hooray for the Union! Victory to the Grants Campaign! And

who wants to volunteer to go there now, break in and start the squat? ME! ME! As I took the applause I looked round to see there was only one other candidate for this heroic venture, a mumbling Stalinist ('Tankie', as he was possibly known) whom I had taken to avoiding, a strategy that was now going to be very hard to enact. Tankie and I gathered some belongings and walked across Norwich. My fervour for the enterprise was already dissipating by the time I lay on the filthy floor in one of the dozen rooms in this dark, decrepit place. It seemed not to have been open since the Second World War – no light, no heat, no hot water and, next morning, no cold water either. It was real hard being a revolutionary.

The first thing that Tankie and I had done on arrival had been to pin a notice on the door announcing that we had taken 'temporary possession of this building to provide accommodation for homeless students, an action endorsed by the University of East Anglia Students Union.' Returning in the evening, I saw our grand statement squashed into the mud in the front garden. Around it, strewn aggressively, lay our clothes and personal effects, looking even more pathetic than they already were. The door bristled with a new sturdy padlock and a peremptory note from the Norfolk Police which seemed not to acknowledge the mighty authority of the Student Union. No doubt Ché Guevara, whose book bore the title I loved the most – *Reminiscences of the Cuban Revolutionary War* – no doubt Ché would have taken the fight to the police, recruited local farmers to the cause, set up a camp in Swaffham . . . but not I. I chose instead to gather my meagre belongings and slink off into the night, dirty pants trailing behind me. Hooray for the Union. But not as much as before – and bollocks to Tankie.

After a couple of frozen weeks camping in Bluebell Woods, I found a cheap room in a house in Norwich with Barney and his wife. Barney was a builder who loved his job so much that when he came home he carried on building – which meant the place was constantly alive with drilling and banging, and every month or so a new extension materialised. One winter morning, after Barney had been up very early, I entered the bathroom to find it even colder than usual. Like Dante, as he escapes the hell at the centre of the Earth, I looked up to see the stars – Barney had removed the roof during the night.

I loved my little room, its strange aroma – musty *and* homely – its ordinary window, flowery curtains and boring view. It reminded me of Philip Larkin's exquisite, dismal poem, 'Mister Bleaney': 'Bed, upright chair, sixty-watt bulb, no hook.' Barney's gaff was a *real* house, not student accommodation where people came knocking without an appointment, and it acted as a cocoon, a kind of sanctuary from the crazed youthfulness of campus. One afternoon in Norwich, in a moment of uncharacteristic extravagance, I bought an old television for a pound. Young people imagine that TVs now are bigger than they were, but in fact only the screens have expanded. My quid telly had a tiny square screen set in the bulk of an enormous wardrobe-sized cabinet. It weighed several tons, was far too big to get on the bus and it took me and three passing friends two hours to manhandle the monster the half-mile between the shop and my room. After I had killed my helpers and stuffed their bodies under the stairs I turned my attention to the first television I had ever owned. I switched on and had a bath while I waited for the set to warm up. I was out and nearly dry by the time an image had formed.

It was black and white, of course, with rather too much black but you could make out a picture. Living in a tent and on campus, I had lost touch with the outside world and so it was with as much surprise as delight that I saw that I had tuned in at the start of a football match between England and Scotland. Excellent. We beat the Scots by some ridiculous score like 9–2. Better. The second programme managed to surpass even that: lying on the thin mattress that protected me from the iron bedstead, my feet protruding into the hallway, I watched Muhammad Ali take on World Champion Joe Frazier in an amazing comeback bout. When the fight was over and Ali had won, I stretched back and reflected that if I never saw another thing on my ancient TV it would still have been money well spent. As if to test this mental assertion, my huge old machine chose this moment to sigh gently and expire.

One drizzling Sunday, when Barney and his wife were away, I spent the day alone reading *The Glass Bead Game* by Herman Hesse. As I went to sleep that night, I realised the only words I had spoken in the previous twenty-four hours had been 'Chicken chow mein, please.' It was a day of solitude and silence and yet it is one of the most intense memories I have of being a student – lying quietly in my humble little room, drinking tea and reading. I was, as is evident in this book, prone to romanticising my life, casting myself in a variety of heroic artistic roles – the freedom fighter, the spurned lover, the showman, the poet, the midnight rambler. My silent Sunday became, in my mind, the brave hermitage of a wise and studious monk.

The friends I made in my undergraduate days are friends still. Phil, for example, I had met towards the end of my first year, when we both had small parts in the Rag Revue, an annual comedy show presented in the main hall of the campus where, more commonly, big-name bands played or EGMs were held. The show opened with the entire cast Tiller Girl-ing clumsily across the stage, while singing witty new lyrics to the tune of 'There is Nothing Like a Dame', e.g. "There's not a thing that's wrong with any man here/Apart from the fact that we're all . . . students." Happily, this is the only couplet I can recall, but I remember the hit of the evening was Phil's vicar sketch. Phil, from a Methodist family in Basildon, Essex, and with a naturally quirky imagination, has a talent for downtrodden small-town characters. 'I'm very unlucky,' he intoned, 'I peeled a banana the other day. It was empty.' We made each other laugh and began a friendship that will end when one of us dies.

It was Phil who introduced me to Adam, who is not as other men. In an era when standard male-student hair was two foot long, unkempt and greasy, Adam's neat short back and sides was outrageous – even more ridiculously, at all times, beneath his short-sleeved cricket jumper, he wore a shirt and tie! Adam was a tornado of energy, rapidly finding positions in the Drama Society and Nexus, the student TV station (an unusual facility now as then) and he soon made a name for himself as a director, gifted magician and flamboyant man-about-campus. When not cruising Norwich on Daphne, his scooter, he was to be seen roller skating around the university, sometimes with his arm clad in plaster and a sling to verify the broken limb that had prevented him handing in an essay.

Adam was the owner of an extraordinary laugh, a peal of un-expectedly loud goose-like honks and snorts, so ridiculous that people imagined it was affected. As the man who tried to get him to reproduce it for comic effect, I can testify that he cannot do it to order and conclude that this really *is* his natural laugh. Were I to make a soundtrack of my life, somewhere within it would be Adam's ludicrous, life-affirming klaxon-honk. He had been head boy at a public school in Cambridge but was an academic in the same way that I was a ballet dancer. His degree was in something like Norwegian Art with a minor in Basket-weaving but he arranged his timetable and his 'injuries' so that his studies, if any existed, didn't distract Adam from the various shows he put on, or appeared in, at university. He had a visual flair and a keen awareness of the physical possibilities of perform-ance; he was practical, organised, determined, danced well, crooned like Bing Crosby and owned a dressing-up box that, unlike himself, seemed to have no bottom. He could balloon-model, saw people in half and claimed, plausibly, to have taught Princess Anne to yodel. You may imagine from this description that he came in epicene form, but Adam was like a stocky bulldog and had been a judo champion. Phil and I could hardly compete with him in most areas but we possessed two skills that he lacked – an ability to write new material and a sensibility that did not date from three decades earlier. Adam's large and interesting record collection featured only one album recorded by a living artist.

During that summer term Adam, Babs, Phil and I began to write and rehearse for the end-of-year revue which we had taken over in a bloodless coup. I gave little thought to my forthcoming year in France, but I filled in a form applying to be an English assistant in a French school in . . . in where? Paris, apparently, was an impossibility. During the previous summer, on my inter-rail trip, I had spent three happy days walking in the Pyrenees. 'Oh, for a beakerful of the warm South.' Yes, south – I'll go south. I wrote down 'Montpelier' and forgot about it.

The title we chose for this show reflected all three of us: '*SwingalongaDante,*' the unbeatable combination of Dante Alighieri and Max Bygraves. I now met Carpenter, a *soi-disant* 'West London Formalist' who sang Dietrich's 'Falling In Love Again', while draping his bulky frame over a piano and pouting like a lipstick navvy. We did three performances, the last to an audience of two hundred and fifty who stayed boisterous throughout the two-hour marathon. Hundreds of forgotten reviews later, I still recall that the *Eastern Daily Press* described my 'Cricket Strip' as 'the hit of the night'. Coming on as a cricketer preparing to bowl, I removed my jumper, handed it to Adam, the inscrutable umpire, and then, as I took off another jumper, the 'Stripper' music struck up and I danced around in a provocative fashion while peeling off several more sweaters and a couple of pairs of white trousers. Adam, his expression unchanged, swathed himself in the surplus kit. On the second night I received a heckle that I have never had since: 'You've got a hard-on!' When the music ended, and I twirled my nipple tassles,* I stood in only a jockstrap baiting the drunken audience, who were now baying for total nudity. The jockstrap *was* removed, but only in the blackout. Naturally, in the last show, the lights did not go off but my jockstrap did, and, lo, it was a third showbiz flash, to add to my streak across the campus earlier in the term and

* Using my fingers to hold them – well, I *am* a bloke. A stripper – sorry 'burlesque dancer' – friend from New York tells me, in some detail, just how difficult nipple-tassle spinning is; copies of this email are available on request.

75

my threepenny display for the two girls at Southwark Park Primary School ten years earlier.

As a former opening bat for *Grumpy Old Men,* it is my duty to look down contemptuously on young people's pathetic desire to be famous, to be a 'celebrity'; however, my diary entry following the first night of our student revue unmasks my hypocrisy.

I loved being a big celebrity.

And now I could see a way of becoming one:

Several of us had the idea of trying to form a travelling revue group in two years after we'd done our degrees and also doing something at the Edinburgh Festival – probably will come to nothing but it's an exciting idea.

SwingalongaDante was a suitable finale to my second year as a student and my ego glistened prettily in the June sun. But on the Monday after the last day of term, I reported again to the Greenwich Borough Council depot in Eltham for another two months on the dust – eight weeks of heavy lifting, sopping sweat and the fine discomfort you feel when maggots are wriggling down the back of your shirt. And, since I did it for three summers in a row and since I still wish to hint at my sexy rough edges, there follows an account of the life of the student council worker.

The era of the black bin bag was only just dawning and we dustmen had to empty the contents of several bins into our own personal aluminium receptacle which we then poured into the grinding jaws of the dustcart. The regular blokes, toughened by years of humping rubbish and knowing every individual bin of the route, set a formidable pace. If I could not keep up I was making them finish later and I often found myself gritting my teeth as I chased the lorry up the road with my heavy metal skip-bin. As soon as I learned some of the idiosyncrasies of a round I would be moved on to another one and had to start from scratch again; one way or another I did a lot of scratching that summer. Falling behind the lorry intensified the resentment that some of the regulars felt towards we temporary workers. Most of us were students, after all, and thus liable to reappear in coming years in the cushy office jobs, handing out orders to them. But the binmen gave you a chance to prove you were not a wanker, especially if the gang had got ahead of the game so well that you all went and had a long session in the pub on Friday afternoon.

 Toiling on the dust was a filthy business, but had its compensations. Wet, stinking and strong – I felt like I was a proper working man. If dogs snapped at us, we snarled back and gave them a kick. I condescended to my feeble friends doing mimsy office jobs, while my Marxist rhetoric now came stamped with a proletarian authenticity. As we drove back to the depot at the end of the day we stood on the tail-plate, clinging to the side of the lorry and posing jauntily. Although I could hear my women's-lib friends' snorts of disapproval, I joined in the good-natured wolf-whistling directed indiscriminately at every woman under the age of seventy. There were financial perks too – 'totting' was the ancient art of flogging off bits of metal and scrap that people were throwing out. Although only the regular gang got the totting money, I was given a share of the cash we made from disposing of people's supplementary oversized rubbish.

The binmen were top dogs at the depot and looked down on the road sweepers, but, although you finished two hours later,

I was always pleased to be put on sweeping for the day. My favourite route ran across Blackheath where me and my chariot crossed the path I had taken to school two years earlier as a tight-arsed prefect. I would stop at this intersection and eat my sandwiches while lying on the warm grass and gazing at the sky. Once when my mother, now the school secretary at Roan, was walking home across the common she found me asleep in the sun next to my cart. The job was not as physically demanding or as smelly as the bins and although I could be visited at random by the supervisor, I was largely alone and independent. King of the Road.

There were other council jobs, the most coveted of which was 'Extra Furn', council-speak for house clearance, a job that invariably took less time than was allowed for it, such that I could be home for the afternoon session of the test match. 'Ratting' sounds bad but was as cushy as Extra Furn since one merely had to go round the borough tipping poison down drains. The toughest job of all was 'paving'. As the lowliest figure in the team, with no skill in laying the concrete rectangles, I had to manhandle them from off the back of the lorry – work that even the big muscly blokes found demanding. The recompense was that, during the lunch hour, the pavers could nip off and crazy-pave someone's garden for cash, using the stones that got broken during council hours and, if need be, some that 'got broken' during council hours.

Towards the end of my summer of garbage and stones, before I set off hitch-hiking round America with two friends for six weeks, I got a letter telling me how, and where, I would spend the next academic year. My application to be an English assistant had been successful and the school to which I had been assigned was not in Montpelier but in the city I had been told I'd never get: Paris. Paris! The year lay out before me and shouted me on. On the flight back from the States I was already picturing myself loping through the Latin Quarter, en route to a glass of red wine and a philosophical debate with a mademoiselle. Yes, that was what I'd be – an intellectual, an existentialist, a poet, a lover, a South London boulevardier in this most grand and elegant city of artists.

Alors, j'arrive en France.

CHAPTER 7. MONSIEUR SMEEZ

Napoleon was the first person to moot the idea of a tunnel connecting England and France beneath the Channel but in September 1975 it was still at the committee stage so I took the overnight train/ferry/train from London to Paris. This journey, with its gettings-on-and-off in the middle of the night, delivered me up at the Gare du Nord tired, depressed and nauseous. It was a fresh Monday morning when I arrived and the streets teemed with smart urbanites walking purposefully along the boulevards, exuding an air of certainty that I could not match.

I found my way across Paris to the *Cité Universitaire,* a campus housing a thousand students from over a hundred different countries in its curious array of buildings. Each of the forty 'maisons' is designed to reflect the country whose students it accommodates. The most glamorous of these is *le Pavilion Suisse* designed by Le Corbusier, the least the *Collège Franco-Britannique* where I was booked to stay. Squat and uninspired, it looked, and felt, like a gloomy provincial public school. At reception I filled in the first of dozens of forms I would be given all round Paris in the coming weeks. As I picked up my bags I learned that I would, after all, be sharing a room. Oh bollocks. Still, at least I had requested to share, if share I must, with a French-speaker. I was determined, during my Parisian interlude, to get my language skills up to the standard of the other students in my French seminars at UEA. The best way to do this, I reasoned, would be to buy a notebook, and fill it during time spent with French people – preferably French females with whom I could also have sex. I did not expect a female cohabitee but I did want a French one.

– Bonjours, je m'appelle Brian.

– Et moi, Jean.

– Vous êtes d'où, Jean?

– Je suis d'Oxford.

– Oxford, Angleterre?

– Bien sûr. Et vous?

– Hello John, I'm English.

– Oh, me too.

The room was small and dingy, John was tall and posh. In so far as there was a best bed, John had it. I unpacked and strolled through the rainy grounds, overawed by this big new foreign city and all this stuff I needed to assimilate. My diary that day declares:

Man, I'm depressed. I feel like the last person on Earth.

The Lycée Janson de Sailly lies in the 16th Arrondissement, the wealthy swathe of Paris between the Trocadéro and the Arc de Triomphe. Its pupils, the sons and daughters of the *haute-bourgeoisie*, included several with famous surnames. My excitement on learning that I would be teaching a Tolstoy turned into open-mouthed shock when Monsieur Lavaud, the avuncular head of English, told me that later in the year I would have the son of President Giscard d'Estaing in one of my classes! Good gracious. My duties as an assistant, I had been led to believe, involved supporting the proper teacher by reading texts out, talking about the British way of life and generally being a live and visible *rosbif*. However, I soon learnt that the English teachers to whom I was assigned saw me rather more as an opportunity to put their feet up in the staffroom for an hour. I was thrust alone into classes of thirty to forty teenage Parisians who, unable to say 'Smith', referred to me as *'Monsieur Smeez'*.* Although I had taken a one-term course in the theory of teaching English as a foreign language, I had very little experience to back up my flimsy notions and manufactured chutzpah. The pupils under my care had the same view of me as their teachers; I was an hour off from normality, as I have been for people many times since. Lessons could be unruly but, *au fond de bout,* we all got on fine – I was, after all, closer in age to *them* than I was to my colleagues on the staff, none of whom could boast an Afro haircut or a Greenwich Borough Council donkey jacket.

This is how to speak English to foreigners. Be clear; use simple grammatical structures; avoid idioms, difficult words and, especially, phrasal verbs. English phrasal verbs (as you obviously know) are usually made of a simple verb, e.g. 'make', with an added preposition like 'up'. These tricky little bastards can usually mean at least two things, as in: 'I made up my mind to make up a story while she made up her face.' Change the preposition and you open up (NB) another plethora of meanings. 'I made out that I needed to think while she made out the small print of an application I had been making out. She had finished her make-up so

---

* If you have a tame Frenchman at home, get him to try and say 'Smith's crisps' and sit back and laugh.

we made up and then made out on the carpet while the maid was out.' And that's enough phrasal verbs.*

I liked to wind my pupils up some mornings by writing something provocative on the blackboard as soon as I arrived. When I scrawled 'English food is the best in the world', I learnt that the French word for 'Eurgh!' is 'Beark!' The English, my students informed me, put jam on their meat and loved baked (pronounced to rhyme with 'smackhead') beans. We are also inveterate gobblers of 'la gelée', by which they meant fruit jelly, a dish abhorrent and comical to any right-thinking Parisian. Feeling an obligation to my nationality, I determined to defend the kiddies favourite party dessert and persuaded my mother to send me some packets, which I prepared and took to school. I'm afraid that the nephew of the President (oh yes – him too), the great-grandson of Tolstoy – the genial Dimitri** – Bruno, a fogeyish sixteen-year-old who took me under his young wing, and all the other kids were unanimous in their contempt for English jelly. My pedagogic initiative earned me only a telling-off from the school cleaner and a messy hour spent scraping morsels of wobbly phosphorescence from the walls of the classroom.

These kids' stereotypical Englishman was reserved, polite – the French for a gentleman is '*un gentleman*' – ate bad food dispensed '*le fairplay*' and, *pace* certain textbooks, lived in thick fog in a world of bowler hats, umbrellas, friendly 'bobbies' and double-decker

---

*Oh go on with me – I'm finding it hard to turn off. 'I turned on the telly where the lady was so sexy that I found she had turned me on. At this point the lady doing her make-up turned on me and turned me out into the street. I turned out my pockets – nothing. Never mind, though, because it turned out the sun was shining.'

** I can't remember now if that was his first name – but Dimitri will do.

red buses. The boys and girls of my classes seemed to have no trouble squaring this image with the groovy English bands they loved, the violent Leeds football fans who had smashed up Paris the previous summer or, come to that, *Monsieur Smeez,* the scruffy extravert who taught them English and jelly. Perhaps they learned the trick of paradox in the philosophy classes that all French school children are obliged to take. One of the first teachers I met told me, when I asked him what he taught, '*Je crois je suis prof de philosophie.*'

This encounter with French wit took place in the *Réfectoire des Profs,* the staff refectory, which served the best food I had ever tasted. The regular three-course meals in this humble canteen featured dishes I had never heard of: artichokes, *hachis parmentier,* avocados, crème brûlée, *blanquette-de-veau.* Every day featured some scrumptious combination of foodstuffs one did not find on the menu in Captain America's Burger Bar in Norwich. Most amazing to me, though, was not the food but the fact that *they served wine with it! And not just one glass, as much as you wanted! For no extra money!* Having come from the land of undergraduate parties, where a bottle of wine was as rare as a student in a suit, it seemed like I had pitched up in a boozer's paradise.

Unable to muster the restraint exhibited by the real teachers, who mixed one or two glasses of red wine with water, I ended up half-pissed every afternoon for two weeks, until it finally dawned on me that wine would definitely be available every day, so I need not neck it desperately before they realised their mistake. Stationed at the bottom of the pay scale, I got these revelatory meals at the subsidised price of two francs. As far as I was concerned, my wage was extremely generous – nearly twice as much as on the bins – and I only had to teach twelve hours a week, spread across four days. There was a dissertation to write in French by the end of the year and I signed up for a weekly language session at the British Institute, but I still had a good deal of time to myself and one of the great cities of the world.

After some failed attempts to find alternative accommodation, I resigned myself to a term at the *Collège F-B* and developed a workable rapport with my room-mate by keeping all my mess to one side of a chalk line drawn down the centre of the floor between our beds. I chummed up with fellow Brits in the *Collège*, and met Lindsay, a large, loud, bullish, intellectual Scotsman who was doing a Ph.D. on Flaubert. Lindsay introduced me to Kasbih and Hassan, two Moroccan friends who prepared fabulous chicken and mind-bending smokes. There was not much incentive to stay in my room, since John was always there and we were never destined to be friends. I went out, out, out in the way that is only really possible in your early twenties, attending films, concerts, plays, lectures, galleries, frequently with Lindsay who considered himself too cool for the tourist sites which I visited alone.

And I walked, walked, walked with all the zest of my days running errands for Lily. It was six years before I could afford my first taxi ride so, if I missed the last metro, I would stride five miles home, checking my route on each passing metro map. I was a modern-day *flâneur* – like Baudelaire, the observer in the shadows, drifting in and out of the crowd and always moving on. Within a few weeks I knew Paris better than London, while my French, now undergoing daily workouts, began to improve to the extent that I was sometimes mistaken for a Belgian. When speaking English I used French phrases with a self-important flourish – an irritating habit which I still indulge. The form-filling finally ended and I started to feel more and more *a l'aise dans mon assiette*. And then – *quelle joie!* – I got a date with a French girl.

Waiting for a woman to turn up, or not turn up, was something I had done often and was due to do many times more. I was ever-prone to making assignations with females at drunken parties for the following day. However keen they might be at two a.m. they were seldom so enthusiastic (and nor was I) on the hung-over afternoon – that is, if they remembered, or bothered, to turn up at all. But this was a bona-fide rendezvous, arranged in sobriety at a seemly hour. And so it was that I stood by the flame of the Eternal Soldier at the foot of the Arc de Triomphe at eight p.m. on a Friday night, three weeks after my arrival in Paris. In hope and expectation, I preened myself: blue jeans, one of Syd's old police shirts and my donkey jacket, now topped by a jaunty red scarf bought from a stall on the Boulevard St Michel. Fifteen minutes went by. And another five . . .

There is a tipping point in waiting for a woman after which you think, on balance, she is likely to be a no-show. At this point my classical technique went:

1. Consider some exciting things I could now do on my own.
2. Rubbish the memory of the woman.

If this mental exercise went well, after thirty minutes I was beginning to hope she might not appear and at forty I would bowl off, happily unencumbered, into my bold new scheme. But, on this occasion, I couldn't pull the trick off. I *wanted* her to come and I couldn't pretend to myself that I didn't. My confident anticipation soon descended into moping and self-pity. Poor old *Monsieur Smeez*, all on his lonesome in Paris. After forty-five minutes I zigzagged through the hectic traffic, remembering not to look to my left, and slouched toward the métro Avenue Kléber.

– Where are you going? she asked, materialising into the November night, just as I was poised at the top of the escalator.

– Oh hello, I was just leaving.

We performed the standard Parisian greeting – an excessive two kisses on each cheek. We spoke in French.

– I'm sorry. Did you think I had presented you with a rabbit?

– Pardon?

– You thought I was giving you a rabbit?

Gosh, she was strange.

It transpired that the French for 'she stood me up' is *'elle m'a posé un lapin.'* She hadn't posed me a rabbit. She was an hour late. We laughed at the confusion and, henceforth, whenever I mentioned her to Lindsay, who was becoming a confidant, I referred to her as *'la Lapine'*. *La Lapine* and I went to a café and talked. She was eighteen, in her first year at the Sorbonne and came from a grand family in the 16th Arrondissement, grand enough that her surname started with a *'de'*. As we chatted, I periodically jotted down in my notebook things she had said – not because they were profound or funny, but because they were French idioms, words or structures that were new to me. At the end of the evening a dozen or more notes appeared under *'poser un lapin'*. On the Monday following my date with *la Lapine*, I learned that Bruno had spotted us in the street. His question to me went straight into my notebook. *'Eh, Monsieur Smeez, est-ce que tu t'es trempé ton biscuit?'* No, Bruno, I did not dip my biscuit. It was to be a while before my biscuit saw any action, and when it did finally get dunked it was not courtesy of *la Lapine* but with a passing Dutch girl from the *Cité Universitaire.*

It was Bruno who reminded me that I had a London accent when I was remarking to him that whereas '*le cake*' refers to an expensive pastry in France, the equivalent in England is a '*gâteau*'.

– I like kike, Bruno announced.

– You mean 'cake'?

– Yes, kike.

Ah, I understood. He heard my London '*a*' as '*i*'. It was the same problem when one of the French English teachers had talked about a tape, adding sniffily, 'or as you call it, "type".' Years later Ned Sherrin liked to introduce me as the man who taught the son of the President of France to speak English with a cockney accent. Henceforth I adjusted my '*a*'s to make them a little more RP and noted that, even in French, my accent could be an issue. Rarely, though. One of the pleasurable aspects of living in a foreign city is that no one knows your background. When speaking French my nationality was evident but my class was not. As a teacher in one of the most famous lycées in France, situated in the '*quartier chic*', the Parisians I met assumed I must be from a much more bourgeois background than is found in Bermondsey or Kidbrooke.

Syd had spent his twenty-first birthday as a prisoner of war in Germany; mine was celebrated drinking wine on the viewing platform halfway up the Eiffel Tower. During the day I roamed Paris with Pat Butcher, a UEA Comp Lit man billeted in Rennes for the year. We drank a bottle of *pinard* at Baudelaire's grave in Montparnasse before ascending the Eiffel Tower to meet Lindsay, a couple of people from Franco-B and Bruno. Back on terra firma, I was bundled into the boot of Pat's car and transported to the Gare du Nord, where Lindsay nicked a metal sign concerning insulating gloves from the side of a train, a sign that hangs still in his toilet at home.

At midnight I was returned to the Trocadéro, so late that *la Lapine* was wondering if it was *her* turn to receive a rabbit. She had written a sweet little poem to me, '*un anglais fou a Paris*'. But after half an hour of muscular snogging, she had to go. I walked the five miles home, stopping briefly to join some Americans for a Thanksgiving Day beer. *Ooh la la*, my early *angoisse* was evaporating, Paris was exhilarating and I was finding my place in its maelstrom of citizens. Gathering confidence, my appetite whetted by numerous 'Franco-is-dead' parties,* I resumed my rôle as a student revolutionary, this time not in the backwaters of Norfolk but in the Mecca of demonstrators. The French have always been more politically *engagé* than the British. In Paris, when they tried to bump metro prices up a huge amount, every Parisian instinctively refused to pay and the authorities were obliged to capitulate. In London, a few years later, when they made a similar proposal for the Tube, there was a deal of angry talk but most people (including myself) paid up meekly and the battle was lost. The French did not forget the 1789 revolution; it was a citizen's *right* to revolt (and to have lunch). The streets of Paris had seen dramatic disruptions seven years earlier and I found, to my delight, that there were demonstrations most weekends, protesting variously about Giscard's heavy-handedness, the scandal of unemployment and the Minister of Education, whose crime I never really understood.

Marching through Paris among thousands of students, chanting

---

* Spanish dockers kept the dictator alive weeks after his body had given up.

and shouting – the opposite approach to that of the *flâneur* – was thrilling until the end of my second '*manif*', when it turned from a gregarious stroll into a fearsome battle. I was enjoying myself so much in the noisy throng that I didn't notice fellow demonstrators melting away as we approached a residential area. Suddenly, the hundred or so who remained started pulling on crash helmets and producing large sticks. This was getting serious. But there was no time to escape because the students beside me linked arms as I was swept round the corner into the square where the Minister in question lived. Now I was in the front line, facing row upon row of riot police. These tough-looking blokes in black, faces obscured by the visors on their helmets, standing behind riot shields, each clutching a huge baton, *un matraque*, were the dreaded CRS, known for their violence but not at all for their conversational skills. Students were tying scarves round their mouths and brandishing their own coshes. Behind me I heard a strange *kerump* and started crying – not, you understand, through fear, but because the CRS had fired tear gas into our midst. As the men in black surged towards us, my glasses fell off and I dropped to my knees to look for them through stinging eyes. Around and above me a pitched battle broke out. Half-blind and grovelling pathetically, I was the perfect try-out gig for, say, a novice CRS man seeking to christen his *matraque*. But perhaps I was just too easy a target; I stayed unbashed and was rescued by a passer-by who crossed the street and gave me back my glasses.

– Ah, *Monsieur Smeez*, you must get out of here or they will arrest you.

It was Dimitri Tolstoy.

– And if they arrest you, they will deport you.

– Thank you, Dimitri. I'll see you on Monday.

I had neither the aptitude nor the bottle to be a street-fighting man and it had become apparent to me that, although I recognised the importance of protest and enjoyed the idea of myself as committed politico, I could not generate the outrage necessary to change the world through direct action. 'I feel bad that I don't feel worse. That is the liberal dilemma in a nutshell,' wrote Michael Frayn. Woody Allen observed that 'the world is run by the people who turn up.' I didn't turn up – I had other things to do. If I had to choose between a documentary about oppression in Cambodia or *Match of the Day*, I went for the football; between a play and a meeting of the local Stop the War campaign . . . well, you get the idea. I made little effort to keep abreast of affairs in England, electing instead to sit with *Le Monde* and a dictionary, so when Monsieur Lavaud asked me what SALT stood for,* I was embarrassed not to know. Nor was I able to give him the inside track on why Prime Minister Wilson had resigned.

After Christmas I said goodbye to the *Cité Universitaire* and moved into a flat with Lindsay** on the Rue St Sébastien, in the 11th Arrondissement just north of the Bastille. It had one bedroom so I slept in the living room/kitchen and went through Lindsay's room to go to the toilet which, inexplicably, had no door. Lindsay

---

* Strategic Arms Limitation Talks.

** Lindsay is a man with whom I associate one word in particular. He would talk about some interesting thing he had been doing which sounded fantastic until the arrival of a sentence that began with the word 'unfortunately'; as in: 'Och, we had a great time, climbing the mountain; we saw the dawn and it was magnificent . . . Unfortunately we got lost on the way down and had to call out the mountain rescue service.' Or, an impressive early example, 'I was all set to interview Roland Barthes. Unfortunately he was run over and killed the day before the appointment.'

and I sat up late at nights smoking dope, discussing literature and girls, both subjects he knew more about than I did. We were both under the spell of structuralism and the new criticism, which meant that all conversations eventually terminated at the question, 'What is the meaning of meaning?' Lindsay introduced me to the idea that he and I were '*marginal*' – outside the general run of things, at odds with ordinariness, 'outwith', as the Scots say. I was pleased to place myself in this camp, imagining myself a misunderstood poet forced to dwell in the conventional world of '*metro, boulot, dodo*' (Tube, work, sleep). We went to see Phillip Glass, Memphis Slim, obscure French movies, art openings (*vernissages*, the French call them because it's something to do with varnishing. What a beautiful word, I thought, '*vernissage*'). At Easter, Pud appeared in his car and he and I set off on a tour of France, picking up hitch-hikers and girls, staying in hostels, meeting briefly with *la Lapine* and her friend, and even crossing the snowy Alps in Pud's little red Mini so that we might say we had been to Italy.

As spring muscled aside the cold in Paris, Rue St Sébastien attracted dozens of visitors – a selection of Lindsay's friends and his mother who competed for floor space with Carpenter, Richard and Lin, Phil, Gary, Adam (who silenced an entire metro carriage with his ridiculous laugh) and, on the weekend of the Rolling Stones concert, for which I had acquired twenty tickets, so many guests that only the emaciated could lie down. When a late arrival knocked on the door at three a.m. and passed straight out on the thin strip of floor where I had been lying, I had to attempt to sleep standing up.

Syd, Hazel and Nick came with Maurice (Syd's oldest friend – his Gary), Maurice's wife Maureen and their son, staying in a hotel on the outskirts of the city. It was the first time my father had left Britain since the War and it was my mother's first-ever trip abroad. Looking after *them* for once, rather than the other way round, brought me a new form of satisfaction. Maurice strutted up the Champs Elysées, reminiscing about the liberation of the city, despite the fact that he had not been in France during the War. I was an expert tour guide, the master of my domain, a man about town, *plus Parisien que les Parisiens.*

My desultory affair with *la Lapine* continued: I took her to see Leonard Cohen in concert and we left during his sixth encore (three of which were 'Suzanne'); at a fair, I won a goldfish which she christened Brian (or 'Brianne' as the French said it); she sometimes came with me as I knocked off the more obscure tourist sights; she taught me how to dance '*le rock*' – an obligatory requirement for dancing with the ladies of Paris, but . . . but the *grande affaire* that should have happened between us never did because, as my French improved and I met other women, she became less interesting to me, revealed some right-wing views and looked, more and more, like a young Princess Anne. She never knew that following a mishap with a condom (known in this era as a 'French letter' to the English and a '*capôte anglaise*' to the French), I had impregnated one of the Moniques that Lindsay and I had taken to Jim Morrison's grave for the obligatory joint. I didn't know this either until three months later, when I returned to Paris briefly and lunched Monique, who, she informed me, no longer bore the child *Smeez*. Or maybe she lied, and maybe there is a thirty-three-year-old Parisian out there with a big nose and poor eyesight who wonders who their father might have been.

My year in France was seminal in my life. I discovered some of the nuances of a different culture, a series of small revelations which threw a new light on my own. Learning French clarified for me the ways that my own language carves off meaning and taught me tricks that I would later employ on stage. I wrote a poem and heard a joke, which both still feature in my one-man show. In Paris, despite my earnings at the lycée, I fell into debt for the first time and became addicted to *Gauloises non-filtres* – the hard man of French cigarettes. I learnt about food and wine, befriended Arabs, found new insights into the endless puzzle of women and, in teaching, acquired a skill that permitted me to work in London for five years without being obliged to go to an office. My knowledge of the city, its poets and its language have, ever since, given people the useful impression that I am sophisticated in a manner that only a Parisian can be. In Paris, I learnt a little *savoir-vivre*. My dissertation, which wilfully and erroneously compared Henry Miller to Baudelaire, was finished and I bade farewell to my classes and to Lindsay (for a while). I phoned *la Lapine* from the Gare du Nord; Brian the goldfish, she informed me tearfully, had just died.

Alors, au revoir à Brian le poisson, à Bruno, à La Lapine, à Dimitri, à Monsieur Lavaud, à Monique, et enfin, à tous les Parisiens de mon beau séjour en France.

'Paris Poem'

It made women go 'aaaah' when I did it in private and for years it was an important strategy in my seduction technique; it seduces audiences too, although it is sentimental, clichéd, and owes a lot to Adrian Henry. In the absence of a title, I have always called it the 'Paris Poem'. It was heard first in 1976, at the Adam and Eve pub, during the weekly meeting of local poets (the definition of poet being someone who had turned up with a poem). Then I took to performing it on stage with the Revue Company to a gentle piano or guitar accompaniment. Occasionally, I still recite it at the end of the evening. I did it on TV and radio several times and even revived it for *Arthur Smith Sings Leonard Cohen*, adding it at the last minute because it fitted in with my Parisian recollections, but principally to please Syd, who always asked me to perform it when he came to one of my shows. Hattie Hayridge loves it too. It is better recited than read on the page but, ladies and gentlemen, in a tiny subsidiary section of its own, here is my 'Paris Poem':

So here we are in Paris in spring
The lovers all love and the *clochards* all sing
But every morning through the eight o'clock blue
The postman comes with nothing from you
There is
    The Boulevard St Michelle
        The Rue St Dennis
            The Champs Elysées
But no you.

So I dip my croissant in my café au lait
I open the window and I call in the day
But in spite of the Seine, the birds, and the sun
It's no fun in Paris buying garlic for one
There is
    The Rue de La Huchette
        The Louvres (shut on Tuesdays)
            The Tour St Jacques
But no you.

Then I heave myself on the Clignancourt line
And the busker there he sings so fine
That I'm lost in the world of the Metro-men
Till I see you're not there and it hurts again
There is
    The Boulevard St Germain
        The Musée des Beaux-arts (also shut on Tuesdays)
            The Marchée aux Puces
But no you.

I ain't gonna live in Paris no more
Get the 9.57 from the Gare du Nord
But whenever, wherever the train may go
You won't be there to kiss me hello
There'll be
    France
        England
            America
                Every place
All of them, without you.

Monsieur Smeez, 1976

CHAPTER 8. BACHELOR OF ARTS

Returning to London suburbia from Paris, my head swollen with
Baudelaire and thoughts of French girls, my glasses replaced by
contact lenses, my pockets empty, I rekindled a romance with a
student, who promptly had a pregnancy scare and went abroad
for the summer. At twenty-one, I had never really had a proper
girlfriend and although I had had a dozen sexual partners I was
a hopeless lover who remained baffled and afraid of the subtle
calibrations of a relationship. I was given to the ancient weak-
ness of wanting the person I could not have, of deifying one
while exploiting the few who desired me. *La pauvre Lapine*. I had
good female friends and was slowly beginning to understand that
women were equal to men and, in most ways, superior, but I still
did not know *how* to be a boyfriend.

There was no casual work for students going at Greenwich
Council but I applied for a job as a door-to-door furniture
salesman around Blackheath. Stan the Man, the ebullient boss of
Furniture Fashion, told me what a great deal he was offering the
lucky public. Then, after a celebratory drink in the pub, he proudly
produced a newspaper clipping in which his previous venture,
selling central heating, had been exposed as a scam. He caught
my alarmed look and assured me, 'This one is bona, Brian.' After
a second pint, he told me about all the randy housewives he had
fucked during his sales career. When I think of him now I see
the face of Benny Hill.

I was one of the advance guard who banged on doors announcing that I was conducting a survey about furniture, the opening question being: 'Do you have any furniture in your house?' Even the most confused old lady had a ready answer for this one, so I would gently proceed, via the crude psychology of Stan's 'questionnaire', to persuade my victim to invite Stan the Man, prowling like a big fat cat up the road, to come round for an immediate 'consultation', whereupon he would 'go for the kill'. It was the Greenwich *Glengarry/Glenross*. After three days I resigned, having come down with a bout of imaginary glandular fever.

In debt, and with no income, I sat in the pub spinning out gloomy shared half-pints with Dennis and Gary, who were similarly skint. I felt adrift in the anticlimactic limbo between the Paris adventure and my return to UEA in October. The one consolation was that we had met the extraordinarily provocative Miriâme, a gorgeous feline French student who was spending summer in London, and whose olive skin glistened beneath the leather hot pants and bra she wore at all times. The tiny hot pants were largely obscured by a thick metal belt, attached to which was a large padlock – a chastity belt, she told us, that had been placed there by her jealous French boyfriend who had made her promise that she would not unlock it for any English boys. It was a hot summer in 1976 but, goodness me, Miriâme in her hot, hot pants was hot, hot, hot, hotter still.

On a walk along the river, I looked at all the tourists gathered around the *Cutty Sark*; couldn't we do something to get *them* to give us money? I proposed that Gary and Dennis join me in some busking at the popular old ship. We would recreate the *Blue Peter* sketch I had written at school and reprised at UEA (it did not occur to me that no foreigners knew what, or who, *Blue Peter* was), do a bit of singing to a music track, take the hat round and retire to Beverly Hills on the proceeds. Reluctantly, Dennis agreed, while Gary was adamant he would not perform but would provide a tape recorder and do the bottling. I hurriedly turned the sketch into a duologue and opened the festering bag that contained my *Swingalonga* costumes.

The next afternoon Miriâme joined us as we set up nervously by the ship's figurehead.

'Good afternoon, ladies and gentlemen . . .'

'I'm sorry – you can't do that here. Can you leave or I'll call the police.'

Poor start. We moved round the corner to the Park entrance, but didn't last long there either. Twice frustrated, we gave up and slouched to the Cutty Sark pub further along the river. In one last attempt to regain Miriâme's respect, I asked the landlord if we could do a turn outside, where drinkers sat overlooking the Thames. To my surprise he agreed, so we fished out our fetid wigs once more and started our comeback.

As we began hesitantly, the women in the small audience smiled in indulgent bemusement and the men stared in evident appreciation, not at Dennis or me but past us to where Miriâme was posing and pouting by the river in her standard sex bomb ensemble. Sensing that a change in artistic direction might increase our profitability, I soon invited Miriâme to dance to some music, hastily fumbled on by Gary. Now the blokes were *really* enjoying it. The whip-round yielded up an ecstatic one pound fifty. We presented our little spectacle six or seven more times and with each successive performance the comedy became briefer and more irrelevant as Miriâme's dance got longer and more uninhibited. By closing time Dennis and I merely provided an introduction to Miriâme's rhythmic writhing. Our roller-coaster career finally ended when the landlord's wife came home, fired us immediately and took her husband to a back room for a talking to. This hardly dimmed our triumphant mood and Miriâme, perspiring like a goddess, declared, in her Bardot accent, that tonight, *mes petits anglais*, she did not feel the need for her chastity belt. I watched as she went home with Gary.

This was not the first or last time that I competed with Gary for a girl and came in runner-up. His 'slits for eyes, long eyebrows' and duck gait notwithstanding, he was more of a looker than me and had some winning chat-up lines. He was a student like myself but he would intrigue women by informing them that he was the 'royal Tube-driver,' explaining that just as there was a royal yacht and a royal train, so there was a royal Tube conveyance at a secret station under Buckingham Palace designed for subterranean escape or if the Queen needed to nip to Harrods during the rush hour. This was why, Gary continued authoritatively to the by now hooked female, there were so often mysterious hold-ups on the Underground.

All male students like to alter their status if placed in normal human society where women are gathered because saying 'I'm doing an HND in mechanical engineering' tends not to impress the ladies as much as being a film producer or a lecturer in Chinese studies, both of which I had claimed to be. Having purchased an East Fife Football Club blazer in a charity shop on a visit to Richard in Edinburgh, I also became, for purposes of seduction, a professional footballer – albeit of a lowly nature.

My friend, fellow comic Tony Hawkes,* told me that he had once posed as an American to a girl in a club. They went on a date, and slept together before Tony realised he was now in too deep to – pardon my French – come clean. I don't know the conclusion to this story but I doubt that Tony comes out of it well.

My last year in Norwich. Many of my friends had finished their degrees while I was in Paris, but Adam, Phil, Carpenter and Babs had also spent the year abroad and we all took up residence on the outskirts of town in the gaff that Adam's dad had conveniently purchased. It was an ordinary terraced house (i.e. to me a place of prodigious luxury), to which we gave the jokily inappropriate name of 'Seaview Farm'. Adam even got 'Seaview Farm' emblazoned on a twee wooden sign and a couple of weeks into term it was featured as an amusing item in the local paper. Adam himself naturally had the big bedroom, which he decorated in extravagant fashion. His proud centrepiece was a kind of tree displaying his vast collection of ties – more ties, probably, than existed among the whole of the rest of the undergrads in Norwich. He had frequent visitors, many of whom were luscious women who clearly wanted more than a conversation about Hollywood musicals. How could he resist them? Ah, the naivety of my youth. Adam's technique with women, which seemed to have them all drooling, was to have no romantic interest of any kind in any of them, a strategy that was way, way beyond my capabilities.

* His name is spelt with no 'e' and when it is, it pisses him off. Which, obviously, is why I have done it.

It disappointed me that our house name was more famous than I was, and I set about rebuilding my reputation as an 'eventist' – a word applied to me by Tom Elsasser, the brilliant polyglot lecturer who had introduced me to the works of Walter Benjamin. ('Fascism aesthetics politics; communism responds by politicising art.') Inspired by the American stuntman Evel Knievel, who flew over improbable numbers of buses and canyons on his motorbike, I publicised a forthcoming attempt to leap the campus pond on a child's tricycle. Evel himself would have struggled to achieve this feat and a small crowd clapped and cheered as I plunged predictably into the water. On my twentieth birthday I dispensed sherry in the university launderette and ostentatiously placed my bed in the centre of the campus, inviting anyone who wished to join me. Friends duly pitched up, dragging their own beds, until about twenty of us coagulated into a large, noisy tribute to John Lennon and Yoko Ono. There can be no doubt that some of the students at UEA had me marked down as a grade-one wanker.

At Christmas Adam produced and directed *Cinderella*, which I helped to write. Phil and I played the ugly sisters while Adam roller skated on in a bright blue bellboy outfit as Buttons, and Babs gave her cool and funky Queen. The late-night version proved popular – although not with the mayor and his wife, who left after I drunkenly accused her of having 'a mouth bigger than a cow's cunt'. Encouraged by the response we began making plans for the next Rag Revue in summer and, perhaps, for the Edinburgh Festival Fringe. Auditioning for another female, we settled on Maxine, a fresh and vibrant first-year in a stripy rugby shirt who sang, danced and was instantly likeable.

Phil was so impressed by Max that, seven years later, he married her.*

After a Christmas spent working in a GPO sorting office in Borough, the final exams loomed, and I curtailed my showing-off in the bar and on campus in favour of revising in the library. I read the first three volumes of *Á la recherche du temps perdu* in French but, improved though my skills in the language were, I fell back exhausted by Proust's transcontinental sentences and continued in English. I toiled away in the world of poetry, linguistics, Robbe-Grillet, the French imperfect subjunctive and Shakespeare, usually while sitting in one of the library carrels – private cubicles available only to postgrads and finalists. If you arrived early enough on Monday you could book one of these for a week; I equipped mine with a thermos of tea, sundry foodstuffs and my slippers to ease me through the days. As the library closing hour approached, I treated myself and visitors to joints and beer, thereby ruining all the good work I had put in buttering up the library staff. What did it all mean, all this bookery and memorising? I wrote a poem in the student paper:

'A quasi-structuralist considers finals'

Consider the word examination
One more syllable than masturbation
The semantic element seems to suggest

* Other early members included Tim Bentink who is now David in *The Archers*, Rick the piano-playing opera singer, muso voice man Brian Bowles and Roger Danes whom I met again years later as a BBC Radio studio manager.

a period of learning that ends in a test
but you know and I know and so does my mum
reductio ad absurdum and fingers gone numb

Consider the phrase finals revision
– phonetically close to urinal precision
and I believe on the same paradigm
as terminal cancer and last pantomime.
But when it's all gone and the structure lies bare
you light up a rollie and pretend you don't care

Consider the notion dehumanised art
the iambic rhythm renders it a part
of the staple diet of English verse
last seen down Bluebell Lane in a hearse.
But as the ink on the last paper dries
some barman in Norwich will be wiping my eyes

Discussions around the theme of 'What are you going to do
when you grow up?' began to proliferate around me, and one
or two of my contemporaries joined the trawl applying for
teaching courses and proper jobs – 'the milk round' as it was
called. I felt I should show willing and consider my 'future', so
I made a half-hearted application for a post as English
assistant/lecturer at the University of Silesia in Katowice, Poland;
they responded with a *whole*-hearted rejection and that seemed
like enough job-seeking for a while. Besides, I had six weeks'
employment lined up for the summer before we all went to
Edinburgh, working nights in a bakery outside Norwich. It was
well-paid too, although my incompetent organisation meant that

my first session as a baker finished at six a.m., three hours before my last exam began.

Opposite the library stood the mysterious Careers Centre, one of the few university buildings I had never entered. I was obliged by the terms of my degree, however, to make at least one visit. When I informed the careers man that, as an 'existential Micawberist' I had no real idea of my ambitions, was not seeking a real job and would rather 'bum around' and see what happened, he rubbed his eyes and sighed wearily, 'Oh, another one of them.' Although we had now committed to performing the revue at the Edinburgh Festival in August, I did not take this seriously as a career option. When one of my lecturers said, 'I expect you'll be going to London to get involved in the media', I was genuinely surprised at the thought. I had a vague notion that I would like to be a writer of some sort, but quite *what* I would write about and *how* I might make money from it were questions I could not answer. I was a big fish in a small pond at UEA but a plankton in the Pacific as regards the world that lay outside the university. My self-confidence and celebrity around campus did not translate into any grand expectations about my future. I revisited my schoolboy fear that I would end up as a teacher – probably back at Roan School for Boys – and again I asked myself, 'What does a quantity surveyor *actually do?*'

My stunts among the scholars were not quite finished. At a university fair I set up a Rent-a-Poet stall, where I wrote poems on any subject for 50p, a game I have occasionally returned to over the years. My last-year set piece was to run for President of the Union, standing on a 'Don't Vote for Me' platform with a radical vision:

The Union Bar to shut, a campus curfew at ten p.m. every night (to be enforced by vigilantes recruited from the National Front); the presidency to become an oligarchy through the male line.

My campaign team let it be known that I was only running in order to boost my already over-inflated ego and that, in the event of my victory, all Union funds would go on drink, drugs and concubines for the president and his henchmen. At the hustings, I unveiled a programme of compulsory abortion for all women students (I can't remember the details of this proposal but I'm guessing that I would be the one responsible for impregnating them to start with). The manifesto on my leaflet was accompanied by a large picture of my arse above two photos of Adam's bulky legs and Carpenter's feet, apparently locked in congress with another pair (see photo page six).

I was not the last nor the best joke candidate at UEA. A couple of years later, an enterprising bunch of nihilists contrived to have a cauliflower elected as Union President. Although, subsequently, many root vegetables have held positions of far greater power than this, the tradition of the bonkers left-field parliamentary candidate seems, sadly, to have died along with Screaming Lord Sutch. Sometimes I wonder if I might not one day revive my search for public office. The 'campaign' was a fine party for me and my team and, in spite of my determination that no one should vote for me, I was secretly pleased to come in a respectable third.

The afternoon of my last A level, you may remember, I had walked into Greenwich boating pond wearing a lady's hat, and smoked a cigar. At UEA, after my final finals paper, I drained a can of beer and got a bus back to work in the bakery. When graduation came round, Syd drove up to watch me collect my 2.1. Hazel, I knew, hated this kind of formal event, but I was amused and pleased that Syd's chum Maurice joined him for the day. I felt foolish in my formal gown and the first suit I ever owned – a thin brown second-hand three-piece, which boasted both flares *and* turn-ups. As the Vice-Chancellor presented me with my degree certificate I produced a bunch of flowers from up my sleeve and gave it to him – which won me my last laugh as a graduand. Afterwards, my fellow new graduates and I took our shoes and socks off to stand around swigging champagne in the campus pond, which had recently been rendered less provocatively deep – possibly as a result of my own immersions in it. When Syd and Maurice left, I returned to Seaview Farm and to hot, hectic nights in the bakery. And that, finally, was the end of my formal education. From the September playground of Southwark Park, via Greenwich and Paris, to a June afternoon in Norwich, it had been a delicious, confusing, and exciting ride. I lent my degree certificate to a friend who needed it to forge a CV and never saw it again. Nevertheless, I was now Brian Smith BA (Hons).

Let me record one last, shameful episode in my university career.

During my finals revision I had developed an interest in political movements of the nineteenth century. My flirtation with the theories of Marcel Proudhon, the French anarchist who stated that 'Property is theft', ended outside the campus supermarket when I was caught shoplifting a Cornish pasty and a pint of milk. This was something I would not have done as a first-year.

Deposited in a back office on my own while I waited for the police to arrive, I pulled out a notebook and wrote a poem. Two plain-clothes men arrived and clearly did not like the look of me

– unsurprising since I was wearing a pair of flared trousers made out of deckchair fabric, a grubby tie-dye T-shirt and odd socks, not an outfit calculated to impress the Norfolk Constabulary. Even worse, the whole effect was topped off by my egg-streaked moustache and my enormous back-combed Afro – now at the alarming apex of its beauty. Fuckin' stoodent. I confessed to my crime immediately, but they didn't seem interested.

'Do you take drugs, Brian?' one of them suddenly asked. They looked on my arms and legs for needle marks and searched me but found only a packet of ten Number 6 and my notebook. One of them flicked through it until he came to the poem I had just written.

– Why have you written, 'This Cornish pasty was inevitable'?

He was good. The real answer, of course, was that I was a modest but incompetent shoplifter (not to say a prosy poet) who thought he was bound to get nicked one day. I couldn't say that but I had not spent all those afternoon seminars analysing poems for nothing:

– Well, the pasty symbolises the discrepancy between our boundless human dreams and the quotidian world of trivia which, er . . .

His eyes glazed over. I had done enough. He moved on.

They eventually took me to the police station where I was told they were going to take me home to search where I lived. I'm not sure if they were allowed to do this but I was by now so cowed and depressed by the experience that I agreed meekly. They would have found, among the turbulent sea of clothes and books in my room, a stubbed-out joint. After a long wait one of them returned.

– Is your dad a police officer?

Oh dear. This was the reason I was so miserable at what was happening. Syd was the most honest person I knew and I could hardly bear to think of his disappointment and anger if he found I had been done for shoplifting. Syd did not believe that property was theft.

— Yes, he is.

— All right, you can go.

It was the most relief I had ever felt. Thank you, Syd, for that, although you never knew about this episode and, if you were still alive, I would probably not have written about it.

CHAPTER 9. FIRST EDINBURGH

In late summer it is the only thing to do. For two of the past thirty years I have missed it and both times I felt like all my friends were having a terrific get-together while I had stupidly chosen to stay home and sulk. The Edinburgh Festival, one of the universe's great parties, was established in 1947 to provide a platform for 'the flowering of the human spirit'. In that same year, eight companies set up a festival of their own alongside the main event, inaugurating 'the Fringe', which welcomes all manner of amateurs, dreamers, drummers and wallowers in the self-indulgent. These days there are also festivals of film, books, jazz, dance, TV and, probably, origami. Together they form the biggest arts festival in the world. The Edinburgh Fringe has provided a ravishing playground for my own imagination and the things I have done in my career of which I am most proud all started, in one way or another, in this stern, dramatic, unique city in the month of August where the streets are alive with young wannabes chanting the performers' mantra:

> I'll get drunk
> I'll get laid
> I'll get spotted
> I'll get paid

My adulthood has been measured out in Edinburgh Fringes and if the event did not exist I would have had a different life.

Whenever for some reason (like writing an autobiography) I wish to identify what year something happened, my first reference point is the roster of stuff that lodges in my head recording, in roughly chronological order, every show (and some of the women) I have mounted in Edinburgh. Not *every* show, you understand. Not all the one-off cabaret gigs, the guided walking tours, or the cameo appearances in odd plays, the benefits, the 'best-of-the-fests', the processions, the sideshows, the radio spots, the press stunts, the state-of-comedy seminars, the TV programmes, the hospital charity gigs; not all of them – no, I mean the ones that inspired me to go up to the festival in the first place, the shows which I (or some sort of me) had prepared, budgeted for and advertised.

All those summers lay before me when we arrived in 1977, buoyant and optimistic with a revamped version of our university show *SwingalongaDante*, subtitled '. . . *dahlings, it's the Divine Comedy*'. We drove up from Norwich in a grubby yellow van stuffed with costumes, props, posters, programmes and hope. If we sold twenty-five tickets a night we would break even; if the audience numbered fifty or more we would make a small profit. That must be possible – after all, we had some great quotes from the *Eastern Daily Press* and the primary school which served as our venue was famous for a wee pupil called Sean Connery. I spent three days failing to do as little as possible in the frenetic preparations for our opening, which first required us to convert the school hall into a theatre. The other members of the team were aware by now that me and carpentry were enemies, but I joined in grumpily sticking up posters, hustling, begging, giving out fliers, borrowing coat-hangers – all the palaver of 'let's do a show right here in the barn'.

On the Sunday morning before our Monday-night première,

exhausted and, in my case, hung-over, we took part in the traditional opening parade in which Adam had secured us a place.
Clutching bags stuffed with costumes, we walked to the gathering
point along a line of waiting lorries until we located the spot
reserved for us where it was revealed that, unlike all the other
local businesses and fringe groups on the parade, we did not have
a lorry and would be obliged to proceed on foot between floats
at street level – the poor bloody infantry among the divisions of
rolling tanks.

The float in front was occupied by members of the Cambridge
Footlights Revue, who easily found room on their commodious
lorry for our bags and shouted down encouragement. The
Footlights had history, experience and a big oily machine behind
them; they had already been on tour with their show, had a large
venue, a guaranteed audience and an air of self-confidence that
we, mooching around the gutter in our cheap wigs, could not
match. Meeting them here, I felt a little of Syd's humility in the
presence of members of the establishment – the officer class.
These young men with their pedigrees and superior A levels were
probably much funnier and much cleverer than us.

Mind you, they had no Babs and Max who gathered the hand-
outs and bravely strapped themselves into their uniform of fishnet
tights and high heels, while we boys pinned up our baggy leopard-
skin underpants. These 'nappies', worn with white shirts and
unconvincing false moustaches, constituted the costume of the
Canaletteloni* Brothers, a frenetic bunch of acrobats – all called
Luigi Cannalleteloni – whose enthusiasm, since none of us *were*
acrobats, outstripped their tumbling skills. To a furious piano

* NB: The number of 'n's, 'l's and 't's in 'Cannalletteloni' has never been agreed.

accompaniment, we would run on, manically shouting in mock Italian, and commence banging each other's heads with tin trays, leaping through hoops and performing extravagant forward-rolls. Adam would drag up a member of the audience to stand on his shoulders, while in one trick I launched myself dangerously over Adam and Phil to crash to the stage behind them. There is a photo of this that still makes me wince whenever I see it. Wagons roll. We canellettolonied along Princes Street to cheering crowds, convinced we would draw enough attention to sell dozens of tickets.

For our début public performance I treated myself to some clean socks. Richard and Lin, with whom I was staying, arrived twenty minutes early with a friend, bought a programme, and took their places, while Rick, 'Banana Fingers', tinkled on the piano. Then Lindsay showed up. We waited nervously in the school toilets that were now our dressing room. After half an hour it was apparent that no one else was coming. Our audience numbered three people, all of whom we knew.

Fucking hell, what a bummer. We felt utterly dejected. What had been the point of the posters, the fliers, the parade? We had been wasting our time and I, at that point, would happily have packed my bags and gone to London – Babs, I think, might have felt the same. But Adam and the others were not going to give up so easily. I was outvoted. We would continue the run, and what was more, we would not cancel this show. Twenty minutes later, during our opening salvo of audience participation, anyone entering the school hall would have seen the cast and the entire audience standing on stage swinging-along-a-Dante to a hundred empty seats.

*   *   *

In the next few years our troupe became known, above all, for our enthusiasm and energy, both onstage and off. Galvanised again by Adam the following day, and every subsequent day of the festival, we returned to the streets of Edinburgh, singing and dancing outside the Fringe box office, cajoling passers-by, button-holing journalists, and doing anything we could think of, however desperate or humiliating, that might increase our ticket sales. By the Thursday the audience at last outnumbered the cast, and on Friday we hit double figures for the first time. Things were improving but I remained disconsolate – I estimated we were each investing six hours' work for every 50p ticket sold – but at least performing the show was becoming less embarrassing and the few people who came seemed to be enjoying themselves. Whenever we could we did a spot at the Fringe Club on the Royal Mile, where performers gathered after their shows to compare notes, watch the cabaret, dance, get drunk and sleep with each other. Nowadays there are too many shows at the festival for there to be one central performers' bar, which is a shame because it was a fantastic place to end your evening, equalled in bibulous exuberance only by the bar at the Gilded Balloon a decade later.

We took time off only to attend other comedies which, I noted, were all significantly shorter than our own two hours of fun. The Footlights boys were good, but no funnier than us, while the Lancaster University Revue presenting *Hayley's Vomit* were definitely worse. Chris Langham's show was the most hilarious and featured the funniest thing I saw that year – Jim Broadbent doing his 'jazz dancing'. Langham cut a dashing figure with his famous girlfriend and his reputation as a TV writer. I heard with amazement how someone would ring him up and offer him twenty quid to write a joke! 'That must be good,' I thought.

Our audience numbers continued to grow, as did the number of pints I consumed at the Fringe Club after the show. During one performance in the school hall I was afforded a foreglimpse of the type of confrontation that awaited me on countless nights to come when a drunk persistently interrupted my Max Miller routine. I did not then have the resources to deal with hecklers but at this, my first public barracking, it did not matter because Rory McGrath, our friend in the Footlights, who was sitting in front of the drunk, turned and, inviting him to 'Shut up, you Scottish cunt!', punched him in the face. A small scuffle petered out as the lights came on and the rueful heckler left, along with twelve others, thus halving our audience. I could not decide whether Rory was a hero or an arse – I still can't really. In the last week we received a good review in the *Scotsman* – no doubt it would have had five stars if reviews had been graded then. Or perhaps four stars since there was one caveat among the heavenly inches of praise. My cricket strip, a *succès d'estime* at UEA, was declared, 'unfunny in the extreme'.

On the final night of our run, hoorah, we sold out to a raucous crowd who laughed and clapped. Afterwards, in spirits as high as Arthur's Seat, I capped the evening by finally copping off with a woman who, I was to discover, became a nun soon after. Edinburgh had supplied a mixture of emotions, the extreme contours of the experience fitting perfectly the geography of the city itself, but when it was all over the only thing I wanted to do was to repair to my new pad in London and lie down. I had gone to the Festival thinking of it as a fun holiday which might pay for itself, a kind of full stop to my university career; I had not bargained for the sheer *hard work* it entailed. There were a lot of funny, ambitious people around in Edinburgh, funnier and more ambitious than me. We had worked our tits and bollocks off, but nothing had come of it and I was more in debt than ever. I didn't expect to return to Edinburgh. However, when I recounted our adventures to Carpenter in a London pub and he asked, 'Will you ever go on stage again?' I could not bring myself to say no. And I guess the only time I ever will say no to that question will be during the endgame of my death.

Unless, of course, I die on stage.

CHAPTER 10. ROCK 'N ROLL HOVEL

Twenty-four hours after our big last show in Edinburgh, drained and hoarse, I opened the door of my new London flat and caught a strong whiff of sweaty men. One of them I knew to be Gary, who had been in residence in Merton Road for a year already. Picking my way past bicycles, piles of rubbish and a dismally predictable traffic cone, I walked up the dark stairs to the sitting room where Gary was one of the six smoking blokes slumped in front of the TV. After cursory hellos and mumbled introductions I climbed more creaky stairs to the bedroom I had been assigned, a thin chamber with a sloped ceiling, lit by a grimy skylight and a naked bulb suspended from the nicotine-yellow ceiling. A partially dressed man, passed out in the foetal position, lay snoring on my bed. Hi honey, I'm home.

My feeling of anticlimax, which had been growing all day, blossomed into outright misery. I had no money, no job, no girl-friend, no prospects and now, it would seem, no bed. My future stretched across the horizon like a vast featureless arctic waste-land. Oh Gawd. What was I going to do? I put my bags down next to the recumbent drunk, went downstairs and joined the silent smokers.

184a Merton Road, South Wimbledon was one of the greatest student-style slums the world has ever seen. On the occasions during my years in residence when I invited a girl back, I invariably felt the need to add the proviso: 'It's a bit of a shit-heap . . .' This would elicit the response, 'Don't worry, I've been in shit-heaps before.' But when confronted with the place, even if they didn't say it, I could see from their expression that they were thinking, 'Christ, this really *is* a shit-hole.' If they were prepared to stay the night you knew they must properly fancy you.

Consider the bath. It was large enough to accommodate a small whale but the apertures of the taps were so unequal to the challenge that it took nearly an hour to fill. In the unlikely event that there was hot water in the tank, it had cooled down to tepid by the time the tub was even half full. Dirty tidemarks ran round the off-white interior, sludge grey lines which resisted the most vigorous scrubbing (that's what we assumed – no one actually tried cleaning the bath). After a hearty game of football or rounders on muddy Clapham Common, everyone wanted a bath and the only way this was possible was if we all used the same water. Being last in was a bad short straw to draw. In the kitchen every surface lived under a permanent layer of oozing grease and the cupboards were full of unreturned mildewed milk bottles. The kettle was so tired of life that in the time it took to boil you could nip to Tom's corner shop, buy tea bags and still have time for a sit-down before its frail whistle struck up. The rarely used oven skulked beneath old chip-wrappings and morsels of discarded kebab.

Syd and Hazel actually stayed one night and I can hardly imagine a greater demonstration of parental love and self-sacrifice. Gary's mum and dad also bravely visited once, managing about an hour before fleeing. They were sitting gingerly on the edge of the settee, a shapeless thing spattered with burn marks and moth holes, when their corgi, feeling more relaxed than its owners, took a crap under the telly. If Gary's mum hadn't cleared the mess up, I'm not convinced any of the floating population of residents would have bothered to do it. The Christmas decorations we put up that winter were still in place two summers later. Every few months someone would crack and make an effort to clean the place, but the most we achieved was to return the flat to the state it had been in a week earlier; thus it deteriorated ever more as time went by. I was one of the five official rent-paying residents but there were usually several more inmates, hard-up friends, tourists passing through and often a bloke who, it would turn out, no one knew. We operated an 'everyone welcome' policy which meant that nearly all of my contemporaries stayed or lived there at one time or another. Three women achieved this feat without noticeable trauma, chief among them Babs, sweet Babs with her free-spirited elegance and her natural bohemian cool.

If there was no bedroom available, a better option than the floor of the sitting room was the 'cupboard' upstairs in which the water tank was housed. The space was not tall enough to stand up in, but it *was* possible to lie underneath the gently humming tank. Darker, quieter and warmer than the bedrooms, out of earshot of the phone, the cupboard offered an arena for sleeping that everyone who spent a night there declared to be the closest they had come to returning to the womb. Simon, a UEA man whom I had forgiven for seducing my girl when I was working at the bakery, Babs and Phil were among the roll-call of cupboard-dwellers but the longest-serving of them was Adam, who furnished it so prettily that it became the most coveted bed in the house.

Adam, the only flatmate with any standards of cleanliness,

stuck a sign in the bathroom – CLEAN THE FUCKING BATH – but to no effect. During his six-month residency he was often absent for several days at a time but if we asked where he had been he was enigmatic – coy, even. Not that anyone cared. One day he sat me down and told me he was gay, one of the least astounding revelations there has ever been. He was enjoying the excitement of his first unfettered love affair with a gentle, softly spoken air steward called Gerald, who generously donated all his old clothes to me.

In the absence of any better plan, and with a pressing need to earn some money so that I would not have to ponce off my parents any more, I phoned Merton Borough Council. My timing was inadvertently judicious and my qualifications in order; I was offered a job road sweeping, starting on Monday. So that was how I spent the winter of my twenty-third year – living in a tip, pushing a thick broom along the gutters of Mitcham wearing a pair of Babs's old tights under my jeans on cold days. I got up at 6.30 a.m. to walk to the 'yard', which became 5.30 when I took on the overtime job of cleaning the depot toilets before going out on the broom. Every morning, even if I had slept soberly for ten hours, I was shocked by the hateful cold shriek of the alarm clock and resolved that *one* day I would find work that did not start so brutally early. The problem for sluggards like myself is that the template for the hours of industry had been established by early birds before we late worms had arrived in the office to have our say.

To my disappointment, I found that I was not a solo sweeper as I had been in Greenwich, but was one of a crew of four in a milk-floaty vehicle. This entailed a lot of time spent in the company of the three other men as we went from road to road and hung around workers' eateries drinking tea. Whenever we

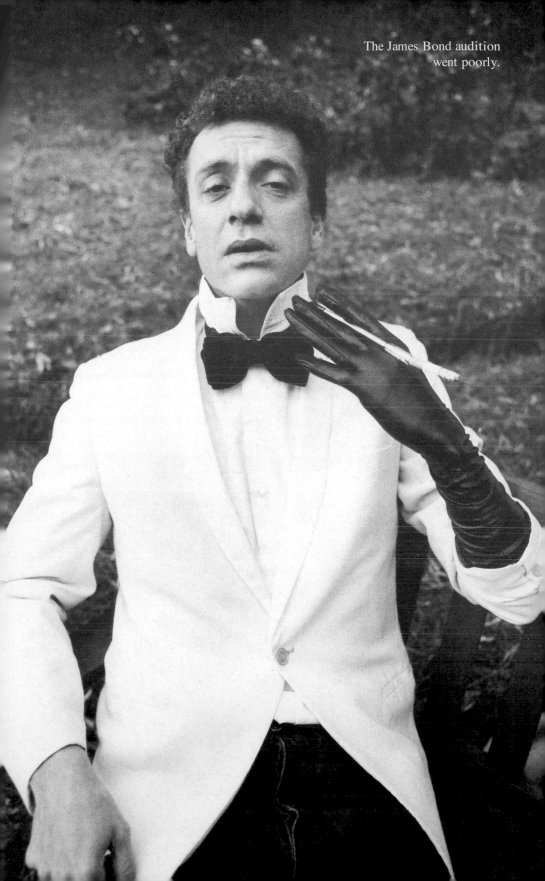

The James Bond audition
went poorly.

My grandmother Kitty was in a dance troupe called the 'Seven Little Rays of Sunshine'. Here she is just the one.

ith my brother Nick. I seem to
vn too much forehead. The boy
ho lived with us turned out to
my older brother Richard.

Even at the age of seven, I had
he face of a twenty-a-day man.

Syd told me he hit fifty that
day and he probably did.

Devon? Camber Sands? I sense
I have just irked my mother.

Facing page) My parents'
vedding, December 23rd 1950,
vhen my very different
randads first met.

With Pud, proud editors of *The Pirate* magazine. Leather patches on the elbow, NHS glasses

With Richard – bad hair days, bad hair lives.

The University of East Anglia graduate gowns were designed by Cecil Beaton. Honestly. That night Syd told a joke that my friends still remember.

Who sent me this, I wonder? I was never a member of the UDR.

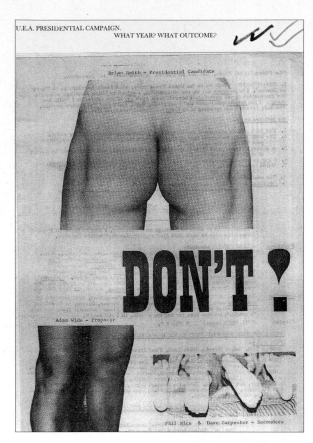

Brian Smith – Presidential Candidate

DON'T !

Adam Wide – Proposer

Phil Nice & Dave Carpenter – Seconders

When I stood for president of the Student Union, this was my poster. Designer's note: the stroke of the exclamation mark is formed by my inverted testicles.

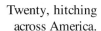

Twenty, hitching across America.

More Dick Van Dyke than [Ja]cques Brel. The National Revue [C]ompany (l-to-r, [...] Maxine, Adam, [...]ne, Babs, Phil).

Poetry reading in the campus pond.

Publicity with Phil and Babs. Enthusiasm was [o]ur strongest suit.

HAM ALONG A YORICK.....

The *Loose Ends* Panto with Barbara Windsor, Ned Sherrin, Clare Rayner, Julian Clary and Rory Bremner.

had a break I took the opportunity to read – *Catch 22* is a novel that I will for ever associate with eating bacon sandwiches in Ethel's café on the outskirts of Mitcham Common. The keenest in our gang was the ever-cheerful Ron, a big, red-faced man in orange overalls. I got to know, and relish, the simple rhythm of Ron's thought patterns. He had distilled all his opinions into two phrases: 'It's a game' followed soon after by 'It's a game and a half'. Either phrase could be supplemented by 'where you are'.

– Morning, Ron.
– Morning, Brian.
  It's cold today.
– It's a game, Brian. It's a game when it's cold.
– It's a game where you are, Ron.
– It's a game and a half where you are, Brian.
Or:
– God, Ron. This chicken was 50p a pound.
– 50p a pound? It's a game, isn't it?
– It *is* a game, Ron.
– It's a game and a half, Brian.
– It's a game and a half, Ron.
– It's a game and a half when it's 50p a pound of chicken, Brian.
– It's a game and a half, Ron.
– It's a game and a half where you are, Brian.
– It's a game and a half where *you* are, Ron.
Or:
– Jim Callaghan, eh, Ron?
– It's a game, Brian. Callaghan? It's a game and a half where he is.

Once we were proceeding past a wake being held in a front garden when Ron startled the mourners by booming, 'It's a game and a half when you're dead.'

The squalor of the surroundings at home was in inverse proportion to the fun we had there. Our regular parties, to which we invited everyone in the country, were uninhibited by concerns about the state of the flat or the reactions of our neighbours (on one side the bloke was deaf and on the other they didn't seem to care). There was always a theme, starting with our Spanish Holiday Night, for which we dyed the water in the bath blue (given its vast size, it accurately represented the Mediterranean) and scattered sand over the floors. Needless to say, no effort was made to clear up the mess after the party and a new, blue mark joined the others circling the bath. Adam's sign continued to be ignored. He was swimming against the tidemarks.

And then there was the post-nuclear party – a popular conceit, since everyone then suspected we would be nuked at any moment. Sundry hideous mutants arrived and took their place dancing in the rubble we had tipped over the floors. In the early hours of the morning I spotted a gatecrasher desperately casting around for something to steal, but seeing nothing worth having, he contented himself on his way out with nicking the Sunday papers that lay by the door. In summer we had a party in our large unruly garden in which we had placed a couple of armchairs that, even by our standards, were too manky to live indoors. Stalls included Guess-the-Weight-of-the-Neighbour's-Dog, and Buy-a Kiss-from-Lovely-Gary, while I sold off my old clothes cheap to anyone who wanted them (which turned out, unsurprisingly, to be no one). We lit a large fire in the garden and when we ran out of wood we burnt the garden armchairs and then selected items of the furniture from inside the flat.

Meanwhile, my long and dilatory search for a partner continued and I established myself as a serial monogamist with a stronger emphasis on the serial than the monogamy. I fell heavily for an Irish/Canadian woman, by whom I was eventually so hopelessly besotted that I became a mooning ninny whom no one would want as a boyfriend. We went out for two years and she even moved briefly into Merton Road. When she ran off with a bloke I knew, I felt again the dreadful, pointless pain of jealousy. Now I can look back on myself then and smile indulgently at my turbulent emotions, but I was distraught for several months. 'He who loves most is the inferior and must suffer,' wrote Thomas Mann; it was a phrase that haunted me for a long time, as I continued to alternate between the girlfriends I worshipped and the ones who worshipped me – who got treated pretty badly. I had plenty of female friends but seemed incapable of forming a grown-up relationship.

Poor Kath was one who suffered my lack of consideration. Simon's girlfriend was a friend of Kath so one Friday we invited the pair of them out on a 'mystery' double date, instructing them to dress glam for a show and not to eat. When they arrived, looking delectable (Kath in stockings and suspenders), we presented them with jam sandwiches and escorted them to the wrestling at Wimbledon Town Hall. This turned out not to be the hilarious joke I had envisaged and demonstrated again my failure to understand the female psyche. Perhaps I was intimidated by the model of my parents whose love affair began the moment they met in the Streatham Locarno and did not end until Syd closed his eyes for the last time fifty-two years later. Theirs was a rare and passionate marriage of equals. They were always there for me and even when we differed or argued, I never, for one moment, thought that they did not love me. To be a stable individual, the most crucial factor is to be cherished when young. In this, as in many things in my life, I have been extremely lucky.

As winter subsided, I finally clawed my way back to a bank balance of zero and consequently gave up the sweeping, let my bones thaw out and joined Simon in a spell of signing on at the DHSS* and reading. I did my best to reassure Syd (and myself) that I was not intending to make a career out of lying on my arse dossing in a slum but, although I enjoyed performing, I thought it unlikely I would ever make a living from it. This was not the greatest period of my life – people's twenties, you come to realise, seldom are – but I'm glad now that I was a road sweeper and then an impoverished 'layabout', because it gave me an insight into life near the bottom of the pile. If you are lying in the gutter, or indeed sweeping it, you can look, not just at the stars, but straight up the world's skirt too.

No one registers street cleaners – commuters on their way to work look right through you and your status is so low that you can observe the universe, untroubled by the universe observing you. I convinced myself that I was again a kind of *flâneur*, one who roamed the roads in thought but who also lived out a solidarity with the manual worker or his unemployed friend. No doubt I was, as usual, romanticising my situation but now that I am handsomely paid and

* Which became the DSS. 'When,' asked Simon Munnery, 'will they drop the "D"?'

recognised by drunks, I tell myself to remember that time when I wasn't. Meeting some of the Footlights boys a while after our first Edinburgh experience, I was envious to discover they all seemed to be working for the BBC or had commissions to write for TV comedy shows, but that humble cap-doffing slice of Syd that lived within me told me that this was the order of things. Look at all the famous Oxbridge comedians; how many comics from UEA could I name? My consolation became that when I *did* get the opportunity, I could talk about having a lowly job or signing on without sounding patronising. It was easier for me to empathise with an audience than it was for those who went straight into showbiz or who never knew what it was like to have run out of money for the weekend by Friday evening. Those poor bastards missed out on cleaning the Council depot toilets at 6.00 a.m.

You need constantly to remind yourself, if you are in a job where people clap you when you stop working, where sycophants and bullshit PR people seek you out, that you are no more important than anyone else. A few months ago I was at Saint Pancras station when a man approached me and said:

– You're a star.

– Eh?

– You're a star.

This was embarrassing.

– Well, no, yes, I've done some bits and . . .

He did not seem to understand, and decided to give it one last try:

– Eurostar?

I have been protesting my humility but in this case my ears at least chose to believe the PR.

* * *

125

Flopping around during the day at 184a in our coats (it was frowned on to turn the feeble but expensive heating on before the evening), Simon and I also had a chance to follow silly fancies. One afternoon we discovered a shared boyhood passion for the athlete Alf Tupper, the 'Tough of the Track', a character from *The Victor* comic who, despite his frequent conflicts with the toffs of authority, always prevailed in the end, usually breaking the world record for the mile in the final frame. Neither of us having bought a copy of *The Victor* for ten years, we fell to wondering how Alf was doing. Did he continue to prepare for every race by eating fish and chips? Did he still have that wolf-head emblazoned on his running vest? Did he still exist? When we failed to find him in the copy of the comic that we duly purchased, we began to despair for Alf. Now one would Google him, but while we waited for computers to be invented we rang DC Thompson, the publishers of *The Victor,* in Dundee. Unexpectedly, we were put straight through to the editor, who told us that Alf was returning to the comic, had left the fire brigade, gone back to freelance welding, abandoned the 440 yards and was once again after the world mile record to add to his 1500-metre time. What a happy afternoon that was.

On another unemployed Monday I saw a small ad from a journalist looking for any trio involved in an amicable *ménage à trois* who might wish to discuss their set-up in a national newspaper. Carpenter and his girlfriend Kim were the resident couple at Merton Road and I persuaded them to endorse my made-up story about the three of us in order to collect the twenty pounds on offer. Thus we spent an evening in the pub with a young journalist called Carol Sarler, fabricating a tale about Carpenter's acceptance of mine and Kim's occasional afternoons in bed together. We kept going as long as Carol was buying the drinks and while I was off in the toilet Dave, in an inspired move, momentarily let slip his mask of stoic acceptance to reveal his true heartache, etc. Great stuff. The article duly appeared in a Sunday rag and ten years later I revealed the truth to Carol Sarler in the Assembly Rooms bar in Edinburgh.

And then I was in a band. You have to be when you're young, don't you? Carpenter had been lead guitarist and Hearnshaw the keyboard player in UEA's top campus band, Jack Plug and the Inputs. The other members lived locally and paid obeisance to 184a which was a kind of mother ship for UEA grads in disarray. The band rehearsed in Carpenter and Kim's bedroom upstairs. On these occasions it was impossible to read or to hear the telly so I took to going to watch The Results, as they were now called, and then to pissing around with the mike. My voice is neither interesting nor beautiful but I can carry a tune. These days I sometimes advertise myself as 'the world's only Leonard Cohen tribute band', having performed a show called *Arthur Smith Sings Leonard Cohen*, but I would be reluctant to inflict my 'singing' on a paying audience outside the realm of comedy. I had no such qualms back then when I still had the remains of a falsetto and an outstanding pair of thin red trousers. By a process of osmosis I became the new singer in The Results.

It was the back end of the 1970s and punk was having its afternoon in the sun. Having long been bored by the self-important heavy-metal stadium-rock bands who had dominated the music scene for so long, I was an admirer of these snarling new boys and became a pogo-er of some standing in the Hope and Anchor in Islington – though I never could bring myself to spit on the bands. I considered getting the full punk regalia but could not face Syd's opprobrium and besides, I was now a relatively agèd twenty-four. Too young to have been a proper hippie, I now felt too old to be a proper punk. My aspirations, in any case, were more Ian Dury and the Blockheads than Johnny Rotten. Dury was a marvellously witty lyricist ('he didn't paint the Mona Lisa – that was some Italian geezer') and one of the songs The Results covered was his uninhibited tribute to 'Blockheads'. Other covers from our eclectic set were: 'Virginia Plain' (Roxy Music), 'Pump It Up' (Elvis Costello) 'Mathilda' (Johnny Mathis), 'Kung Fu Fighting' (can't remember), 'All Over Now' (Rolling Stones), 'Sunny Afternoon' (The Kinks) 'Lazy Sunday Afternoon' (Small Faces), 'Saw Her Standing There' (The Beatles) and, for reasons of comedy, 'Puppet on a String' by Sandie Shaw. We also performed our own songs, for which I wrote the lyrics and we all concocted the tune. Often my instinct for the comic overrode the rock requirement to be mean, moody and magnificent. There was a reggae number about an enormous pimple that took over London, and a song which started gently . . .

> We wandered together along by the cliff.
> In my mind I lived a Rod McKuen riff.
> You ran to me, I knew you'd hug me,
> I looked at you, I thought 'Christ, you're ugly!'

The song then degenerated into shrieking guitars over my screaming demand that the world should be united in ugliness and proclaiming myself the ugliest of all. My favourite song in our repertoire had the title 'I lost my ticket to the Bruce Springsteen concert', whose epic lyrics I made up as we went along.

A number called 'Kleptomania' began:

> On a video screen, in an office upstairs,
> A figure is seen, stealing some wares.
> The store detective, risking his life,
> Hurries downstairs to arrest his wife.
> Kleptomania – take it away . . .

'Joelle' was a ballad I attempted to perform in the style of Jacques Brel about losing out in love to a window cleaner from Bethnal Green. In the last verse, I plucked a woman from the audience and sang to her, which helped disguise the fact that the tune owed less to one of the Fench *chansonniers* than to Dick Van Dyke's 'Chim-Chiminey-Chim-Chiminey-Chim-Chim-Cheroo'. It was one of two songs we did in the band that overlapped with the Revue – the other was a ditty about a new tax on sex, whose chorus ran, 'I wish I was paying more tax . . .'

In the closing years of the 1970s, The Results played over a hundred gigs in and around London, including the slightly prestigious Dingwall's in Camden (now, significantly, part of the Jongleurs comedy club chain) and the Rock Garden in Covent Garden. Every Friday, it seemed, we found ourselves in some urban corner of Essex – Dagenham, Romford, Chadwell Heath. Our audience, when we had one, could be unruly, as on the night where a man ran amok brandishing a table above his head or the gig in the Seagull pub in West London where, after our last song, a roomful of sweaty skinheads with swastika tattoos raised their arms in appreciation and shouted what *I* thought was the name of the pub, 'Sea-gull. Sea-gull.', but which turned out to be a far more sinister chant . . .

My dominant memory of those nights is not the excitement of the performance or the roar of the crowd, but the tremendous *fag* of it all. Those of us who finished work early or didn't work at all met at 184a about five hours before we were due on stage in order to manhandle all the necessary equipment – including enormous speakers, seemingly hewn from lead – down two flights of stairs and into the van. Then, squashed into any space available between the wires, speakers, drums and putative rock stars, we set off into the grinding London traffic, picking up strays en route. If it was one of our Far Eastern venues, we faced the certainty of an interminable crawl along that most miserable of London byways, Leyton High Road. On arrival there was an hour of unloading and setting-up before the soundcheck, a musical necessity that is almost as tedious as the technical rehearsal for a stage show. After an interlude of lounging about in the venue, munching on stale sandwiches and counting the arriving punters, we at last took the stage. As ever in the world of rock, there were groupies around – well so I read, though none of them ever seemed to come to *our* gigs. The set usually ended at closing time and, if I was not with a girl, I would do a perfunctory lap of the bar to see if I could find one for the night. She would have to agree to wait an hour while we packed up, then to travel many miles wedged in the van, dropping people off round town, before finally arriving in South Wimbledon to wait in our squalid front room while I helped lug all the equipment back upstairs. You'd be surprised how often I found a woman to agree to this. Not once.

By now I had signed on with an agency as a casual labourer – a lump of muscle available for hire – which meant I was back to grim dawn starts. I have never really understood why the working man starts even earlier than the office wallah, but it meant that on nights when we had a Results gig, I was doing nineteen-hour days. So were the others, of course, though Carpenter's position as toilet air-freshener installation man seemed to involve spending every afternoon at home in bed. Exhausting though these times were, I enjoyed being the frontman in a band. I had seen The Who, the Stones, Elvis Costello, The Boomtown Rats and sundry unremembered punk bands, so I knew the correct procedure for the rock singer – lots of jumping around, air-punching, microphone-jerking, macho posturing and, wherever possible, some cool sneering. The musicians in the band all played their part too. Little Dave was a funky bassist, Pete the drummer was frenetic, Hearnshaw earnest on his beloved synthesiser and Carpenter the hairy superstar lead guitarist *par excellence*.

We acquired a small if not particularly loyal following and when we got a residency at the Two Brewers in Clapham, Richard and Lin became our most ardent fans. Lin was convinced we were bound for stardom but, while we certainly put on a lively show, we were just one of innumerable pub-rock bands seeking attention. After a favourable review in the *NME*, we were encouraged to put out a single, a portentous piece called 'Shot Down in Tears', which portrayed the decline of a heroin addict, despite the fact that none of us had ever knowingly met anyone who took heroin. The preferred stimulant, for those of us that did, was the hash joint, and occasionally some speed. If amphetamines had been taken before the gig it could mean our set lasting ten minutes shorter than normal, which was in accordance with Carpenter's maxim:

Second verse, same as the first
– Little bit faster, little bit worse.

Our delight when little Dave brought the six hundred copies of our single to a rehearsal one evening was increased the same night by a phone call from an A-and-R man who wanted to sign us. Another good review; I began to believe Lin might be right about our potential. During the days, as I unloaded lorries and humped lumps of metal around warehouses in Acton, I dreamed of an appearance on *Top of the Pops* and long lines of sexy groupies forming outside my dressing room.

The optimism soon made its excuses and left. Following their ill-advised storage next to a radiator, the black discs converted themselves into six hundred curly vinyl ashtrays; the A-and-R man never called again and I fell out with Carpenter over money. We were occasionally paid for gigs, yet a lot of the cash was swallowed up in upgrading our equipment. Carpenter has always been shrewd and I ended up feeling that some of our investment went into upgrading the bulge in Carpenter's wallet. In retrospect I overreacted but I was growing tired of the deprivations of being in a band. Following a row about cash, Carpenter threw ten quid at me, and that was the only money I ever earned as a rock-'n-roller. Enthusiasm waned, someone slept with someone else's girlfriend, I continued to complain that I hated the name of the band ('How about Fiasco Job Job?'), Leyton High Road began to take its toll and, pretty soon, that was the end of The Results.

We just never really had the haircuts.

CHAPTER 11. SONG AND DANCE MAN

And so my twenties ricocheted along, with me rebounding from woman to woman, from scrape to scrape and from job to job. I may have been in a band and a stage show but, for money, I did *proper* work – as a landscape gardener, a postman, a market researcher, a labourer and a failed warehouseman (I was fired from the Lord John clothes company for falling asleep one afternoon in a large pile of trousers). Some jobs suited my skills better; I spent several days in supermarkets on the South Coast stalking the aisles dressed as a fox. My rôle was to detain shoppers long enough for them to watch my nice lady colleague prepare a tasty new brand of chicken burger, which they would then certainly wish to buy. Whoever thought this job up was clearly an idiot. The fox is not known for its sophisticated approach to preparing chicken, while the costume with which I was provided made me eight feet tall and, far from attracting people towards me, it alarmed them or, if they were very young, terrified them into screaming flight. Wherever I walked in the supermarket, you could hear the sound of small children crying. There were other peculiar theatrical employments; one evening, dressed as a policeman, I entered a pub in Charlotte Street and 'arrested' the advertising executive celebrating his birthday. Some of Syd's policing skills must have rubbed off on me because the chap was taken in despite my plastic helmet, purchased an hour earlier from a tourist stall. Before it turned ugly, I ripped my shirt off to reveal the words 'Happy Birthday, Doug' written on my chest, earning myself a five-quid bonus. It was low-grade stuff – but hey, it was showbiz.

Merton Road was becoming even less and less recognisable as a place of human habitation. One evening in the street outside the flat, Gary and I noticed a large discarded dentist's chair, complete with big arm and spittoon. We carried it home, where it joined the papier-mâché lamp-post and the dead-goldfish bowl as an eccentric accessory to the sitting room. The wallpaper had started to wilt and on the occasion of Lindsay's front-room lecture, 'Time and the Novel', we stripped it off, so that Lindsay could write explanatory notes on the walls with a marker pen. The rubble from the post-nuclear party, meanwhile, and the sand from the Spanish extravaganza meant that the floors looked as though they belonged in a bombed-out house in a war zone. If only the Turner Prize had existed then . . .

When I tired of my tawdry London life and the search for a form of work that would allow me longer in bed in the mornings, I visited Syd and Hazel in their new house in Bath for a taste of normality. Syd had now retired from the police and found himself a job as an usher in the courts in Bath. My parents had lived all their lives in London, so it was a big step for them to move to the small, pretty town in Somerset, with its genteel Georgian atmosphere and World Heritage status but they eased smoothly into this new milieu. Syd, predictably, became extremely popular among his new colleagues, including a camp solicitor and a clerk, known, apparently universally, as 'Wanker Watson'. Hazel, having worked as a secretary for ten years at Roan School for Boys, now did the same job at Bath High School for Girls (her conclusion was that single-sex schools suited boys less then girls), she tended her garden, read novels and dragged Syd on country walks. It is to Hazel and the Scouts that I owe my love of rambling in the country – Syd went along because he loved his wife but he *strolled* rather than walked, stopping frequently to investigate anything unusual, as though the lanes of the Cotswolds were his copper's beat in Lambeth.

At the first opportunity I hitched down to spend a glorious country weekend with them, the first of many congenial visits to the town. It was an ideal place to escape the rufty-tufty scumbag life of South Wimbledon and smoky, crapulous nights in pubs and clubs. For a year or two after finishing college, Nick stayed in Bath working at the Ministry of Defence while Richard and Lin, supplemented by their first child Freddie, and then by James, were also frequent visitors. We spent jolly Christmases *en famille* and created the brief tradition of the Smith Family Pantomime. I was the Narrator, Lin usually played Mary, Richard an obstreperous Joseph, leaving Nick, Hazel and Freddie to be the three wise men, with James as the baby Jesus. Syd had a specially created starring role as 'the Black Ram of Bethlehem'. When Freddie grew older he found these charades beneath him, until he was permitted to terminate the show abruptly by appearing unexpectedly in the nativity scene and shooting everyone with a plastic machine gun, screaming 'Eat lead, motherfuckers!'* One year I took the boys, or rather Batman and Spiderman, to busk outside the Abbey, where their superheroic qualities proved not to extend to street performance. On another, later Christmas,

---

* This is a character whose early appearance would improve many other productions I have seen.

when wee Florence was born, the cramped sleeping arrangements allowed us to finally test which of us older male Smiths was the most prolific snorer. The standard was very high, but at the end of the final snore-off, as the roof rattled alarmingly under Syd's tremendous barrage, Nick conceded defeat to the patriarch's titanic hooter.

As the 1970s came to an end, I wondered how much longer I could delay my answer to the question 'What are you going to do when you grow up?' It had become apparent that I was not going to be a pop star, and to become a writer you needed to do something I had no time for: you had to *write* something. However – what could I lose other than most of my money? – I decided to stump up with the others and return to the Edinburgh Fringe with a new show. We kept the 'alonga' in the title in the hope that people might remember us from the previous year and, surprisingly, some did. *HamalongaYorick* was a loose retelling of *Hamlet*, in the form of close-harmony singing, acrobatics – the Canalettelonis were already hardy perennials – literary parody, monologues and, unfortunately for me, dancing. In this first immature wrestle with *Hamlet*, I wrote a soliloquy that I still trot out occasionally:

'Torquay, or not Torquay, that is not Wrexham.
Wigan 'tis Newcastle-upon-Tyne to Suffolk the Hastings and
    Harrow
Of outrageous Morecambe, or to take Barnes against the sea
    at Peebles and, by opposing,
Eltham. Torbay, Ruislip, Ruislip Penzance to Sheen – aye
    there's the pub!

For in Ruislip of death, what Cheams Kingston, Wembley have
  Sheffield off this Bootle
Coil? Fife on 't. 'Tis an UnWelwyn Garden City.'

Generously received, well attended and pleasingly reviewed, the show was a big enough hit to ensure that we didn't even lose money. After a couple of appearances on Radio 2, in an activity now known as schmoozing,* I showed off to the BBC Light Ent people who produced the *News Huddlines* and *Weekending*, the topical comedy shows on Radio 4 . . . We were further thrilled to learn that we had been booked to perform the show as part of a short season of Fringe comedies at the Duke of York's Theatre in the heart of London's glittering West End. **

Wow, this made me feel tremendously important – the West End! We would be in a proper theatre, near Charing Cross station, like the ones that Hazel had taken me to as a schoolboy. It was not a school hall or a disused church but a big solid purpose-built Victorian theatre with a proscenium arch and numbered dressing rooms – intimate chambers that contained mirrors framed by light bulbs. You entered through a Stage Door, complete with Stage Doorkeeper. Before the start, a voice came over the tannoy – 'Act One beginners to the stage, please.' The little rituals stirred my blood. This must be what it was like to be a proper paid entertainer. *HamalongaYorick* played to a large partisan audience

---

* Years later in Montreal I interviewed a classically grizzled Broadway agent, Howard Lapides, who told me he had invented the word 'schmooze'. ('Well, actually it was my buddy, but he's dead, so I invented it.')

** 'London's glittering West End' is a phrase that still affords me a glimmer of camp excitement and I shall be repeating it too frequently throughout the rest of this book.

made up of pretty well everyone we communally knew and was described by Sheridan Morley in the *Spectator* as 'appalling amateur rubbish'. This was simultaneously our first review in a national publication and our first stinker (though Adam was chuffed with a description of him as 'a youthful Danny Kaye'). I was enraged into starting a feud a few years later with Sheridan M, a feud that, now he is dead, I rather regret. In truth, by the standards of the West End, I now see that the show *was* amateur rubbish. In the end, enthusiasm and 'boundless energy' (a phrase applied to us more than once) was not enough for the Duke of York's, where, in a coincidence that provides a self-aggrandising end to this paragraph, I returned fifteen years later to perform my solo version of *Hamlet*.

Morley's opinion may have been shared by the people who booked small-scale shows since no offers of work followed our performances in Edinburgh and London and I found myself back in the badlands of Merton Road without a job. Same as the previous year. Razzin' it up in Edinburgh was exciting but it meant I never had a summer holiday or any money. Was I just wasting my time? Someone's dad said, on meeting me, 'Ah yes, another one from the University of Messing About.' He was right. I owed it to Syd and Hazel to make some use of the education they had paid for. The thought that had filled me with a sense of dread when I was a schoolboy was that, one day, I would be a teacher. But when Simon suggested I should apply for a job at the language school where he was teaching, I put on my one white shirt – normally worn by Luigi Cannaletteloni – brandished my certificate from the Lycée Janson de Sailly, and did my head-boy act for the interview. Teaching English to foreigners wasn't like *real* teaching, where you faced thirty or forty potentially hostile kids;

my students were adults who had paid for their lessons and were, accordingly, industrious and eager.

The Oxford School of English was connected to Oxford not by any relationship with the university, although that was the implication, but because it was in Oxford *Street*. The students, at varying levels in their abilities, were an interesting, eclectic bunch drawn from all over the world. In my first class I had a Yugoslav dentist, a Japanese fashion designer who wanted to be a clown, and a Brazilian pilot. I learned some of the ways of languages that weren't English or French; for example, just as Chinese people have trouble with '*l*'s and '*r*'s in spoken English, and the French with '*th*'s, so Arabic speakers cannot distinguish easily between '*p*'s and '*b*'s'. I devised a trick whereby I asked the Arab students to say 'big pig' at my lighter so that they blew the flame out with the second word but not with the first. Something to do with 'plosives'. Not all of my protégés, it transpired, were as diligent as the rest. One Turkish-Cypriot lad, installed at the school at the insistence – and expense – of his father, attended eighteen months of lessons with myself and Simon, at the end of which he could manage two words in English – 'lager' and 'minicab'.

The next Edinburgh came and went without me and the Revue team and as I entered my second year of teaching I began to hear that pedagogic voice a little louder – '*Be a teacher, be a proper teacher, you'd be good at it and it's paid. You've got nowhere as a performer. In three years' worth of shows you have earned a minus amount of money and are as obscure as when you started. Teaching is worthwhile – a profession, not like poncing around on stage . . . and think of the holidays . . .*' Eventually, I grudgingly filled out an application to do a postgrad teaching course. Although I have no memory now of why, I picked Wolverhampton Polytechnic to send it to. A week after my interview I received an offer of a place, which disappointed me almost as much as if I had been rejected. I put the letter to one side for a few days to consider. It was a crossroads: did I carry on with my shambolic theatrical endeavours? Or did I abandon all that to pursue a more conventional life, the one for which my upbringing and education had prepared me?

That was on a Thursday. On the Saturday something happened that made up my mind. Among a number of highlights in my showbiz life this one stands high; I was squatting in a car park in Wimbledon, trying to find some reception on my small transistor by waggling it about. At last I could make out the words 'written by . . .' and then it was gone. Bollocks! But again it sputtered, 'with additional lines by . . .' more interference, more swearing, and then, *then* it came through loud and clear . . . 'and Brian Smith.' I had sold a joke to *The News Huddlines* on Radio 2! I would get seven quid for it! I was a professional writer! Well, anyway, I'd sold a joke. If I win the Nobel Prize tomorrow I would not be more pleased with myself than I was then. Boys, throw your shorts out the window. It's a game and a half where you are, Ron.

I sent a letter declining the offer from Wolverhampton Polytechnic.

CHAPTER 12. STAND-UP

I am a stand-up comic. Even now, after a thousand gigs, making this statement gives me a bristle of pride and a bump of self-importance. 'That must be the hardest job in the world,' people say routinely to stand-ups. It is not, of course, but it is the most *singular* job in show business and, in some ways, the most glamorous. The stand-up comedian is a solitary warrior, ignoring the theatre's fourth wall in a direct Brechtian assault on his (or her) audience, the one performer whose success or failure is determined instantly and *audibly*. He does not sit down in timid informality, he *stands up*, like you stand up against bullies or for your rights. He has come to banish cant, bullshit, hypocrisy and the straight face. He does not hide behind costumes, music, cameras, props or masks, he relies on no one but himself, he is not edited or enhanced after the event, he strides onto the middle of the stage and addresses the crowd, like a politician with no party on his back, like a preacher without God, a gladiator come to slay a roomful of lions and Christians. He 'kills', he 'rips the room apart', he 'storms it' and the world applauds at his feet. I am a stand-up comic. Who would not be proud to be such a creature?

But when he fails, when no laughs come, when he 'dies', 'goes down the toilet', why, *then* he is an arse and he must get the first train out of town. The stand-up is a con artist who will dance to any tune that gets him a gig and pander to any prejudice that keeps him in the spotlight. He distributes prejudice with a smile, disseminates the lie that laughter redeems or that it is, as Nietzsche said, 'the one true metaphysical consolation', when really it is a way of hiding from the serious business of life – the tragedy of existence.

The first time I tried stand-up I died. I also went down the pan at gigs numbers five, twelve, thirty-seven and so on, until just a few months ago when, in a large, bland businessmen's hotel near Derby, my quips left a roomful of car salesmen indifferent to the point of belligerence. To add to my shame, the shape of the room meant that after my public humiliation, when every part of me screamed to get out quick, I had to skirt around the edge of my former audience to reach the exit. They turned in their seats to consider me. Every comic knows this walk of shame. You try to avoid eye contact with anyone. You know what they are thinking: they are thinking that you are a useless, unfunny cunt. They are wondering how much you've been paid for pissing them off and how the hell you ever persuaded someone to book you. Like the golden-duck batsman's long walk back to the pavilion, or the defendant's grim passage from the dock to the cells, the cry of 'Take him down' pounding in his ears, it is a head-down procession of despair.

In stand-up comedy when you die you are a zero but when you kill you are, briefly, immortal. Mostly, though, it's somewhere in the middle.

In the Revue company's first appearance at the Edinburgh Fringe in 1977, I had done a turn impersonating the stand-up comedian Max Miller, 'the Cheeky Chappie', a massive music-hall star in the Thirties, Forties and Fifties, *so* famous and popular that they would hold the London–Brighton train for him if his show came down late. Wearing an outlandish suit, plus fours, co-respondent shoes, tilted trilby and a seductive twinkle in his eye, he delivered a brilliant patter of jokes and songs, laced with racy innuendo. He had been a hero to my Grandad Jim, and remains one to Tony, the elegant cove who works at the porter's lodge where I live. Maxie's catchphrase was bold and true: 'There'll never be another.' The routine I learnt came from a record that belonged, of course, to Adam but it was only when I came to write this book that I realised Miller's breakneck pace and cockney Jack-the-lad pose might have informed the stand-up style that I eventually evolved. Max was hugely talented, famous and rich in a way that I will never be (though I notice they *do* hold the train for me and frequently long after I have got on it). But by 1977 Max Miller had cracked his last gag and variety was dead. As far as I was concerned, my tribute to 'our Maxie' had no bearing on my own performing aspirations (whatever they were).

There were twenty-four revues – similar to what we now call sketch shows – in the Fringe programme in that eye-opening year at Edinburgh, but zero stand-ups – nor would there be for four years. The template for the British stand-up comic then was the sort of act you saw on telly in *The Comedians*, the show which gave us Bernard Manning, Stan Boardman, Frank Carson, etc.* This genre of performer did not play Edinburgh, just as Edinburgh-flavoured acts were not seen in Blackpool. I felt no affinity with these chubby blokes in their frilly shirts and glittering jackets, slickly marching their jokes by in single

* In stand-up comedy, Billy Connolly and Victoria Wood were, and are, glorious exceptions.

file. 'Sparklies', a TV booker I knew called them. Jokes to me then were for old blokes in the pub, ready-made narratives displaying no individuality, belonging to everyone, and so to no one. They told of a world I did not know, of nagging wives, stupid Irishmen, seaside boarding houses and salesmen travelling in ladies' underwear.* They might once have been the staple diet of my grandad's era but now they were the laborious weapon of pub drunks.

Unlike some comics, I was not a comedy obsessive as an adolescent but I absorbed what was around. On TV, the performers I admired were to be found among the Oxbridge set – *Monty Python*, *Beyond the Fringe*, *Pete and Dud*. I was also fond of *Hancock*, *The Goons* and, especially, Spike Milligan (I once put on his song 'I'm Walking Backwards for Christmas' twelve times in a row on the jukebox of a pub and left after the second playing). These guys did sketches and monologues, they did not lower themselves to cracking cheesy gags at a microphone – indeed, they parodied the performers who did. Eric Morecambe, it was hard to deny, was the funniest natural comic of that and possibly any other era but the archetypal comic at that time was, to me, a conservative, uninteresting figure.

Stand-up, then, was not initially a form that it crossed my mind to try, though, as the Edinburghs went by, I became increasingly frustrated with the Revue material – it was the 1980s and we were still doing a *dance* at the beginning, for Christ's sake. Adam always succeeded in spurring me into action, but his muse was a 1940s musical film star whereas by now I had tight red trousers and pogoed to The Jam. I had been the lead singer in a band

---

* I loved Syd's jokes, but principally because I loved Syd.

that had played in hip London venues, shouted loudly at CND demos and Rock Against Racism concerts – how could I wear my pencil tie and my Elvis Costello sneer with any conviction when I was still to be seen on stages around Britain in a big yellow curly wig exhorting people to wave their shoes in the air and sing 'Monopoly – the Wondergame!'? How could I, who wrote poems in the style of John Cooper-Clark and had once snorted cocaine, be performing whimsical parodies of Stanley Holloway poems?

Within thirty seconds of seeing Alexei Sayle step onto the stage at the Comic Strip in the Raymond Revue Bar, Soho in 1981 I finally knew I wanted to try stand-up comedy. What ferocious attack he had. ('I don't just do this. I'm also the editor of a newspaper called *What's On in Stoke Newington*. I don't know if you know it, it's a big sheet of paper with "fuck all" written on it.') He swore masterfully through tirades about social workers, muesli, Marxists, Mrs Thatcher and real ale – polemics which frequently span out into demented whimsy. The antithesis of the Sparkly stand-up guy, whose persona tended to be genial and straightforward, Alexei was also scornful of the privileged Oxbridge types who dominated TV. He was *angry*. Fuck you. This was evidently comedy's version of punk and it even came to adopt the terminology used by bands; comics didn't do shows, they did a 'set' at a 'gig', while ad libbing became 'riffing'.

In his shiny undersized suit and his pork-pie hat, Alexei looked to me the coolest dude in London. Scarcely less impressive were the other acts: the charismatic Rik Mayall with his shrieking sidekick Ade Edmondson; the dry, laconic Arnold Brown – a Jewish Glaswegian ('two stereotypes for the price of one'); Nigel Planer and Peter Richardson in a weird double act; and Pauline Melville, who played an extremely right-on old lady – she wasn't especially funny but, like Alexei, her subject matter was refreshingly contemporary. It all seemed so *modern*. Every sketch, every song, every monologue I had ever done suddenly acquired the odour of formaldehyde. Stunned by what I had seen, on the night bus home I announced to Kath, who had forgiven me for the wrestling incident, my intention to try stand-up. She nodded encouragement and looked doubtful. When we got to hers, I sat down, synapses firing, and wrote a routine which by morning had congealed into a thin pastiche of one of Alexei's.

Nevertheless, I was at last motivated to ring the Comedy Store,* opened a year earlier by Don Ward with charming insurance agent, dentist, dude-around-town Peter Rosengard, which had become the first arena for what was soon to be known as 'alternative cabaret'. I booked a five-minute try-out spot for a month's time on a Saturday night and sat down to consider what I might do. I had been on stage on my own many times, but only within the comforting confines of the Revue Company or the band. At this, the first Comedy Store, on the third floor of the Gargoyle Club in Soho (a strip club during the rest of the week), accessible only by lift, I felt exposed and terrified. I arrived at eight, to be told that open spots went on at two a.m. at the end of the second show. In the interim I went round to Richard and Lin's in Clapham, always a haven in my chaotic life; I ate glumly, tried not to drink too much – and failed, which was the first of several basic errors made on this maiden stand-up outing. The others were: poor microphone technique, a glazed look born of concentrating

---

* The Comic Strip was made up of successful Comedy Store acts who had formed a collective and moved round the corner.

too much on remembering my lines, an overreaction to a heckler and an inappropriate script. Phil came to cheer me on but ended up consoling me.

Tony Allen, the man who invented the term 'alternative cabaret' and acted as its unofficial guru, was the compère that night. A regular speaker at Hyde Park Corner on Sundays, Tony – tall, stooping and wild-haired – was an anarchist and a natural contrarian, whose take on the world was unfailingly provocative. For example, he would not endorse the imprisoned Nelson Mandela – an obvious hero to the left – on the grounds that he was a politician, and politicians, by definition, were corrupt. During the miners' strike he refused to join all the other comics in doing benefits because he did not wish to help send men back down into those dark dangerous holes. He set the tone (a comic I knew called him 'Lofty Tone') and it soon became unacceptable to do material that was casually sexist or, one of the Sparkly staples, racist. Swearing onstage was *de rigueur* but for several years the word 'cunt' was outlawed unless it was used to denote the beautiful genitalia of woman. Tony's namesake Keith Allen only did stand-up for a couple of years but his fearless modernity was also a big influence on the early cabaret scene. His most daring monologue, delivered in skimpy leathers, mixed two disparate contemporary iconic figures as he strutted on stage as a gay miner.

A compensation of my debut death was a first sighting of the great John Hegley – then in his early glasses period, when every quirky poem and joke returned to his love of spectacles. ('I've got my glasses on my face/I haven't got my glasses in my glasses case/I've got my glasses on my face/I've got my glasses in the proper place.') John is a one-off – a raw, multi-talented troubadour who is one of the genuine originals of comedy. But that night I did not appreciate this. That night I could only be jealous of the comics who had done well. The gong that ended my act sounded in my head for four months before I tried stand-up again.

By then the Comedy Store had closed while its owner, Don Ward, sought out newer, bigger premises to house these increasingly popular shows. In its wake a number of other venues opened; as more new acts appeared and audience numbers grew, I got booked to compère the Hemingford Arms in Islington, on the strength of my Edinburgh appearances. My opening spot was, initially, a disaster; any humour in my first line was undermined by the microphone not working. Except that it *was* working. A member of the audience shouted helpfully, 'Try turning it on' and when this proved to be outside my range of skills he kindly came onto the stage and did it for me. At the Comedy Store, I would have already been gonged off but here, in the relaxed back room of a small pub, with an audience of polite urbanites, my vulnerability worked in my favour. 'You've got to say that is an undistinguished start,' I said and when they laughed, my confidence ignited and I took my first step forward, standing up.

My success that night earned me a run of Saturday gigs at the Hemingford where I began to learn, imagine and improvise the arcane art of the compère. It is a peculiar job and a peculiar word with its irritating accent (it sounds French – yet they hardly know the word). The Americans say MC or 'host', and so do we more and more. The traditional British version did ten minutes at the start of each half and otherwise briefly introduced the performers, but I chose to do less at the front and more between acts so that I would be constantly engaged throughout the evening. As a kind of liaison officer between audience and acts, the compère sets the rhythm and tone of the evening and is therefore liable to be extrovert and upbeat. His job is akin to hosting a party – he introduces people to each other, makes sure guests and performers know what's going on, where the toilets are, when the interval is due and, as the last performer on stage, he has the final word of the night. At the Hemingford, when some audience members assumed that I was the manager of the pub who'd got up to have a go himself and ended up being quite good, I was pleased. Low audience expectation and the knowledge that I need never be on for longer than five minutes gave me the courage to ad lib and experiment, to chat to the audience and tease laughs from their responses. In pursuit of this I invented games and quizzes that I could, if I wished, return to ('Who can name five people with the initials J.C.?'* 'How many men can you name called Shane Atwoll?').

Most of the acts I introduced at the Hemingford Arms had, like myself, a background in fringe theatre. There was a French mime artist who actually *did* do 'inside the box' and 'walking into the wind'; Pierre Hollins was able to juggle apples and eat them at the same time; Fascinating Aida was a formidable trio of women in sequinned ball gowns who looked thoroughly incongruous on the tiny dusty stage in the back of a pub – but their witty, scurrilous songs (written by the divine Ms Dilly Keane) had

* e.g. John Craven, Jesus Christ, James Caan, Jacques Cousteau, Judith Chalmers, John Cleese. Never Jeremy Clarkson who mercifully didn't then exist. Now you try . . .

the crowd slobbering for more. The cabaret scene was flour-
ishing, but was still so small and poorly paid that no performer
yet considered playing it to be much of a career move. The
Edinburgh revues offered me the best route out of the nine-to-
five vortex. We had evolved a style by now that reflected our
personalities: loud, warm, clean, tuneful, witty, old-fashioned,
inventive – a curious synthesis of Adam and Babs' camp and
mine and Phil's more modern sensibilities. Max stood brashly
between the two, often in a pair of fishnets.

At our second Festival we had met a tall, stooping, itchy young
man called Rupert Gavin, who, I was astounded to learn, was
earning *eight thousand pounds a year* as an advertising executive.
Rupert was laconic and fun, a man with a department of showbiz
in his businessman's heart, and one of those people who arrives
at his office at seven a.m. and leaves twelve hours later, having
done more work than most people manage in a month. In subsequent visits up north he was our producer and fifteen years later,
by which time he had been head of BBC Worldwide, owned
several London theatres, become the boss of Odeon Cinemas
(etc.), Rupert was still producing shows of mine.

It was Rupert, or maybe Adam, who had the outstanding idea
of changing the name of our troupe to the 'National Revue
Company', using the same type font as the National Theatre. In
these more litigious times we would probably be gagged, sued
and made bankrupt, but we went unchallenged then. There is no
doubt that some people were seduced into thinking that the
company was, in some way, attached to the big theatres on the
South Bank. The *'alonga'* shows became bigger and bolder, if not
more contemporary, and we did little tours, requiring interminable
hours spent driving back at night from venues far afield so that

we might slumber for a few hours before commuting to our day jobs – in my case seventeen long stops (two changes) from South Wimbledon to a language school in Turnpike Lane. And, finally, we earned the Actors Equity cards. Being a member of a union, I felt, validated me, even though I nearly ended up as Captain Wanker* and did not yet bother to advertise that Brian Smith had become Arthur Smith.

The persistent enthusiasm and popularity in Edinburgh of the National Revue Company, the show we did (without Adam) that dispensed with camp, and some fine flirting by Babs and Max, at last made the producers at the BBC take a look at us and eventually commission a radio series. There was whooping and kissing in the back of our old yellow GPO van when we heard the news. Maxine dug out the paper cups from our *Famous Five* sketch and we toasted each other in lemonade. It began to seem plausible for us to turn properly professional soon.

I was now 'gigging' more in London in the expanding collection of venues which had become known as 'the circuit' and earning myself some small renown as a specialist compère. As MC you see a lot of acts and I began rapidly to find my place among them, as well as to sleep with one or two. I generated more workable material, some of it culled from sketches we had done, some that I had written, others I had just 'found' or relocated from their original context ('Always heed the words of Lothian Council: "Tuesdays and Fridays are rubbish days."') Like many male

* There are some great Equity names. The Chairman of the Equity Thames Variety Branch – in some fashion my representative on Earth – is called, marvellously, 'Rhubarb the Clown'.

stand-up debutants, I was aggressive – during a parody of a punk poem I twice nutted the microphone with such commitment that blood ran down my ranting face. I was confident enough to do a solo spot but it was a long time before my set was more than a ragbag of compèring conventions. There was no time to rectify this because now, if I wasn't MC-ing, I was performing with Fiasco Job Job, the new double act that Phil and I had formed. At the Hemingford I appeared several times in both guises – 'Ladies and gentlemen, that was Fiasco Job Job with Phil Nice and er, me.'

The double act was more formal, more artful than my early knockabout MC act. Phil's and my stage relationship was an extreme version of our real friendship with me the aggressive self-important wide-boy intellectual to Phil's put-upon man of reason whose wanky sleeveless jumper turned out to be knitted from his collected belly-button fluff. Having spent much time on stage together in the Revue, Phil and I had an easy rapport, the act coalesced rapidly and soon Fiasco Job Job was known as one of the best double acts in town, an accolade easily earned since there were *only* about ten.*

The essence of the double act is bickering status disputes . . .

ARTHUR: . . . I'm sorry, Phil, I can't do that. I'm going to my handsome classes.
PHIL: (*Incredulous*) Handsome classes? What, you're learning how to be handsome?

---

* Here are the names of the others I remember: the Devilfish Horn club – who became children's TV stars as Trev 'n Simon, the Oblivion Boys, Dusty and Dick – one of whom was Harry Enfield – the Flaming Hamsters, the Vicious Boys, the Wild Girls, the Port Stanley Amateur Dramatic Society and Skint Video. Actually there are more comics now but not many more double acts.

ARTHUR: No. (*Pause*) I teach.*

At this point I instructed Phil to pretend to be female so I could demonstrate to him how to talk to women.

PHIL: I can't be a woman. I've got a penis.
ARTHUR: Well, give it here then.
(Phil produces sausage which Arthur pockets)

This sophisticated conceit meant that before every gig Phil and I had to consult over which of us would purchase a sausage. Buying them individually was not possible, so after the gig I would arrive back in South Wimbledon on the last Tube, half-pissed, gee'd-up by the applause, clutching three or four sausages. I fried these up into a Phil-penis sandwich in our greasy kitchen before picking my way through the socks, newspapers and half-eaten chips that lay between the kitchen and my bed. One night an article protruded from the litter. Gary had placed it there for my attention before turning in. It was a review in that day's London *Evening Standard* which, I'm afraid, I'm going to quote from:

---

* Comedy nerds may note that this exchange is based on a Woody Allen line. I loved the urbane intelligence of Allen's work and listened to his stand-up routines on cassette. Reading his biography, I learned that he had been part of the famous team of writers who worked on the Syd Caesar Show on NBC in the 1950s, a group that included Mel Brooks, Neil Simon and Carl Reiner. Aged twenty-six, when Allen was earning fifteen hundred dollars a week, he jacked it all in to be a stand-up. Although, initially, he died most nights, he ground on until he became a sell-out Las Vegas act. And then he retired from stand-up and made some films . . .

Alternative Comedians take it in turns to compère the shows. At the Hemingford Arms it was Brian Smith's turn. He is a formidable and aggressive comedian of immense assurance. No one ever dared tell HIM he was boring.

He fixes his audience with a lopsided grin, demands names, introduces everyone to everyone. 'Jeremy, Tim, Vicky?' he said, 'You can tell we're in Islington . . .' and moved at breakneck speed into a joke in French, a Rastafarian on Wordsworth, a Shakespearean knock-knock.

He cropped up at the Earth Exchange too this time as half of an excellent duo Fiasco Job Job. Yes, they are good but don't sit in the front row. I suspect a young man called Ralph wished himself far away . . . Fiasco Job Job were a smash but the star of the evening was young Mr Hegley again . . .

My 'material', such as it was, was clearly not in the mould of the great Alexei who never really played the comedy circuit, despite his influence on it. The 'Rastafarian on Wordsworth' to which the reviewer referred was another piece I'd done in a Nat Rev Co show. Adopting the Jamaican accent of Napthali, a smoking Rastaman chum, I intoned:

'I . . . and I wander lonely as a cloud,
Him float on high him move and dance
when all at once me see a cloud
– a host of golden ganja plants!'

At a left-wing benefit gig there was an uncomfortable moment when someone shouted 'Racist!' at this; I sensed immediately that a white man impersonating a black man (a favourite device of the rabid comedian Jim Davidson) was not on any more and I never did the joke again. The phrase 'politically correct' had entered the English language, followed not long after by 'It's political correctness gone mad.' Comedy was an arena where battles over language and ideologies were being fought out. At another benefit – for John McCarthy, the journalist who had been taken hostage in Beirut – I referred to the people 'manning' the information desk, provoking the heckle, 'That should be *staffing*!'

An Australian feminist comic at one of our gigs was outraged into heckling at the Fiasco Job Job penis/sausage exchange.

'Just because he hasn't got a penis that doesn't make him a woman – he should have a *vagina!*'

This seemed a reasonable point so, following a discussion with the audience, we continued with a peach representing Phil's vagina. The debate over what was 'acceptable' and what wasn't continued (and still continues). I had a little run of one-liners based on well-known scraps of language, e.g.:

'Red sky at night, shepherd's delight. Red sky in the morning, shepherd's warning. Red sky in the afternoon, shepherd – stoned out of his head.'

'Tyger tyger burning bright – vandals set the zoo alight.'

'You can lead a horse to water, but you can't make it throw Princess Anne in.' (These days, pleasingly the joke can be revived with Zara Phillips in place of her mum).

One night I tried a new one:

'The Grand Old Duke, he had ten thousand men – he got AIDS.'

This received a small laugh, but a big heckle: 'That's horrible! I've got friends who are dying of AIDS!' It was Simon Fanshawe, the only openly gay comic in Britain. Any attempt to confront him would have looked as though I was anti-gay, which I most certainly was not. And he was right: it was a cheap shot that tapped into a national homophobia that had grown more virulent since the appearance of the AIDS virus. Again, as when I was challenged about the Rasta joke, I crumbled and mumbled an apology. Simon was brave that night and, if I didn't thank him then, let me do so now. I was given pause once more to consider my attitude and my material. I didn't want to get laughs at the expense of some poor bastard with AIDS.

Attitude, according to the American David Letterman, whose TV chat show various people attempted to emulate on British TV throughout the 1980s and 1990s, was everything. If there was a consistent strong attitude fuelling your performance, you could talk about anything and get away with it. Whilst I felt that if your 'attitude' was racist, sexist or homophobic and you did it as yourself rather than as a character comic, you were playing a sad or dangerous game. It was the attitude I observed in John Dowie that inspired me. Dowie was a Brummie comic and to my mind the funniest stand-up in London at the time. His anger at the world was genuine, unlike, say, that of Jasper Carrot, whom he resembled. Dowie's fury was not manufactured, even when he was talking about everyday stuff: 'I see now you can buy milk in *boxes*, and it says 'open this end'. Listen, it's *my* fucking milk, I'll open it *whatever fucking end I want*.' I looked up to John and his invigorating cynicism; in later years, I was chuffed to collaborate on shows with him.

Yet more clubs were opening, and by the time I returned to the new Comedy Store in Leicester Square I was a paid act called Arthur Smith (unless, of course, there was anyone in from Streatham tax office, in which case I was Daphne Fairfax). The Falklands War was under way and the Comedy Store was one of the few public places where you could escape the outpourings of jingoism that accompanied it. The Falklands provided a lot of weak material for comics although, mercifully, I cannot recall any of my own. Phil and I attempted a kind of childish squabble, inspired by Borges's description of the conflict as 'two bald men arguing about a comb', but it didn't play well.

It is hard now for young people to understand the fierce divisions that existed in British politics in the 1980s when Thatcher and her followers pursued their brutal agenda, when Tories felt no need to be touchy-feely, when dockers, miners, shipbuilders and a multitude of other workers were discarded and there were three million unemployed, when greed became heroic and City boys swanked their wealth around the West End.* 'Is he one of us?' Thatcher liked to ask, and so did those on the left. Thatcher once remarked that 'Any man who rides a bus to work after the age of thirty can count himself a failure.' We hated the woman and all Tories and we took the bus. One of my own sacrificial gifts to the Labour Party was a refusal to sleep with any Conservative voters, however sexy and alluring they might be. It was a resolution that was only tested once but, amazingly, I held my nerve, and went home to pleasure myself in a socialist way.

* cf. the period leading up to the current economic crisis.

There is an irony about the comics' opposition to Thatcher, of course. What could be more Thatcherite than a stand-up comedian? Self-employed, un-unionised,* unsupported by any namby-pamby arts grant, he has got on his bike and got a gig. As she won the next two elections, the jokes and the vitriol continued, but I am not persuaded that the routines of a small number of obscure comics troubled Conservative Party 'think-tanks' for long. Alternative cabaret's tiny contribution to the left was the shaking up of the cosy conservative world of 1970s and 1980s light entertainment.

None of this affected the Nat Rev Co, marooned as we were in the 1940s. Our style was an oddity, inhabiting a different showbiz universe from the one to be found on the London comedy circuit – or anywhere, really, except on our radio shows. Nostalgic, dotted with mid-century pastiche, the shows were nevertheless 'tirelessly inventive'. In one, we gave the audience scratch-and-sniff cards to enhance the sketch they were watching. In another, an audience member sounded a buzzer dictating an immediate improvisation, long before *Whose Line Is It Anyway?* did the same thing on TV. In the awfully titled *Piccalongadillygo*, performed at the newly opened Assembly Rooms, a comic or musical item existed for every square of the Monopoly board and was performed in the order dictated by a throw of the audience dice. We yodelled, tumbled, introduced the Intensely Experimental Theatre Company, sang in Norwegian, Hawaiian and French and learned to sing 'Jingle Bells' backwards – a trick I still dine out on.

At Edinburgh, if nowhere else, we had a following but we

* No equity card was required for stand-up.

were still concocting wacky publicity stunts to boost numbers further. We played golf down the Royal Mile, performed a Kung Fu version of *Gone With The Wind* on top of an empty plinth outside the Fringe Box Office – competing with the youthful Ian Hislop of the Oxford Revue – and then there was the painful Batman incident.

The hook from which we hung *Satalongamatinee* was the local morning picture shows we had all attended as children, so to raise press interest we performed at the one cinema in Edinburgh that still ran one. It was soon apparent that even *our* sketches were above the heads of this restless audience. Dressed in my Batman outfit, I determined to save the day. Super-heroically, I laid down the challenge, 'All right! Who wants to fight Batman?' A dozen small arms shot up. They formed a queue on the stage and then took turns to punch me, very hard, in the guts. This would have been a good story had there been any TV crews or journalists in the auditorium but, alas, the only adults watching were the manager of the cinema sniggering into his moustache and Rupert, smiling wryly. I acquired a stomach-ache and the wisdom never again to invite violence from ten-year-old boys.*

An extravagant approach to audience participation was the signature dish of every Revue Company show. Thousands of people were persuaded to wave a shoe in the air and sing 'We are the Gaumonteenies', to impersonate farmyard animals or to rub their tummies and pat their heads while repeatedly chanting, 'Rumpty Tumpty-Tum'. We infiltrated the audience even as they were entering the auditorium – 'slick mingling', as we called it –

---

* I reminded Rupert of this story recently and he said, 'Yes, I own that cinema now.'

which was potentially dangerous for Babs who, despite being an excellent dancer, is so clumsy and gaffe-prone that she earned one of Adam's fizzing soubriquets – 'Clitter-fingers'. During one slick-mingle, 'Clitter' inadvertently pulled out a man's tracheotomy tube and, later in the run, harried an old chap onto stage with the line 'Come on! What's the matter with you? Have you only got one leg?' 'Well, actually,' he said apologetically, 'I have.' 'Still,' he added gamely, 'it *is* the year of the disabled.'

The radio series was recommissioned but as we reached our late twenties enthusiasm for the live shows was diminishing, and enthusiasm was our strongest suit. In a shopping centre in Swansea, where we were seeking to drum up trade for our show at the local fringe festival, an old lady had delivered a stinging, heartfelt heckle, 'Why don't you go back to London and leave us all alone?' Agreed, Madam.* Stand-up comedy had begun to colonise the Edinburgh Fringe programme and the festival would never be quite the same again. We all had, as they say now, 'other projects to pursue', and while none of us regretted the end of the era of the live Nat Rev Co, we knew it had been a robust episode in our lives, that the intimacy born of hours spent in the back of cheap vans, frantic scrambles from rubbish job to gig, anxious minutes searching for costumes backstage, sunny afternoons rehearsing bad acrobatics by the river in Hammersmith, cramped dawns in caravans, sexual escapades uproariously recounted, we knew that these shared adventures would create a bond between us that would not be broken. And it never has.

* I try to have an answer to this whenever I do a show out of town.

And now I was going to get a go on TV. One afternoon in Edinburgh, during the run of the last-ever National Revue Company show, *ClapalongaCurtaincall*, I was visited by a London Weekend Television researcher who told me that they wanted me to appear in a new late-night stand-up comedy programme called *Pyjamerama*. Good gracious.

– How long will my spot be?

He smiled.

– No, we want you to present the whole series.

Blimey. It was barely three years since I had first stepped on stage at the Hemingford Arms and my reaction to the news was less delighted than horrified. I wasn't ready for this – I had barely twenty minutes of material; I felt more apprehensive than I had since those schoolboy Saturdays waiting to go in to bat. But I did it and they didn't ask for the money back. You may judge the impact I made on *Pyjamerama* (why did these ghastly titles follow me around?) from the one offer of work that resulted from it: I was asked to be in a re-enactment of a murder for a TV crime programme, on account of my resemblance to the suspect. The character monologues I performed at the front of a late-night Thames TV (London only) chat show caused a similar lack of fuss among agents. Acting seemed an area I could explore. I saw myself as a 'character actor' (as Nicholas Crane, the eminent thespian, points out, this actually means 'ugly actor') although I knew that the only real character I could play would have to be rather like me and, given my inability to do accents, he would have to come from South London too.

The Nat Rev Co was no more and my teaching career was ending too. The appearances on TV of 'Mister Brian', their teacher at the Language School, amused my students, whose ribald reactions led me to introduce them to the idiom 'to take the piss'. Many nationalities filed through my classes but I never found one that lacked humour and my years of teaching emphasised for me the essential similarities between cultures, the *sameness* of us all. My income from comedy now outstripped my wages from teaching and it was time to become a professional, if not full-time, comedian. After handing in my resignation at the language school, I took my favourite class out for an evening in the West End to say goodbye to them and, I hoped, to teaching. A photo records the evening: Mansour, a lanky Iranian with a flashing, mischievous smile, is standing in Trafalgar Square, beaming away like a lighthouse, with six struggling pigeons shoved up his jumper and all my class, from all over the world, are laughing around him.

Writing and performing comedy on stage and radio had allowed me to achieve a major ambition. I did not have to get up *before I wanted to* any more. Oh most wonderful! For months after my retirement from teaching I set the alarm for seven a.m. in order to savour the thought of all those poor saps, slogging it out on the Tube. And then, hmmm, turn over and back to sleeeep. Laughter, marvellously, had offered me a lie-in. I am a stand-up comic. I do not get up early.

CHAPTER 13. PANTOMIME DANE

When I was offered the chance to understudy Frankie Howerd in a revival of *A Funny Thing Happened on the Way to the Forum* I was flattered, but not enough to accept the booking. I imagined the announcement from the front-of-house manager: '... and so Mister Howerd's part will be played tonight by ...' (she looks down at a piece of paper) '... Arthur Smith,' followed by a chorus of 'Who?' and the unmistakable sound of people leaving. Thank you, but no.*

Around the same time, Adam and I travelled back by train from Cardiff with Kenneth Williams. Kenneth spoke wistfully about his sexy exploits as a sixteen-year-old lad during the Blitz. He seemed indifferent to his own huge talent and, having formed the impression that Ad and I were intellectual heavyweights, was eager to discuss two esoteric books that he had read but we had not. I sometimes think the best thing about having a degree is that you don't have to worry about *not* having one. Kenneth seemed disappointed by his profession and by life in general. Like Frankie Howerd, he bore the sadness of having conducted his career at a time when being a male homosexual was effectively illegal and when Simon Fanshawe's material would have had him lynched. There was a tradition of camp comedy but its exponents

* Later, I wrote for Frankie in the *Loose Ends* panto.

had to promote the fiction of their own heterosexuality. Ah, the good old days.

You wait for one old-timer and then three come along at once. A few weeks after I met Kenneth Williams, I supported Ken Dodd at a corporate event at Beverley race course. Dodd is an extraordinarily durable comedian who knows so many jokes and is so eager to tell them all that his shows are liable to end in the car park long after the exasperated techies have turned the lights out in the theatre and gone home. I wonder if he is one of those entertainers who is only really happy when performing – stage junkies, for whom a night away from the microphone is a dull prospect indeed. In the big marquee by the racetrack, true to form, Doddy was overrunning and the disco had been paid off. The audience, male businessmen, needed a piss and a chance to chat up the 'hospitality girls' (it was a very 1980s affair) before the local Cinderellas got on the coach home. However, when the MD of the company paying for the event asked me to go on stage and, er, pull Ken Dodd off, I refused. One owed respect to the comics who went before, although I maintained my animosity to the racist right-wing brigade and when, at the same event the following year, Stan Boardman started his set with a couple of 'paki' jokes, I boldly contrived to be nowhere near him at any time during the evening.

Photos of Frank, Kenneth and Doddy were among the gallery of comic heroes who looked down on me as I descended the steps at the Paris Studio, the large velvety basement venue on Lower Regent Street where BBC audience-comedy shows were recorded. When rehearsals started for *The Good Human Guide*, the National Revue Company radio series (the title of our pilot,

Whizzalongawavelength, was rejected, thank God), I wondered if my photo would ever join theirs? The correct answer is no, and not just because the BBC sold the Paris Studio shortly after this. *The Good Human Guide* ran for several series, was nominated for a Prix Italia award – whatever that might be – and saw us dubbed 'the Young Sound of Radio 2', six words that, at the time, instantly rendered us the least cool group of people in Britain. Cool or not, the shows failed to make enough of an impression at the BBC for any evidence of them to exist in their sound archive.

Radio allows you a freedom as a writer and/or performer that is not available on TV, in the theatre, or on film where there are numerous filters between the script and the final result – set, costume, lighting, camera angles, make-up, and some young bloke in a jacket who knows more than you. Radio starts from nothing – from silence – but can then go anywhere with a few words or sounds. It enables listeners to access their own imagination and it is cheap enough to make that it encourages experimentation. In a screenplay, a plane crashing into the side of a mountain would cost tens, probably hundreds of thousands of pounds to film.* On radio it's a couple of sound effects (known in the trade as FX) – price, about seven quid. Radio can transform your perceptions in a second.

My association with BBC Radio had begun properly on the magical occasion of the sale of my first joke to *The News Huddlines*, the first of about twelve. Then Phil and I flogged a few quick sketches to *Not the Nine O'clock News* and later to *Alas Smith and*

---

* This becomes less true every day. Soon they won't need scenery or actors – it will all be done on computer.

Jones, often managing to palm off any rejected material onto *Hale and Pace*. I also had bit parts in TV shows. I was beaten to death by Rick Mayall in *Filthy Rich and Catflap*, the one-series successor to the *Young Ones*, after which I returned to being the programme's audience warm-up man. In cult sci-fi sitcom *Red Dwarf*, I played the manager of a club on a planet where everything went backwards and my part was to be run in reverse – thus making what I said incomprehensible. I proposed to the writers, Rob and Doug, that, given the nature of my part, it didn't really matter *what* words I spoke and they agreed that I could come on swearing like Gordon Ramsay (although he had not yet been invented). The studio audience were suitably shocked by the filthy tirade that I delivered to my fellow actors in the scene, which ended with the words 'I'm not actually addressing you. I'm addressing the one prat in this country who's bothered to get hold of this recording, turn it round and actually work out the rubbish I am saying. What a poor, sad life he's got! I hate the lot of you, bollocks to you!' The show duly aired and I thought no more about it until three years later when a man shouted out at me on Wandsworth Common, 'I know what you said on *Red Dwarf*!' Running my little scene backwards is now, I gather, for the Dwarfies who inhabit the internet in large numbers a nerd rite of passage.

With the radio work, the stand-up gigs and further bit parts on TV – once you had an equity card it was *de rigueur* to make an appearance on *The Bill* – I had now accrued enough money to buy a flat and to do a pantomime in Denmark.

Merton Road had provided a splendid and forgiving arena for several years but to call it dilapidated would have been a compliment. Now, at the end of my twenties, its tatty, fetid charms began to fade, as the mice scuttling across the grimy kitchen linoleum began to multiply: Brian, you must stop living like a teenage runaway. Neither Lindsay nor I could afford to buy a place but, between us, we could scrape up enough for a deposit. And so I moved four stops up the Northern Line to Balham and, looking at my surroundings now, I remark that Lindsay is long gone but I am still here. There was a famous sketch about Balham, written by Frank Muir and Denis Norden, which became a short film narrated by Peter Sellers. 'Balham – Gateway to the South' remains an epithet beloved of taxi drivers and makes my manor the only one in Britain with its own catchphrase.

Now that Balham is the most fashionable place on Earth, it is hard to imagine its tawdry reputation in 1984, a reputation that dated back to the eighteenth century when it was known as 'a brothel on the way to Brighton'. The prostitutes who once lined Bedford Hill have moved on to Streatham and beyond, while the Bedford Arms is no longer a place of murky couplings but home to the Banana Cabaret, one of London's longest-running comedy clubs. 'With its broad boulevards and its pulsating nightlife, Balham is like a cross between Paris and Rio de Janeiro,' someone wrote in the London *Evening Standard* once. It was me. In the same article I also proclaimed myself the mayor ('Night Mayor – I don't do days').* I continue to bat for Balham which, despite its recent gentrification, still retains a certain comical identity. As does the whole of South London for the lardies of the North.

* A joke stolen a few years later by William Hague, a long-forgotten Tory-boy leader of the Tory party.

George Melly, a committed North London man, referred to us in the South as 'transpontines'. My own joke runs thus: 'In North London they have little blue plaques commemorating famous people. In South London we have big yellow signs saying 'Did you see this murder?'

Du Cane Court is a large block of thirties flats near Balham Tube. Syd had pointed it out to me once as we drove past, assuring me that 'that was where Hitler was going to live'. Even at the age of ten this struck me as unlikely. The theory, endorsed by older Balham residents, comes with no real evidence but several embellishments. From the air, the flats resemble a swastika; the Court was used as a navigational aid by the Luftwaffe and, significantly, was never bombed; Mrs Goering had tea here before the War; the seventh floor was full of spies . . . and so on. I even met an old lady who believed that Lord Haw Haw was broadcasting, not from Berlin, as historians and the people who caught him believe, but from Du Cane Court in Balham. Was there a kernel of truth in any of this? Had the Germans designated my flat as the new 10 Downing Street? Or rather, Buckingham Palace? Was Adolf really going to drive up the A23 in a removal van with Eva Braun? More plausibly, had some Nazi committee somewhere taken a look at the place, brand new and secure, and earmarked it for something? A barracks, perhaps? I paid my nephew James to investigate it a few years ago and he concluded that the only real way to find out would be for him to fly to Berlin, stay in a nice hotel, and look in archives. I didn't want to find out that much and promptly transferred James to another department of UBE (Uncle Brian Enterprises).

I had lived in the flat a few months when I was offered the

role of Nurse Nelly Nightcap, playing opposite Adam's Sheriff of Nottingham, in an English-language pantomime in Copenhagen. Three months in a European capital all paid for? Acres of liberated blonde Nordic hotties? I cancelled the few gigs I had and set off for Harwich in the back of the retired London taxi that was Adam's car. While casual conversation between us meant I had to bellow and Adam got a stiff neck, we cut a dash as he put on his chauffeur's cap to drive us off the ferry through immigration control into Denmark. The Danes knew of the Hackney carriage but had never seen one. I waved graciously, leading the man on duty to remove his hat and declare, 'Ah, it is the King of England!' This remains the only joke I have ever heard a customs officer make.

Adam and I had adjoining rooms in Copenhagen in a flat in one of the big dark houses up a broad road, drooping with brown trees. The owner was Magda — a heavy-lidded old woman who smelt of melancholia, sat in her kitchen drinking all day, and soon, predictably, conceived an overwhelming passion for Adam. But there was no time for romance. Rehearsals got under way and, although I was merely a member of the cast, I could not stop myself engaging in script battles with Vivienne McKee, the onlie begetter of London Toast Theatre's annual *Crazy Kristmas Cabaret*. The show bore some relation to *Babes in the Wood*, but in tribute to the striking miners back home contained several references to Arthur Scargill and Mrs Thatcher. I cannot recall now how Nurse Nelly featured in the plot but it wasn't crucial. My task was to parade around the forest displaying a rapacious sexuality, flirting and duetting with the Sheriff in a range of colourful outfits — each more hideous than the one before. Panto dames fall into two categories: the *actor-dame* who has his own costumes, does his own make-up and looks like a woman, and the category which welcomed me – the *comedian-dame* who is just an ugly bloke in a skirt.

Pantomime is a uniquely British entertainment, so a proportion of our audience were Danish professors of English and anthropologists stroking their goatees and pondering the cultural significance of all the cross-dressing, outlandish costumery and audience participation. What did this peculiar presentation tell us about the British psyche? The programme contained background notes on the history and the form of this esoteric Anglo-Saxon entertainment, so that when a character said, 'Oh yes, he did,' there was a brief pause while the audience consulted their notes to find the correct response. All credit to the Danes, they played their part with gusto. 'OH NO, HE DID NOT,' they hollered back. The rest of the audience contained intrigued couples, schoolchildren and pissed-up day-tripping Swedes who seemed to understand the shouting-out principle *without* recourse to the programme.

One of the reasons I loved doing stand-up was that it had freed me from the irksome business of dealing with stage costumes, a duty where my ineptitude bordered on the dyspraxic. You cannot, however, play dame without the obligation to be constantly wrestling backstage with a big dress and oversized high heels. In this area, as in many others, Adam and I were opposites. His talent for manipulating buttons, hooks, Velcro, sequins and cloth is world-class but, even by his own vertiginous standards, Adam surpassed himself during our six-week run in Copenhagen. In our big love scene at the end, while I tottered around with my frock hanging off and my false tits at half-mast, the sheriff made his entrance every night and every matinée in an outfit of his own design that was as ludicrous as it was superbly ironed but, more amazingly, was different *every single time!* It became a joke between us as to how much he could make me laugh when he entered stage right in some new ensemble that he had spent the morning chasing down and sewing up. On the last night he arrived to seduce Nurse Nelly in a full suit of shining armour. If the run had gone on much longer I would not have been surprised to see him come on painted gold and astride an elephant.

Performing two shows a day was tiring – and pretty boring too after a while, which was why Adam and I would depart from the script in an unending quest to upstage each other, sometimes to an extent that led me into further artistic conflict with Viv. I was always interested in finding ways to lighten the tedium of regurgitating the same old stuff at the same old time in the same old place every day, and on one occasion, when I was backstage executing another imperfect costume change, I accepted a cigarette – a cigarette that, I now realise, contained no tobacco. As the curtain opened on my next scene, I was in my correct position – one foot resting jauntily on a low table in another sensationally maladjusted costume – when I experienced a very strong sensation which, I have since learned, is known in certain circles as being 'stoned out of my bonce'. This feeling was accompanied by the revelation that I was an absurd creature. Here I was, a grown man, standing on stage in an ill-fitting dress, confronting two hundred Scandinavians who were staring at me, clearly expecting me to *do* something. I had no idea what that thing might be – the script had joined me in going out of my mind. A prolonged, embarrassed silence followed while the audience and I blinked at each other. We all wondered what was going to happen. And then I found myself launching into an *a cappella* rendition of 'Blue Moon', a number we had sung in the Nat Rev Co. This, mercifully, seemed to satisfy them, until at last the sheriff arrived wearing a ten-gallon hat to rescue me and guide me through the rest of the scene. My hero!

Alas, neither Nurse Nelly nor Magda would ever be of real interest to the sheriff, who preferred to hang out with fellow leather cowboys in Copenhagen's gay bars. Sometimes he would bring home a ranch hand and on a good morning his leathery hunk would enjoy breakfast with my blonde, while we prepared for the matinée. Danish women were open, liberated and direct – seeming not to understand notions of flirting or romance. Either they were going to go to bed with you or they weren't. They would tell you which if you asked, and sometimes if you didn't. One morning I woke up in bed with a woman in her flat to find a man mending the door to her bedroom. She smiled, and introduced him as her fiancé's father; he and I exchanged polite greetings and he went on with the door while I put my clothes on.

Other than the occasion when I got locked in Elsinore Castle with a Danish model, my favourite night in Denmark came halfway through the run of the *Crazy Kristmas Cabaret* when Richard, now the assistant editor of the *British Medical Journal*, showed up with various other important medical journos from around the world. These high-minded doctors had all been at a conference on alcoholism and, perhaps in the spirit of research, were all superbly pissed. The man from the *Chinese Medical Journal* did not understand anything about the nature of the show that he was seeing but had a rollicking good time anyway. At the end Richard and I went for a drink together and on the street outside the Tivoli Gardens, we embraced in pleasure at the coincidence of the date of our reunion. It was my thirtieth birthday.

CHAPTER 14. ROOMS ABOVE PUBS

In the comedy listings in *Time Out* this Monday (26 January 2009) there are nineteen venues where you can see stand-up comedy in London – and there will be dozens more advertised on the internet and outside the M25. In the mid-1980s, before stand-ups swamped the singers and speciality acts, before 'alternative cabaret' became 'alternative comedy', when the shows were listed in the theatre section of *Time Out* and tended to be at weekends only, there was but one Monday gig – in a small vegetarian restaurant misleadingly called the Earth Exchange on the Archway Road. It had no lights and no stage but Phil and I tried out material there since we knew, however poor our new gags might be, we were unlikely to be barracked by thirty North London vegans. This was not an evening for shoutiness and dick jokes.

Kim, who ran the gig, was a generous, gentle man with a quizzical look, and the Earth Exchange was warm and hippie-ish in his image. Every successful club reflected the character of its creator: The King's Head, a dark basement in Crouch End, was friendly, experimental and smoky, like its boss Peter Grahame; The New Variety CAST shows, which occupied various pubs round town, represented socialism in shambolic action – as did its organisers, Roland and Clare Muldoon, who went on to rescue the Hackney Empire from bingo and decrepitude. But the most striking example of the overlapping of venue and person was to be found down the rough end of Greenwich, the natural habitat of one of the most remarkable people I ever met.

The ironically named Tunnel Palladium was situated in the Mitre pub at the southern entrance to the Blackwall Tunnel, isolated in wasteland and flanked by a gasholder. The Sunday shows were run and compèred by small-time legend Malcolm Hardee, whom I had come across in Edinburgh when he was living in a tent and performing with The Greatest Show on Legs – an amateurish, knockabout outfit whose don't-give-a-fuck attitude and surreal visuals were a refreshing antidote to some of the more austere and earnest acts on display at the Fringe. That was the year when, in a dispute with the American comic Eric Bogossian, he had retaliated by driving naked through Bogossian's show on a fork-lift truck, trailing his audience behind him.

Malcolm, who resembled a debauched Eric Morecambe, was a one-man affront to sobriety, cleanliness and good order. He had been a pupil at Colfe's Grammar School, a nearby rival of Roan, my old school in Greenwich, but had been expelled for blowing up the school organ. His true alma mater was Exeter Prison where he spent several years at Her Majesty's pleasure, though it is hard to imagine anything Malcolm did that might have given the queen pleasure. His career as a car thief and drug dealer having stalled, he decided to go into showbiz with his friend Martin Soan, who had created a pornographic Punch and Judy show to perform around south-west England. This eventually became The Legs, who scandalised the nation (and several others) with their nude cha-cha-cha balloon dance.

Phil and I played the opening night at the Tunnel which, under Malcolm's influence, became the arena where London's top hecklers gathered every Sunday to slaughter open spots and established acts alike. Some punters even met up before-hand in a kind of heckling seminar and one night, when I was performing solo, a voice in the dark interrupted me with a Latin phrase that turned out to mean 'show us your tits'.* The word 'notorious' soon attached itself to the Tunnel which is now remembered as Alternative Comedy's equivalent to the previous generation's Glasgow Empire – a place for confronta-tion, raucousness, multiple comedy pile-ups and deaths. It was not uncommon for the acts to be booed off with such effic-iency that the whole show was over in twenty minutes, an occasion that was greeted by the regulars as a great success. Malcolm, instinctively anti-authoritarian from his thick black glasses, down his naked hairy body, to his piss-stained odd socks, liked to encourage the mayhem by the frequent exhibi-tion of his titanic testicles, which he advertised as 'the second biggest in the country – after Jenny Agutter's father's'. (Apparently, they had once compared notes.) If the mood took him he would urinate over the front row and, such was his charisma, the victims cheered rather than remonstrated.

The Tunnel's uproarious air of unpredictability was encour-aged by what seemed like a deranged booking policy. Possessing a natural affinity with the under-rehearsed shambles, Malcolm showcased acts others feared to: the sensational Chris Lynham who ended his set by removing his clothes, lighting a firework he wedged up his arse** and singing 'There's no business like show business'; a tap-dancing Swede (badly let down by the

* *papillas tuas nobis ostende.*
** Malcolm tried this trick himself and ended up in hospital with a singed anus.

carpeted stage); Madame Poulet and her Singing Chickens (don't ask); the Ice Man, whose whole act consisted of increasingly frantic attempts to melt a large block of ice; Sylvie Bottle-Knocker, a busty lady able to open a bottle of beer using only her breasts and, once only, a transvestite dressed as Myra Hindley, who told the story of *Little Red Riding Hood*. Malcolm's compèring style was fair but ruthless. He would warn the crowd, 'The next act is liable to be shit', but then praise them if they were entertaining. If a performer had bombed badly there was always a laugh available to the MC afterwards and Malcolm would take it with glee. Remembering my own first try-out, I preferred not to compound the comic's misery when I compèred, but I hinted at their failure with a line borrowed from the novelist Anthony Powell: 'Well, I think the best we can say about him is that he is a rich testimony to the infinite diversity of the human personality.'

Every week at the Tunnel Palladium, and then at its successor Up The Creek, the audience chanted joyfully along with Malcolm's handful of old one-liners and clapped indulgently when he set off on his inevitable rambling harmonica solos. He had already created the phrases which defined him – where other people said 'Hello' or 'Goodbye', Malcolm dispensed a loud 'Oy Oy!' His philosophy of life was encapsulated in his other two catchphrases – 'Knob out!' and 'Fuck it!' – both of which he enacted with little encouragement. His reckless appetite for adventure, his dislike of being on his own and his genetically programmed rejection of the sensible course of action meant that every comic had a Malcolm story. If Tony Allen was the theory of anarchic comedy, then Malcolm was its cock-eyed embodiment.

Forty minutes round the South Circular from the Tunnel, in newly gentrified Battersea, stood Jongleurs, a big new venue above a pub, described by Arnold Brown as looking like 'a disused Bavarian castle'. The audience here, who sat at candlelit tables in authentic cabaret style, was well-heeled and high-heeled, containing a consistent smattering of braying men in blue shirts with white stripes and women sprouting shoulder pads and big hair – City boys and girls, Eurobond traders, Big Bang babies: this was not a lefty-liberal joint like the Earth Exchange. Jongleurs was dreamed up, and set up, by Maria Kempinska whom I had also met in Edinburgh. I took her out for lunch before her big opening in Battersea, retrieving her from the department store where she was demonstrating vacuum cleaners to bolster her funds.

Other venues paid a 'door split', which rarely amounted to more than a few pounds (once at the Hemingford I was given an envelope containing 50p), whereas Maria offered a guaranteed fee commensurate with the size of the room, even though she could hardly afford it.* In these early days Maria had an eclectic booking policy appropriate to the name she had chosen for her club – though her tastes were less earthy and more professional than Malcolm's. A combination of disparate performers complemented the comics – apart from the inevitable singers, magicians and jugglers, she hired trapeze artists, fire-eaters, heavy-metal bands and, on the opening night, a lasso-ist. The shows were full of novelty but the standard of the 'spesh acts' was uneven and as the months went by it became apparent that the

* No need for too much sympathy, though, because eventually they shot a TV series there, she and her husband John opened other Jongleurs in other cities and they sold up in 2000 for £7 million.

audience preferred comedy to contemporary dance and laughter to lyricism.

My new opening stand-up gambit (after Daphne Fairfax, obviously), inspired by my recent sojourn in panto and the mass rallies we had overseen in the Revue, was to cue the audience to shout at me, 'FUCK OFF, ARTHUR. I HATE AUDIENCE PARTICIPATION!' The deep, broad stage at Jongleurs and the closeness of its audience encouraged me to experiment with the guinea pigs in front of me. I offered money to anyone who would come on stage and rip my T-shirt from my back, or break an egg over my head, or cut my hair during the interval. The repetition of this last invitation, partly motivated by a reluctance to pay for a haircut, provided me with a succession of bad hair years and culminated in an encounter with a Dublin drunk wielding scissors designed to slice the tops from boiled eggs. Following his well-meaning but delirious assault on my barnet, a rumour circulated among comics that I had been undergoing chemotherapy.

Its proximity to Balham, the certain fee and the possibilities offered by the post-gig disco made Jongleurs one of my favourite venues to play. In the spirit of the place I invented a half-time competition (the first of many) in which I invited the audience to invent films remade for the Yuppie market. My yellowing joke book contains examples which recall some of the obsessions of the times:

Dow Jones and the Temple of Doom
The Man with the Golden American Express Card
Oklahomeowner
Dirty Henry

Around the World in Daddy's Jet
The Gucci, the Bad and the Ugly
Nightmare on Sloane Street

Jongleurs began to sell out on Fridays after LWT chose it to preview the American comedians booked for *Saturday Live*, a new comedy and music show on Channel 4. As compère I found myself going through their material with them to ensure it was comprehensible to a British audience: ('Hey, Arthur, do you have Weetabix here? What is a sausage roll?') The huge US comedy scene was deemed to be ten years or more ahead of its British translation – which had only recently extended outside of London – and the comics had a transatlantic swagger which eluded the average shuffling London comic. Where the US comedians liked to be introduced with a tour of their television credits and theatrical achievements, the British comedian would say, 'Oh, just say my name,' and acts who had been in the Cambridge Footlights specifically asked me *not* to mention their pedigree. 'What is the difference between American and British stand-up?' is a stock journalist's question. Greg Proops, who should know, has stated that the only real difference he notices is that British comics give the audience longer to laugh. The Americans come in slightly quicker, making for a higher tempo.*

* The distant guiding lights to alternative comics were Americans – Lenny Bruce, Richard Pryor, George Carlin – who brought a subversive intelligence to their brilliant acts. Bruce was so radical that he had been arrested at gigs for his views and his 'obscene' language. Hounded and haunted, he had died in 1966 of a heroin overdose in a toilet. Tony Allen used to say, 'And that's how I'm *starting* my career.'

'Alternative Comedy' now had its own listings page in *Time Out*, compiled by Malcolm Hay, who was instrumental in the growth of comedy in London. It had coalesced into a kind of movement, although there was never a meeting* and, among those who bore the title 'alternative comedian', many never met and a substantial percentage hated each other. It is not unreasonable to suggest that alternative comedy, if it ever existed, lasted for only a few months. But, even if this is the case, I am persuaded by all the people who have asked me about it, or reacted against their imagined version of it, that it was an identifiable presence in the zeitgeist.

When the new comedy's commercial flagship, *The Young Ones*, starring most of the cast I had seen that night at the Comic Strip, had appeared on BBC 2 it had seized the imagination of teenagers around the country and TV began to pay the genre more attention. The Comic Strip, under the guidance of Peter Richardson, formed their own production company, and began making one-off comedy dramas, several of which are small classics of the genre. Other TV shows, including *Saturday Live*, followed and, although the number of acts was still small, producers, agents and journalists began turning up to gigs. The Comedy Store back-room bar at one a.m. became a very cool place to be.

'Alternative *to* comedy, more like,' was the standard response of the traditional comedian to what they saw as hostile competition. As far as the Sparklics were concerned the new comics

---

* Actually, there was one once, convened by the patron saint of Jewish alternative stand-ups, the great Ivor Dembina. Even Ivor couldn't coordinate a second.

were scruffy herberts who shouted 'Fuck Thatcher' over and over, while raving Tankie Stalinists hooted indiscriminately in the front row. But what they – we – were was an alternative to *them*. If they had us down as loony lefties and lovers of lesbian whales, we retorted that they were gay-hating, xenophobic and sexist. Bernard Manning was racist, Jim Davidson was a wife-beater, Frank Carson peddled stereotypes, they all played golf and voted for Mrs Thatcher. They were the enemy.*

There is no doubt that some of the acts reacting to these dinosaurs were 'right on' to a ridiculous extent. One popular

* Coincidentally, after I started writing this chapter Bernard Manning died. I knew what this would be likely to mean for me and, sure enough, I soon got a phone call from a TV show asking me to comment. My initial instinct was to decline, because being rude about someone – even him – immediately upon their death is not very gracious, and because I don't enjoy being censorious. I also anticipated the usual sour retaliations. But I did it because I felt *someone* ought to and it might as well be me. Here are some highlights from one of the letters I received soon after. You may insert your own *sic*s.

'He made *everyone* laugh at his bawdy type of genuine comedy that we understood. And what have you done? In the last twenty years or so people like you have introduced this awful alternative comedy. Alternative to what? You and your lot have never made any of our lot laugh!
I expect you all read the *Guardian* and like Tony Blair your ideology is to appease the audience who are also *Guardian* sandal wearing, vegetarian, PC pratts like yourself . . . you are about as funny as a dose of piles! Along with Jo Brand, Reeves and Mortimer, Ant and Dec and so on . . .'

The best response to Bernard Manning's death came from Trevor McDonald who put on a silly wig and said, 'I didn't think Bernard Manning was racist. I thought he was a fat white bastard.'

all-male group, whose name escapes me for legal reasons, performed full-length shows devoted to the proposition that men were irredeemably awful, violent and stupid and we should all shape up. Offstage this pose was considerably undermined by one member's towering piles of porn and another's tireless pursuit of every woman under the age of thirty. Sensible Footwear was a trio of women who sang a similar anti-male tune; a comic called Michelle Reid did her entire (very funny) twenty-minute set about how rubbish periods were; Ian Saville, 'the Socialist Magician', demonstrated the Marxist theory of alienation using coloured hand-kerchiefs; the Spare Tyre Theatre Company praised the qualities of the larger female; there was another feminist company called Monstrous Regiment – I never saw them but did witness the shocked look on audiences' faces as they emerged from their shows. The best-known female stand-up on the circuit (French and Saunders had already signed up for telly) was Jenny Lecoat, who ended her set on a sweet song with not-so-sweet lyrics in which she imagined boiling her boyfriend's penis, 'till you become your true consistency at last.'

At some venues, merely to be a heterosexual male was a provocation and although Fiasco Job Job were only parodically sexist, we were not booked initially at Roland and Clare Muldoons' socialist CAST gigs because we were 'too male'. Or perhaps they objected to the moment in our act where I adopted an expression of pious self-importance, stepped forward and declared, 'You know, Phil, if men cried more often there'd be fewer nuclear bombs in this world.' This was a time where most of the women I knew described themselves as feminists and so did the liberal men, if we were allowed. Numerous male comedians had self-deprecating routines about their gender and sexual encounters that entailed premature ejaculation or oafishness in bed. 'If the five-minute warning went off I would have sex and then boil an egg.'

A female stand-up – one no longer said 'comedienne' – advanced to me the theory that a joke re-enacts the male orgasm: a brief bout of foreplay (the set-up) culminating in an even shorter orgasm (the punchline – already a suspicious compound). Female comedy, she argued, was like the female orgasm and, well, like the female – more complex. There may be something in this analysis but, in the case of the comedian in question, it served additionally as a useful excuse for why she never got any laughs from men *or* women.* Following this discussion, I stated the theory on stage, following it with a joke where I blurted out the punchline too early. '"A man goes to the doctor and . . . give it a Mars Bar, then." Oops, I'm sorry. This doesn't usually happen.' It didn't get much of a laugh and went into the black hole of the tried-and-failed.

Where the Sparklies cracked gags, the alternative scene encouraged observational comedy, the have-you-noticed style exemplified by Jerry Seinfeld or the altogether more surreal approach of Paul Merton. There were a few comic poets around, though none as inventive or distinctive as Hegley, whose mastery of bathos was *sans pareil.* The funny ones, like Porky the Poet, Eddie Zibbin and Jenny Éclair, eventually became sufficiently emboldened to drop the security of verse and revert to their real names – Phill Jupitus, Pat Condell and, er, Jenny Éclair. I injected my own poetic parodies into gigs:

* It is true, nevertheless, that the female comic has more obstacles to jump than the male.

The other day upon the stair,
I met a man who wasn't there.
I met that man again today
– I think he must be a hologram

Or, for the more literary audience:

'If' (by Arthur Kipling)

If you can roll along at a decent pace
And you find that your rear contains lots of space,
If you have windows at the front, yet none at the side
And offer a smooth, unflashy ride,
If you have a red and white flag on your bonnet
And could never imagine doing a ton;
Then yours is the road and everything on it
And, which is more, you'll be a van, my son.

The staple subjects of the trad comic were either ignored, denounced or satirised. Ian Macpherson declared he was going to tell an Irish joke and then spoke a line in Gaelic. John Thompson did a hilarious character based on Bernard Manning called Bernard Right-On: 'An Englishman, an Irishman and a Pakistani . . . what a wonderful example of racial integration.' Where the Sparklies did charity shows for apolitical causes – cancer, holidays for disabled children, etc. – we alternatives were more likely to be on stage in support of Amnesty International, the Cuban Solidarity Campaign, the Birmingham Six, the striking miners, the Anti-Apartheid movement. Backstage at a gig for Nicaragua, as Billy Bragg and Kirsty McColl performed the hit he had written and she had sung, 'New England', Harold Pinter told me a joke. 'I wouldn't open with that, Harold,' was my advice. MC-ing these nights (and attending them) could demand formidable powers of endurance, since inexperienced organisers usually booked too many acts and too many speakers. At one gig (at the Hackney Empire) raising money and support for the imprisoned Israeli nuclear scientist Mordecai Vanunu, three hours into the show, after an impassioned recollection from a Holocaust survivor, I was obliged to come on and present the raffle. There were uplifting moments too. At a benefit for striking ambulance workers at the Dominion Theatre, headlined by Paul Weller, I announced, to ecstatic cheering, that Nelson Mandela was now free.

Political satire was an area untouched by the old guard, who had hitherto left all that stuff to the toffs of *Beyond the Fringe*; I had little aptitude for it either. My imagination doesn't function that way and I just couldn't get *worked up* enough. The true satirist is full of outrage at important events but, while I was of the left, my own ire derived from more trivial concerns – the chirpiness of breakfast DJs, the manufactured chumminess of dinner parties, the fatuity of TV, futons. I had my obligatory raft of Thatcher material but it showed no coherent criticism. Satire can, paradoxically, boost the standing of its targets; John Lloyd, the producer of *Spitting Image,* argues, plausibly, that his programme gave Mrs Thatcher an extra two years in power. There were comics, more *engagé* than I, notably Jeremy Hardy, Linda Smith and Mark Steel, who all became stars of Radio 4's *News Quiz*. During the IRA campaigns, Jeremy described the British government as 'the political wing of the British Army' and opined: 'People say they aren't political; that just means they get other people to be right-wing on their behalf.' Linda tutted about the Middle East: 'It's rather annoying the way *our* oil's ended up under *their* sand.' She thanked her audience with the line, 'You are the difference between a performance and an affliction.' Mark Steel, an alumnus of Swanley Comprehensive, rages at injustice in exhilarating rants of unexpected erudition and is a determined, if not gifted, middle-order batsman.

Jokes about dope were a commonplace. 'Now, a word about drugs,' I would announce sternly, then breathe out '. . . nice.' I mused on the ridiculous claim of the politician to have smoked a joint but not inhaled it. 'That's like buying a hamster and not shoving it up your arse.' Paul Merton came on wearing pyjamas and read from a notebook as a policeman giving evidence in court. The bizarre, hilarious routine that ensued made sense when he revealed he had been given a sweet, 'a sweet I now know to have contained a hallucinogenic drug.' As MC, I sometimes dispensed a 'joint' to an audience member at the start of the gig and, between acts, returned to them to monitor its effects.

The majority of routines have a victim of some sort, but on the comedy circuit these were more likely to be the government, cheesy entertainers or the Royal Family. Nick Revell slagged off the royals and then added, 'Mind you, I won't hear a word against the Queen Mother . . . because a friend of mine's fucking her at the moment.' Establishment figures were the chief object of derision, which is not to say all was fair and reasonable – once Malcolm had identified a Northerner in an audience he would say, 'Here's a fiver, go buy yourself a house.' It's having a bit of fun with stereotypes, or, if you're *un homme sérieux*, it's a form of displaced racism.

It was a matter of pride to the comics that we wrote our own material and it was (still is) an offence to nick someone else's (unless the thief was Malcolm, in which case, somehow, it didn't count). The Comedy Police could find you at any time. By contrast, on the Northern club circuit, jokes belonged to everybody, such that before a show the stand-ups would consult over which comic was doing which joke. You could sometimes see a comic on TV doing lines you knew they had stolen. My own comic question, 'Whatever happened to white dog shit?' was performed by several Sparklies. At first I found this infuriating, but I came to see it as a kind of flattery and to understand the great Barry Cryer dictum that 'jokes are not owned but rented'. Barry, one of the old-school comics who offered a hand across the comedy divide, distinguishes, however, between 'jokes' and 'material'; material is your own work and should be respected, but jokes are formal events that involve men going to the doctor's, or gorillas to pubs, and these are up for grabs. Having once disdained these constructs, I now began to find a quaint charm within them and these days, on stage, I have a penchant for telling them.* Sometimes I have repeated jokes told to me by Syd when I was fifteen. It is a peculiar fact, universally agreed among comics, that jokes of this type spring from a mysterious hidden source – no one has ever met anyone who has actually *written* one.

Jerry Sadowitz, the Glaswegian comic and close-up magician,

---

* Here is my current fave: A man goes to the doctor for his annual check-up. The doctor says, 'Well, I'm afraid you're going to have to stop wanking.' 'Oh no,' says the man. 'Why?' 'Because,' says the doctor, 'I'm trying to examine you.'

was the first act at the Comedy Store to challenge some of the new orthodoxies, reintroducing the word 'cunt' with such ferocity that it was hard not to sit back and applaud. I was there when he first did the line which he had written for maximum offence: 'Nelson Mandela – what a cunt! You lend some people a fiver and you never see them again.' It *would* have been genuinely revolting if it had been '*black* cunt' but by now racist material, thanks in part to the new comedy, was beyond the pale. The old guys knew that well enough to refrain from doing it outside sympathetic clubs and police dinners. This was the small achievement of 'alternative comedy' which, in *Time Out*, now came without the 'alternative'.

Since my maiden death at the Comedy Store, the comedy circuit had developed and expanded more than anyone on it had anticipated and I had performed hundreds and hundreds of gigs around London and beyond. For long periods I compèred at Jongleurs one weekend and the Comedy Store the next (two shows a night). On Sundays I might be down the Tunnel, guesting with the new improvisational group the Comedy Store Players or MC-ing a benefit. My timetable was out of joint with my friends in more traditional jobs – when they played, I worked, and when they were at the office or school or on the forecourt, I was at home, mooching and dreaming. There were dozens of dinner parties I never attended, house parties at which I arrived too late, weekends away I could not make, women I let down, lads' nights out I missed, and always because I was *doing a gig*. All those hours on stage hardened into the backbone of my professional life. I still think that if everything else fell around me but I was still capable of speech, I could, if need be, go back to doing twenty minutes in the back of a pub.

And that would be all right.

CHAPTER 15. ME AND PHIL GO OFF

'Sorry, mate, I ain't goin' sarf of the river this time of night.'

Taxi drivers rarely use this phrase in London any more, but this was 1985 and it was the second time I had heard it in twenty minutes. Wet, one o'clock in the morning, Charing Cross station, the last Tube gone, and I could not face the night bus. It was the end of a day's filming that had started at this same spot nineteen hours earlier. Phil had already gone home to Max and the newly born Laura. I *really wanted* to get back to Du Cane Court – Balham Towers as Adam calls it – where, now that Lindsay had moved out, I lived alone. Phil, me and the crew had taken the ferry to Boulogne, filming on board both ways, plus twelve hours of shooting around and about the French port. The footage was in the can for our pilot TV show *Arthur and Phil Go Off* or, if you are Phil (which Phil is – hello, Phil!), *Phil and Arthur Go Off*. The last scene, on the concourse of the station, in which I accidentally dropped and smashed my duty-free bottles of wine, was in the can and I was plum-tuckered. My kingdom for a taxi. A third South of the River refusenik earned an inaudible 'Fuck you!' before, at last, an angel cockney in a hackney carriage took me into his dark back seat.

The London black cab is the best taxi in the world in my experience, and I am the sort of chap who has hailed cabs in dozens of foreign capitals. (The worst are the jagged yellow boxes of New York.) At night, when I am heading to the local shop for milk or fags and one passes me in the street, fat amber light shining, promising an invitation to anywhere in London, I have to stop my arm from rising up and to still the cry of 'Taxi!' that starts forming in my gorge. Sinking into the leathery black expanse of this beauty, I reflected that the day had gone well enough that we surely had a reasonable chance of earning a series on Channel 4. I allowed myself some weary fantasy: the show would be a hit, we would become celebrated, produce groundbreaking work, the drugs would get better, the girls hotter and Phil would be able to support his family without going on the game. I might soon get to hang out with Isabelle Adjani . . . hmmm . . . well, at the very least I had earned a wodge today worthy of the loadsa-money 1980s . . .

Past the Houses of Parliament, along Millbank, following the Thames westwards . . .

The comedy circuit was continuing to grow and my solo work had expanded outside London but at this stage, after my unedifying showing on *Pyjamerama*, Fiasco Job Job interested the TV people more than my silly stand-up. The commissioners at Channel 4 were impressed by our live shows and the idea we had presented to them was a mixture of our bickering double act and a new style of performance that I had been trying.

In 1983 Phil and I had done our first non-Nat Rev Co Edinburgh Fringe, sharing a late bill with John Dowie, so late it meant not coming on stage until 1.30 a.m. Liberated from the rigorous timetable of previous years and finally relieved of hand-outs patrol, I was free to find it painfully hard not to have a drink in the long hours before we took the stage. I needed something to distract me from the lure of the venue bars, the town pubs, the launch parties, the awards ceremonies, the invitation from an old friend to share an afternoon dram in the Meadows, a glass of someone's first-night sparkling wine – all the siren drinking songs of the city. The Director of the Fringe, Alistair Moffat, suggested that I set up as a rival to the official tour guides who worked the Royal Mile, a casual remark whose possibilities I am still working out twenty-five years later.

Most comics do not go in for outdoor performing. The stand-up's natural home is within a windowless club, clutching a microphone under a spotlight. Outside is for bellowing street-performers with their props, their costumes and their absence of subtlety. Yet street theatre, which bred Eddie Izzard, is a challenging form requiring an élan and a flourish that can conjure magic for all the world's passers-by. The memory of that triumphant afternoon with Miriâme, Dennis and Gary on the terrace of the Cutty Sark pub, and the outlandish stunts we had executed to publicise the Revue meant I could *do* alfresco – give me the Batman costume, let's get cracking. And being a tour guide had always appealed to me – no theatrical set is as big or various as a slice of city. People are more good-humoured in the open; an audience becomes a small clique in the midst of a townful of citizens, conspiring together in larks aplenty in the fresh air.

So, on a couple of afternoons a week I advertised free 'alternative tours' of the Royal Mile, commencing, like all the proper tours, at the entrance to the castle, where I delivered a couple of standard facts about its history of witch-burning, noting that the last witch had been incinerated three years earlier. The castle, I explained, was a failure since it had never withstood one decent siege or housed a violent royal death and went unhaunted by famous ghosts. I continued to distort facts and invent them as we made our way down the hill to Saint Giles Cathedral (named after Giles Brandreth). By the Camera Obscura I pointed across the city beyond the Firth of Forth to . . . France: I enforced a by-law requiring that the punters hop for ten yards and disregarded the large statue of David Hume in favour of nominating the adjacent roadworks as 'the World Première of a new Samuel Beckett play'. The reaction to this parade was at the intersection of amused and baffled. Bamused perhaps. As an accompaniment to the tours, I produced a slim guidebook to Edinburgh and the Fringe with funny photos and spurious history. It also included the names of every influential figure attending the Festival, under three headings.

1. People to sleep with if you want to become rich and famous.
2. Sleeping with these people won't make you rich and famous but it might be fun.
3. Really, there is no point.

These lists were much scrutinised in the Assembly Rooms bar and an appearance on the second made several ladies warm to me. It was a jolly little idea – though not in the opinion of Harry, my new accountant, since the 50p I charged for each copy was 25p less than it cost to print. Harry, a genial soul, both sensible *and* stage-struck, no doubt also anticipated that I would lose interest in flogging the stupid booklets and start giving them away. There is still a pile of the little bastards under my bed.

On our day off from the double act, I conducted a midnight rendition of the Royal Mile tour where the audience was as drunk as me and the distortions consequentially racier. This was a more muscular affair than my daylight meanderings and ended with my audience of thirty in a random Mile-dweller's house singing the Marseillaise. Thus began a little tradition that grew into a full-blown, small-scale, cult annual event. *Arthur Smith's Late Night Alternative Tour of the Royal Mile* has erupted sporadically ever since – and if you skip forward ten chapters you will see how one of them concluded in my arrest.

The contempt for historical accuracy and the wilful perversity of these tours informed the series of *Arthur and Phil Go Off,* which was indeed commissioned after the Boulogne pilot transmitted. We chose unlikely, unrelated subjects – the Loch Ness Monster, the M1 motorway, the town of Marbella in Spain, 'Oxbridge' University and the forthcoming 'Big Bang' in the City of London. In the 'documentaries' we also sought to exploit the comic possibilities that lay in the discrepancy between what TV would *like* you to believe and, for want of a better word, the 'truth' of a situation.

In the pre-signature tune scene of the Loch Ness show, Phil and I shuffle into a shot of the Loch:

PHIL: *(earnest, like an investigative journalist on a mission)* Does the Loch Ness Monster exist?
ARTHUR: No. Good night.
SIGNATURE TUNE

Phil suggests to me that since we are being paid three thousand pounds each to try to find out about the creature, we would be advised to at least *pretend* to have an open mind about it. At one point I unexpectedly push Phil through a window but at the crucial moment he is replaced by a stuntman, a chap who is seen, from a subsequent slow-motion replay, to look nothing like Phil.

On the M1 episode I am raffish and cool at the wheel of a speeding car, until the camera pulls back to reveal that the car is on the back of a lorry; in voice-over Phil sneers at my inability to drive. Our intention was to constantly undermine the viewer's perception of what was happening and 'pull back to reveal' was our most deployed technique.

Back in the taxi from Charing Cross to home, I am anticipating exciting trips away and funny times, as the lights of Vauxhall, Stockwell and Clapham flow by. Nearly to Balham.

What I failed to anticipate that night in the cab was that Channel 4 would lose interest in *Arthur and Phil Go Off*, put the transmission time back, cancel the last two shows and abandon us for ever. Phil and I persuaded ourselves that we were the victims of TV politics but now I attribute the curtailing of the series to our own delusions of grandeur. The 1980s was a decade in which arrogance was a mark of character and, in the spirit of the times, I had begun to believe that Phil and I, especially I, knew most of what there was to know about comedy, that it was our right to be on TV and that no one else could improve on our work. I was wrong.

We needed a script editor, a more experienced producer and director, we should have compromised more and we should have listened to the comments of the people who had commissioned us. Perhaps then we would not have made daft decisions like the one that saw us choose not to be in the first episode of *Saturday Live* for fear of being overexposed. It was not long before we were so *under*exposed that Fiasco Job Job no longer existed. We persevered for a while, had a failed radio pilot, did more circuit gigs, but our number was up; the doors that had been open now swung shut and the commissionaires went home. The double act went the way of the band, the Revue, the radio series and the

TV show. Returning to the clubs of London as a solo act and compère, I tried to reduce my levels of self-importance. Phil set off on his own theatrical journey and, although we have worked together a few times since, and been lovers on and off, I have not for twenty years asked him to give me his penis on stage.

But sod all that for now because I was arriving home in the taxi at the end of that thrilling first day's filming, on the cusp of success, happy at what might be. The cab pulled up outside my front door. The fare was ten pounds. Grateful to have finally made it to Balham and flushed with my own incipient flash, I shook the driver's hand.

'Thanks for coming south, mate.' I gave him fifty quid.

Before Phil and I began the TV series Edinburgh cropped up again. But at this festival, given the frantic filming round the country and in Spain that awaited me, I felt no pressing need to create anything new. So when Rick, formerly 'Banana Fingers', the pianist in *SwingalongaDante*, now a journalist at *Time Out*, asked me to be a chat show host, I laughed and said 'Go on.' The show, to be co-hosted with Muriel Gray, would take place at midnight in the large tent in the 'Hole in the Ground' (now the site of the Lyceum Theatre) where, five years earlier, I had performed in *Satalongamatinee*. The idea was for *The Time Out Chat Show* to become the gathering point for festival-goers at the end of the day. Muriel and I would interview some of the big names who passed through Edinburgh in August in front of a large, informal house of discerning late-night cognoscenti. That, at any rate, was the intention. A number of factors, however, conspired to render the project one to be filed under Do Not Repeat.

* * *

1. <u>The guests</u>. In the manner of chat shows, the early targets – Sean Connery, Madonna, President Carter, Michael Jackson, Billy Connolly, etc. – proved to be unavailable and were soon downgraded to a more plausible selection – Nicholas Parsons, Timmy Mallet et al. (Al? Is she available? Book her.) When word got round that the show was all risk and no reward, Rick managed to recruit a whole new level of nobody. Since some of these people were booked only hours before the event, I was poorly researched indeed.

2. <u>Me</u>. Muriel was an excellent interviewer but I was new to the game and rather diffident. While guests were answering my first question, I was desperately thinking about what my second might be, and thus failed to listen to whatever they were saying. Not listening is a basic error that a surprising number of interviewers continue to make; I was terrified of a repeat of an early encounter, where an old jazzman – good-natured, but evidently bored by language – answered my enquiries with such brevity that I had run out of questions to ask him within three minutes of the start of our fifteen-minute exchange.

3. <u>The weather</u>. It was cold in Edinburgh that year, but when the heating in the tent was turned on it sounded like a cruise missile being launched – far too loud to be used during a show. By the time we started at midnight, the only warm place in the tent was on stage under the lights.

4. <u>The lights</u>, for their part, were angled such that they shone straight into the eyes of the guests. Lord Elgin, poor sod, conducted the whole of his chat about marbles with his hand held up to shield his eyes from the ferocious beam. Unfortunately, it looked from the auditorium as though, throughout the interview, he was giving a Nazi salute.

5. <u>The audience</u>. Over the two weeks of the run the tempera-
ture in the tent continued to plummet and the paying audience,
alerted to the parade of obscurities and arctic temperatures,
became increasingly sparse. A lot of free tickets were handed
out, but only those who were still awake, had nowhere else to
go and could endure the cold – i.e. drunks – showed up. *The
Time Out Chat Show* became a place where you could go for a
good shout, where you could work out your belligerence publicly,
by barracking whoever happened to be squinting in the hot
stage lights.

On the last night the winner of that year's Perrier Award was
to be announced from the stage of the show. Rick had also
managed to book Carl Davis, the celebrated band Amampondo
and Michael Grade, then Chairman of Channel 4. The Ice Age
had retreated for the evening and there was quite a large, if not
healthy, crowd, a reasonable percentage of whom were neither
drunk nor on smack (this was during *Trainspotting* days). My first
guest was Ruby Wax who had been in the French, Saunders and
Tracey Ullman sitcom *Girls on Top*, but was still relatively unknown.
When Grade arrived Ruby was overcome and turned the
schmoozing up to a level only an American could aspire to.

After I had introduced her, I lobbed an easy opener:

– So, Ruby, are you anything like the character you play in *Girls
on Top?*

– Oh, Arthur, *what* a boring question!

I was a little riled by this.

– All right, what was the best fuck you ever had?

Big laugh.

– Well, the most important fuck I ever had . . .

– Not the most *important* fuck . . . you've just done that with Michael Grade in the Portakabin . . .

Even bigger laugh.

– Oh, Arthur, I don't want to talk to you, I want to talk to *Michael.* Get *Michael* on . . .

Grade was standing laughing in the wings and gamely trotted on stage. It struck me as an amusing novelty to have a chat show where the host had left and the guests chatted among themselves, so I left the stage. Ruby had a lot of fun with Grade and not long after fronted her first TV show, *Wax on Wheels,* on, of course, Channel 4.

Yes, I can reasonably claim to have started Ruby Wax's career.

It was one of my most undistinguished Edinburghs but I managed to forget all about it until a couple of years later when someone said to me, 'I was at that chat show you did the night someone shouted out, "Get off, you bald old cunt!"' I laughed ruefully at the realisation that that could have been on any one of half a dozen nights. Rick eventually distributed badges to everyone involved in the debacle which declared 'I Survived *The Time Out Chat Show*.'

CHAPTER 16. WHEN I WAS THIRTY-FIVE IT WAS A VERY GOOD YEAR . . .

Stand-up comedy can be the world's most sociable work. Few workplaces are filled with so many people drinking heavily (although this was not true of the Arsenal changing rooms at the time) and in most jobs when you knock off you are not clapped loudly, nor approached by people who want to be your friend or have sex with you. There is no doubt that an ugly bloke (i.e. me) is more attractive to women after he's been dazzling the multitudes on stage than when he is sidling up to them from shifty obscurity. There weren't groupies on the comedy circuit in the rock-cliché style but there were, and are, sexy, suggestive women who like to hang round comedians – hardly surprising given the female preference for a man with a GSOH.* When Janet Street-Porter declared that 'Comedy is the new rock and roll' stand-ups became cooler and sexier. A whole industry was growing around the scene – bookers, agents, drug dealers, production companies – and 'gag hags'. The gag hags were not often, alas, gagging for me, but for younger, fresher comic blood – acts like Sean Hughes, clever double act Lee and Herring and poor Robert (then Rob) Newman, a

* Unfortunately for women comics, the reverse proposition is not true. Many men are intimidated by funny women but, for me, it was a prerequisite for a girlfriend. Beth is about the funniest woman I have ever met.

sensitive and brilliant man who was almost *embarrassed* to be so handsome.*

Sarah appeared at a gig in Brentford. Opinionated, funny, and pleasingly bossy, she was new to London and had fallen for the comedy circuit like a teenage girl swooning over a boy band (which in the era of the Bay City Rollers she had also been). Much later, she told me how excited – 'made up' – she had been to be invited to the Comedy Store the following night. 'The Comedy Store! I'd only read about it.' As a gag hag she was a pitiful failure; it took six months of ardent wooing, a holiday in Tenerife, anguished letters delivered late at night and straightforward begging before she finally joined me between the sheets (sheets, she felt, which could do with a wash). Sarah, from Cardiff via Cornwall, with fashionable big hair and an infectious laugh was a secretary at BBC Radio News, where she bullied reporters and curtsied to guests. To ring her at work I had to say to the BBC switchboard, 'Could I have *The World Tonight*, please?' Not much to ask. Since I was a regular at Broadcasting House in the Light Entertainment department, 'the corridor of mirth', we would meet for a smoke and a chat on the roof terrace, with its capacious views across London. Sarah was in permanent pursuit of a tan and if there were any suggestion of sun, her eyes closed and her face, like a flower, turned up to catch every available ray – as if the world was an hour away from eternal darkness.

She came to Edinburgh for *Arthur Smith Compères Himself*, in which I played a selection of acts. The quietest of these, 'Brian, the Winsome Poet', recited some of his (my) own work, including

---

* It has only been recently that comedians have been comfortable presenting themselves as rock stars: cf. Russell Brand, Noel Fielding and Simon Amstell.

the 'Paris Poem' written thirteen years earlier. This was a more introverted, lyrical Arthur than had been seen in public, and the appreciation of the audience reminded me that chasing laughs need not be my sole ambition. Otherwise, I crammed in virtually all the material I had accrued since starting stand-up, sang a couple of songs and introduced the cantankerous misanthrope 'Mister Crappy', who sullenly adumbrated all that he found crappy (pretty much everything) and who, I suddenly realise, was a prototype Grumpy Old Man. *Arthur Smith Compères Himself* was a mid-table kind of an affair and persuaded me that character comedy was not my *métier*; Mister Crappy had his afternoon in the sun but after the Festival I quietly murdered the miserable whiner.

By now I had a proper agent in the sleek shape of Vivienne Clore at the Richard Stone Agency. There had been opportunities to sign with a more aggressive rival who promised to 'market' me, beef up my PR, 'improve the brand'* – all phrases which made me shudder. I could have gone further and acquired a manager, who would, no doubt, have made me richer and more desired. A full-on manager, like Addison Cresswell (who guided Julian Clary and Jack Dee to fortune and fame), probably instructs you on what to wear, which gigs to do and which to swerve, whose arse to lick, how much saliva to use and when to do it; they become a friend, a confidant – even, in the case of Michael Barrymore's manager, a wife. Vivienne alerted me to offers that she thought might appeal and had an instinct for those which wouldn't. An invitation to try out as a breakfast DJ on Radio 5

* On reflection, I don't think all the guff about 'branding' existed then.

never reached my ears because Vivienne decided, correctly, that I had no desire to burble between records and, anyway, the pain of my dawn risings for Greenwich Borough Council had not yet faded from my memory. The early bird is abhorrent to me; I am a late-worm kind of a guy. My perception of myself is as an amateur* – a dabbler, a dilettante who takes on projects that interest me, irrespective of their financial or profile-raisng possibilities. Which is not to say I don't do ads and voice-overs which are the sponsors of my outré byways. Vivienne negotiated fees fiercely but did not promote me or tout for work – and that was how I liked it.

It was generally agreed that I was the best compère in London, or that's what the people at LWT told me when they booked me to present *First Exposure*, a series showcasing new comics and indie bands. The shows were filmed in front of a full house at the Theatre Royal Stratford East, in East London. Between acts I chirped up around the theatre – in the stalls, at the bar, in a balcony and, occasionally, on the stage. My approach was more acquiescent, my material club-tested and I ceded centre stage to the acts. My one-series TV curse was lifted when *First Exposure* was recommissioned, this time at the Hackney Empire. Some of the comics who made their TV debuts on *First Exposure,* I note from a cursory Google, have since done quite well for themselves, e.g. Paul Whitehouse, Charlie Higson, Eddie Izzard, Steve Coogan, David Baddiel, Jack Dee and Frank Skinner. None of the bands, on the other hand, were ever heard of again. These were late-night programmes that only transmitted round London,

* The word 'amateur' comes from the Greek word 'amatur' which means 'lover of', as every professional amateur will tell you.

but presenting them improved my status, my bank balance and, following a re-kit for the TV, my wardrobe. Now I was occasionally recognised in the street, an experience I found thoroughly agreeable.

My hair was beginning to leave my head only to reappear through my nostrils and ears. Approaching thirty-five but looking forty-five, my standing as a funny man was secured for the time being. Now was the time to do that thing I had been delaying for years: I would write my fifth play. The success of the previous four need not intimidate me. The first, my interpretation of *Peter Pan* was, you may recall, rejected wholesale by my primary school teacher. Five years later, my second effort, co-written with Mister Brooks the economics master, was a half-hour entry to the House plays competition and mapped the declining years of a famous footballer; it was placed third out of four on the night. In the sixth form I co-wrote an entertainment, inserted between the two acts of the school play, about how selfish we all are, but instead of watching it, the audience, selfishly, left *en masse* for a fag and a drink. At twenty, as part of my thesis in France, I wrote a fourth play in the form of a monologue delivered by a hitchhiker stranded on an empty road and was impressed to learn that it was to be graded by Malcolm Bradbury. Malcolm, who had seen me cavorting comedically in the university square, wrote sparingly on the last page, '*B minus — stick to comedy.*'

Before starting work on the second series of *First Exposure*, I had taken a small acting role in a Fringe play by Nick Whitby called *The Columbian Cousin* and had struck up an instant rapport with the leading lady, Caroline Quentin, who recounted scabrous tales of her spell as an end-of-the-pier dancer. Caroline was, even here at the start of her career, an exceptional actor — full of passion and humanity, graceful, witty, although, as I said in a speech at her second wedding, fifteen years later, 'very bad at having small breasts'.

One afternoon, during a lull in rehearsals, as Caroline picked blackheads from my neck and I dropped them into the roll-up under construction, I mentioned my ambition to write a play. 'You must,' she insisted, 'and I'll be in it, even if it's shit.' She continued to encourage me – nag me, even – throughout the ensuing months, and rang me the night after my last recording of *First Exposure*. All right, Caroline. I had a muse who wouldn't shut up and now I had some time – all I needed was a subject.

The most pain I had experienced in my adult life derived from the shattered love affairs that littered my path. I have been flippant about some of the break-ups, but the intensity of the anguish they caused shocked me, as though I had glimpsed my own death through a curtain. During my early courtship of Sarah, I had written deluges about my unrequited ardour, to add to the thousands of words in which I had contemplated earlier cataclysms. At ease now in my partnership, I looked back at this impassioned verbiage and decided to make a portrait of a relationship in late-1980s London – a two-hander. The action would centre around a large versatile bed, which is the most significant of all items of furniture – the small arena in which we are born, in which we dream, procreate and die. It would mix duologue and stand-up soliloquies and . . . and, well, I had to write it to find out.

How do you write a play? Two years after *Live Bed Show*, I signed up for the three-day course/lecture on 'story structure' given by the American Robert McKee – completion of which, it seemed then, was a *sine qua non* for screenwriters both in the United States and Britain – Charlie Kaufman's film *Adaptations* contains a scene that recreates McKee giving his talk. He has been doing it in cities round the world for so long that if you commission or write drama for the screen, you have probably attended the marathon lecture: a mixture of academic theory, historical example, practical advice and anecdotage which, taken together, forged a template for how to write a story – be it a film, a TV serial, a sitcom, a play, or even a novel. It was informative and useful, but far too long. When, in the final session, he unexpectedly stepped forward and crooned 'As time Goes By' from *Casablanca*, I wondered if the whole thing was an elaborate ruse to persuade two hundred people to listen to him sing. In order to save you the four hundred quid the course costs, I will now boil it all down to a paragraph for you. Here is how to write a play.

Sketch out the plot in enough detail so that when you write the first scene or sentence you have a clear idea of what the last will be. You need a protagonist whose world is transformed by the story's 'inciting incident', launching us into the meat of the first act, in which our hero begins his struggle and meets the girl. At the end of Act One, his situation changes and deteriorates, his task grows harder and he loses the girl. In Act Two, liable to be the longest, his problems worsen, his self-doubt grows, the jeopardy becomes greater and he is brought to a point where he must perform an almost impossible, character-defining action, failure to achieve which will lose him everything. In Act Three, in the big climax, he pulls it off against the odds, gets the girl, and there is a pay-off which makes you reconsider everything that has gone before. The end. A story is a series of detonating surprises. Or you can ignore all this and do it how you want. Regarding dialogue, McKee warns against writing 'on the nose', i.e. the characters express accurately how they are feeling when, as we all know, the interesting truth of a scenario is in the nuances, the hesitations, in the subtext, in what is *not* said.

When do you write a play? is an easier question. Act One, Scene One of *Live Bed Show* was completed during an afternoon in a pub in Bath; subsequent scenes continued in a hammock in Antigua, on a balcony in Mallorca and, eventually, back at my desk in Balham, early in the morning after gigs, half-pissed. That alcohol can help you create is not a theory liable to be endorsed by the Home Secretary, but my experience then was that when I was the-right-amount-drunk I could write, as Henry Miller sought to do, *without fear.* Darker, edgier moments found their way into the beer-stained script: a scene depicting the ignominy of a one-night stand with a single mum and another that transformed into a rape nightmare.

In the sober early afternoons I edited the previous night's ravings and continued to rewrite throughout rehearsals under the eye of Audrey, a young, thoughtful director recommended by Caroline. Rupert produced the play with his customary laid-back élan and I now met Ali Duncan, who became my stage manager of choice for many more shows. Ali is unflappable, resourceful and as bossy as an SM needs to be (i.e. *very bossy indeed.* She taught me that the SM's favourite word is 'no!'). The first try-out took place in the tiny Quay Theatre in Sudbury, Suffolk. None of us had any idea how *Live Bed Show* might play but, in order to inure us against the pain of a bad review, I wrote my own pre-emptive stinker to amuse Caroline, Audrey and Ali at our last rehearsal: 'Self-indulgent, pointlessly vulgar, confused, unfunny, and downright embarrassing . . . contract syphilis rather than see it.' We laughed nervously.

Actors get bored by the question 'How do you remember all those lines?' but failing to remember mine was the thing that worried me most – more, even, than the reception my first play might get. As we travelled up on the train to Suffolk, Caroline and I were filled with dread – dreadful, I suppose. It was a beautiful spring afternoon and we looked across at the indifferent distant cottages receding into the faraway East Anglian horizon. 'Let's just get off at the next station,' I said, 'and go and live in one of those houses for the rest of our lives and never tell anyone where we are.' Caroline played along and we abandoned going over our lines to spend the remainder of the journey imagining the relief of an escape to our rural retreat, where no one would know, or care, that we had chickened out and done a runner. It is a fantasy I have indulged since, in the run-up to the first showing of some new project, or in some particularly disagreeable period of my life. Sod all this, I'll buy a big jumper and go and hide in Cornwall. Maybe one day I will.

A bollocking from the author for forgetting my lines, I reasoned, was something I could endure and when the lights went up my heart stopped racing and the words arrived in my mouth in roughly the order I had written them. I remembered my lines *and* Caroline's which, apparently, I mouthed as she said them. The audience, largely made up of elderly ladies, showed little enthusiasm but did not seem to hate what they were seeing – well, not until we arrived at one of Caroline's speeches:

MARIA: Me and the prospect of soothing oblivion. No one hurts me when I'm asleep, I don't make any mistakes, I don't smoke or spend any money when I'm asleep, I don't have to pretend I know what I'm doing. No one rings me up or embroils me in their plans. No one tries to sell me anything or have sex with me against my will.

I love it when I am awake but not for long and the rain is tapping on the window and the wind is blowing and I know there are people outside in that – drunks from the night and milkmen from the morning and me lying unmolested and relaxed and nothing. Nothing to do but lie there and wank.

There had been some fruity language leading up to this, but a woman saying 'wank' – and, indeed, recommending masturbation as a pleasurable pastime – was an outrage too far. Some huffing rose up from the auditorium and several ladies left loudly, if politely. There was a palpable sense of relief when the drama ended but, as we all embraced in the dressing room, we chose to be positive: the play had hung together, we had got through it without any major cock-ups and, well, this was hardly the audience the thing was written for. Nevertheless, in the rewrite, I dropped Caroline's wank.

In Bath, nurtured by Syd and Hazel, cheered on by Sarah and in front of a younger crowd, the play began to cohere and to find its rhythm. Even so, we were surprised by the reaction in Edinburgh, where *Live Bed Show* sold out, was nominated for two awards and got brilliant reviews. ('Inspired comic writing' – *Guardian*. How Syd loved that.) My proudest moment of the festival came during the scene where I played drunk and boorish, when a woman in the audience, her disbelief sturdily suspended, was moved to shout out, 'Leave him, he's just a drunken bastard!' The laughs flowed, more plaudits followed and Caroline was feted, as she should always be. On our day off I made my annual ascent of Arthur's Seat and, finding a spot just below the summit, out of view of anybody else but with Edinburgh displayed before me, I sat in a smug, green hollow and said to myself: 'Well done, Smiffy. You did it. You wrote a play.' And had I been writing this down I would surely, for once, have allowed myself an exclamation mark – 'You're a playwright!'

At this festival I went running and swimming, but I did not forget to burnish my reputation for excess and devilry. One afternoon Malcolm Hardee plodded into the Pleasance Bar. 'Oy Oy!' The show he was putting on and compèring was playing to tiny audiences but Malcolm had a plan. 'Will you do a rave write-up of my show for *The Scotsman*?' Malcolm had put some of his criminal skills into discovering the system used to file reviews in the paper. Now he needed a plausible two hundred words and felt that I was the man for the job. Outstanding scam artist though Malcolm was, I didn't expect him to pull this stunt off, but two days later there was my review, ascribed to the young critic William Cook who must have got a shock to see the unreserved praise he had ladled over Malcolm and his chums.

'Malcolm Hardee shambles onto the stage and initiates the funniest show I have seen this year. Malcolm, who looks like he slept the night in the bus station . . .' and so on to my pleasing last sentence about Terri Rogers, a sweet-looking lady with a foul-mouthed dummy: 'This is alternative ventriloquism of the highest order.' When Malcolm and I met on the day the review came out, he was unable to stifle long bouts of his peculiar half-whistled snigger. Even by his lofty standards this had been a good gag, especially when all the other papers proceeded to report gleefully on *The Scotsman*'s embarrassment. The paper duly issued a hurt statement and Malcolm, at the towering summit of his mythomania, was described by Mark Borkowsi, a doyen among Edinburgh publicists, as 'a master of the dark arts of PR'. During that same festival Malcolm cajoled me into doing a benefit on behalf of a young friend of his from Greenwich who had been burgled while he'd been away in Edinburgh. Poor lad – they'd stolen his video, his stereo and his camera. Two years later, as I sat precariously aboard Malcolm's boat, phutting its uncertain way along the Thames, he revealed to me that, although his friend *had* been burgled, his possessions had been returned to him on the morning of the benefit, so the money raised went instead towards the considerable cost of, er, Malcolm's boat. I liked to say afterwards that I had been conned into doing a benefit for Malcom's yacht.

The playwright does his job, makes his thing and then waves goodbye to it on the first night. The poor bloody actor has to go over and over it again and again, night after sodding night. During the run of *Live Bed Show* at the Donmar Warehouse, I realised that an actor's life was not for me. On show days, when I woke up (at lunchtime), I felt so oppressed at the prospect of having to go to the theatre that the only reasonable course of action was to mope. This was not how I felt on the afternoon of a comedy gig. Stand-up was simpler, more profitable and more *fun* than theatrics or perhaps it just comes easily to me. Compèring by now felt like a trip to the pub, interrupted by the occasional visit to the stage. I resolved to write another play, preferably without me in it, and stowed *Live Bed Show* at the back of a cupboard, where it waited obediently for five years until its next outing at the Garrick Theatre, in the heart of London's glittering West End.

* * *

The 1980s ended for me where they had started – on the comedy circuit, now expanded beyond anything we early settlers had envisaged. Every city in Britain and every borough in London boasted at least one comedy club and opportunities arose to play abroad. I was the first English comic to do a gig in Stockholm where I gathered my biggest laughs by reading out a Swedish menu. In Paris I did a terrifying ten minutes in French and confirmed my suspicion that the French are highly amused by the word 'cock-a-doodle-do'. In London, where once I had dragged up volunteers from the audience to be the open spot, rookie comics now had to wait months for a five-minute slot, and if you didn't show, sorry darling that's your lot. If you did turn up and were brilliant, the most you could hope for was a five-minute booking in an early show, way into the future. Everyone, it would seem, now wanted to be a comedian. Of course they did. Who would not wish to be such a creature?

The adrenalin of live performance continued to animate me. I relished especially the late show at the Comedy Store, the oldest, best-known and sexiest of all the circuit clubs. Playing within its laugh soaked walls is a rite of passage for the modern comic and doing well grants a comedic status you earn nowhere else. When disc jockeys tickle their posses or journalists write a funny column I think, 'Yeah, but could you do a ten down the Store?' At five past twelve on Fridays and Saturdays the procedure was the same. Kim Kinnie, then Don Ward's right-hand man, gives me the nod, the house lights go down, I start the short walk up one side of the audience; and the three hundred people, packed into the large, low-ceilinged, smoky subterranean room, many drunk and combative, turn to consider the small stage as Kim announces over the PA: 'Ladies and gentleman, welcome to the midnight show at the Comedy Store,' adding, to amuse me, 'in the heart of London's glittering West End.' The hubbub abates. 'Please welcome to the stage your compère tonight, Mister ARTHUR SMITH!' Music, loud applause, jeering; I step into the light, take my place in front of the microphone and feel that this is just about the most exciting place in the world to be.

Life was sweet. Sarah and I now lived together in Balham, while the reception of my first play, small appearances on TV and radio, and my showing as presenter of *First Exposure* allowed me some swagger in the world of funny. These times don't last. Just as I toppled out of trees as a child, I was about to take a fall in a show that would change the direction of my career and acquaint me with the horrible taste of a big, ugly turkey.

CHAPTER 17. BBC MAN

– Go on, Arthur, on you go.

   – Eh?

   – It's five past, we'd better start.

   – But Steve, the audience . . . ?

   – What about the audience?

   – Well, there isn't one. There's no one there.

   – Yes, but when you start, people passing by in the street outside will hear you and know there's something happening in here.

Trotting on, I acknowledged the imaginary applause.

   – Good evening. Thanks for coming – even though you don't exist.

It was hardly surprising that the auditorium was empty since the gig kicked off at three o'clock on a Sunday afternoon, a time at which no plausible comedy show in London has ever begun. As if the event needed any further impediment, it was also taking place at the same time as Run the World. Outside, on Shaftesbury Avenue, hundreds of virtuous joggers padded by in the afternoon sun, leaving me, smoking in the dark room, feeling, and no doubt looking, like a down-at-heel pimp.

Paramount City, bang in red-light Soho, had seen more glorious days as the Windmill Theatre – nude tableaux, Peter Sellers, the War, 'we never close' – all that. In the late 1980s, it was owned by Paul Raymond, who had heard tell of the new wave of comedy, seen the success of the Comedy Store up the road, and wanted a piece of the action. In addition to comedians, as a concession to his more traditional fare, Raymond had also booked Hot Gossip, an undulating girl dance troupe. Backstage, the dancers stood around unapproachably, pouting into mirrors while I blethered on pointlessly until, eventually, Steve's theory was lent credence by the appearance, at the back, of a solitary Japanese businessman.

– Good evening, sir – come in!

What did he make of this? Did he imagine everyone who came to Paramount City got a whole show, indeed a whole theatre, to themselves? Where were the girls? Who was this man standing talking to nobody? Was I mentally unwell? I beckoned him in. He waved back politely, turned and left. It transpired that Hot Gossip had played in Sun City in South Africa in defiance of an Equity ruling, so I was doubly pleased to decline further gigs at Paramount City.

Two years later and I'm back again, standing outside the entrance, looking now into the lens of a TV camera. In under a minute I will be cued by the floor assistant standing next to the camera operator and, as I start talking and walk forward, these two will walk backwards, their paths cleared by two scurrying men behind them. This is the opening shot of *Paramount City*, BBC 2's would-be answer to Channel 4's *Saturday Live*.

– Thirty seconds, says the assistant.

I am fighting self-doubt, I am trying to think about what I'm going to say, where I have to walk once I'm through the doors, the name of the act I am going to introduce, but I am also trying *not* to think about these things because I want to feel like my words are coming spontaneously as I speak them. Relax, Brian, relax. I jiggle my fingers like a sprinter before a race. God, I hate this suit. Relax.

– Twenty seconds.

But I cannot relax. On this Friday evening in March, Paramount City is filled with a large audience and has been refashioned by a set designer to look like a set designer's idea of a glitzy London comedy club. More cameras, lights and women with headsets are waiting inside for me to burst through the doors and introduce the first act on the show. At least at the last empty gig I played here, I could shrug and amble off into Soho in search of fun. Here the world of comedy and a million other people are watching me.

– Ten seconds.

There are some things about the TV series that I am about to present that make me uncomfortable – literally, in the case of the asphyxiating designer three-piece suit I am wearing. There has been an attempt made to render me younger-looking, prettier, more like a BBC 2 presenter. Grudgingly, I agreed to have a sunbed session and go shopping with the wardrobe people. Now, though, I am trying not to pay attention to one absurdity in particular that has arisen today. I have to deliver topical jokes, but there is only one topic that anyone is talking about and that is the one I am not allowed to touch on.

On the other side of Windmill Street a jolly lady in suspenders invites punters into the dark opening of her clip joint.

– Five seconds.

The cameraman braces himself, the crew go quiet but you can still hear the chatter of Soho and, above that, the noise of shouting and sirens born of the thing I cannot mention, The Poll Tax riots are reaching a violent climax in the streets behind me. None of this, of course, will be in shot.

Two . . . the assistant's hand comes down.

Everything about *Paramount City* felt ersatz, from the setting to the topical gags and bonhomie that I dispensed. At the end of the British show, which was transmitted two hours after the recording, I introduced a shorter version called *Live From London* that went out on cable TV (whatever that was) in America. There were some terrific acts – Dusty Springfield, the B-52s, Harry Connick Junior, Denis Leary – but I was not one of them. *Paramount City* never acquired an authentic identity and that was a lot of people's fault and one of those people was me. My material was tampered with by several different people, there were frequent last-minute changes, incomprehensible directives (I was not, for example, allowed to use the word 'crap') and a continued lowering of my confidence. I never stamped my personality on the show – but who cares now?

At the time I cared. It was the most profitable, and the most miserable, ten weeks of my professional life. I nodded when Paul Merton told me he had found appearing on the programme 'a soulless experience'. After three weeks I turned up drunk to a rehearsal. After four I hated it so much that I discussed with Sarah the possibility that I might just run away and hide, like the fantasy escape with Caroline en route to the opening of my play, except that I designated Belgium rather than Suffolk as my sanctuary. Vivienne dissuaded me, advising me to grit my teeth and get through it – think of the money, think of when it's over. Yes, I'll book a holiday, create a cordon sanitaire around me, empty my fraught mind, be nothing, watch the World Cup ... One of the ways I coped with the anxious months was to devote the hour off I had during every show day to slumping in the back row of a cinema, where I tried to lose myself in the big screen. There wasn't time to see the whole film but, after the series finished, part of my convalescence was spent seeing the second hour of the movies whose first half I had watched in the grim tension of those apprehensive afternoons.

Paramount City was a bruising experience and put a halt to my TV career. Addison Cresswell is quoted in *Ha Bloody Ha*, a book about the comedy circuit by William Cook, as saying:

> *Paramount City* drained the acts of any confidence before they went on the telly. The acts were so fucked off with all the script changes. Arthur Smith was completely fucked after that show. He didn't know what he was wearing, what he was doing, it was a fucking disaster — the guy was lost.

Addison's next sentence shows how bad it got for me during this period:

> He had to go into play writing!

Yes, that bad.

> His fucking career was fucked! You try to sell Arthur Smith as a compère for a TV show now, they'll say, 'I saw him on *Paramount City* — he fucked it!' Arthur Smith was the best man for the job at the time, by a long chalk. He was storming it round the clubs. What went wrong? He was not the same guy! What the fuck had they done to him? They put him in some horrible pastel colours. He looked a right fucking lemon!

TV ignored me for a time but radio, for which I am aesthetically and temperamentally more suited, revived me. *Loose Ends*, a new 'lively arts' show on Radio 4, recorded a short feature about a game of rounders that I organised among comedians in Edinburgh. The man behind the programme, Ian Gardhouse, wrote to me recently explaining his thoughts on that day:

> . . . it was in Edinburgh during the Festival one year and I'd gone down with Craig Charles to cover the rounders match that you organised. I took one look at you standing there swinging your bat in one hand, holding a fag in the other, and a can of beer in the third, casually ordering the others around with a merry quip or two on your lips, and I remember thinking, 'I want to work with this fella.'

And we did work together. TV gigs have come and gone, but *Loose Ends* has endured. Ian concocted the programme but *Loose Ends* was presented and embodied by raconteur and *homme de théâtre* Ned Sherrin. It has been the constant in my Radio 4 career, and permits me to write the following sentence without fear of litigation:

Julie Christie had not replied to the invitation, so I had a bath with Kate Adie instead.

We were in Ned's flat in Chelsea, recording the four hundredth edition of *Loose Ends*, on this occasion from his dining-room table. More usually, it was done from studio B13 in the basement of Broadcasting House. The show went out live for an hour at ten a.m. on Saturday mornings for ten years, at which point it started to be recorded in the morning and broadcast at 6.15 p.m. (in which slot it remains today). As one of Ned's regular sidekicks,

I did dozens of interviews with the great, the peculiar and the desperate – though only the one in a bath. I wore swimming trunks, Kate perched daintily on the rim.* In my early days on the show I would introduce a six-minute pre-recorded 'package' from one of Britain's eccentric gatherings. I entered the world sandwich-making championships, got pissed with a trio of students who had wangled a grant to drink vodka and play darts, and attended the AGM of the Test Card Appreciation Society where people from round the country congregated in a hotel in Wales to listen to the music that had accompanied the TV test card.**

Together Forever was a collection of individuals who believed themselves to be immortal. What fun. A number of questions arose in my mind when I met their guiding light – a middle-aged computer programmer from Raynes Park. 'How comes you've only been alive for forty-five years and yet you're already bald? What on earth will you look like when you're 752 billion years old? And will you still bother with birthday cards?' 'Surely you can make a killing if you take out a big pension?' But he was doggedly earnest and it was impossible to elicit from him anything other than New Agey platitudes. His faith in Together Forever had not been dented by the death of two of its members. As I left, I said encouragingly, 'You should write a book about it.'

* On the Monday after, the *Loose Ends* office received a note: 'I would love to have had a bath with Arthur Smith, Julie Christie.' As any man of a certain age and calibre will understand, I believe this to be the sexiest letter ever received.
** The test card, for those of you under thirty, was a photo of a young girl with long hair that preceded programmes on BBC TV. You may be astonished to learn that there was a time when TV was only on for a few hours a day.

'I would,' he replied, 'but I don't have time.'

'Surely,' I thought, 'time is one thing you *do* have.'

Or I might be out and about reporting in to Ned in the studio. Following a decision about the future of the BBC wavelengths, which would have affected listeners overseas, I was sent to do an outside broadcast, 'live from the Radio 4 riots'. Since being gassed and nearly beaten in Paris, I had attended more demos in London (not, of course, the big Poll Tax bust-up), but none of them resembled the polite clusters congregating at Hyde Park Corner. Embarrassed magistrates, doughty teachers, well-dressed diplomats and retired brigadiers shuffled gingerly towards Broadcasting House carrying the only banners I have ever seen with 'please' and 'thank you' written on them. I may snigger, but in these solid burghers lies real muscle. They won the day and taught me never to mess with an enraged Radio 4 listener.

Ian Gardhouse liked incongruous combinations, which was how I came to interview Barbara Cartland. I have not met the Queen, but I doubt if she is as grand and self-important as was the agèd dame. I was surprised to discover that her chauffeur-driven Rolls-Royce had been sent to take me and Jane, the producer, to her home — an enormous old pile somewhere in a leafy segment of Essex. We were welcomed by several epicene young men who fawned and fussed around Ms Cartland, displaying a courtesy so extreme that I wondered if they were taking the piss. I felt a little uneasy that Jane and I were both wearing leather jackets. 'That's good,' Jane said, 'I like it that we don't conform to the usual idea of BBC people.' I think she was relishing the imminent exchange.

It was easy to see why so many hacks had treated the Dame with such deference. We were swept into the pink presence like important envoys from a foreign court bringing our respects to the Empress. Her thick make-up made any facial expression indecipherable although she obviously only trowelled the cosmetics onto the part of her face that was visible to her in a mirror. In profile there was a clear border where the make-up stopped and grey skin began.

'I wonder what I should call you?' I asked with due humility. 'Dame Barbara?' Pause.

'Or perhaps – just Barbara?' Still nothing.

'Babs?'

Did I observe, deep down in the cliff face of her maquillage, a narrowing of the eyes? The interview proceeded stiffly around the subject of Romance. She had recently written a book on what constitutes a romantic hero and ran through his necessary qualities – the usual mix of Darcy and Heathcliff – only, for Barbara, he would also need a title. It was dull stuff and I felt the need to throw her off her pat responses.

'Who is your idea of a *real* romantic hero?' I asked.

'Oh, Lord Mountbatten I should say, he was so dashing and powerful.'

I uttered the follow-up question to this without much thought, but it proved to be the one that generated a genuine reaction and achieved what had seemed impossible – something very like an expression crawled across her face.

'Does it matter that he was gay?'

Loose Ends made for a bracing start to Saturdays. I was picked up by a cab at 8.45, frequently with a hangover – and twice having not slept at all. Before I had properly come round, I found myself sitting along one side of a long table with Ned at the head, genial but gleaming with mischief, surrounded by five or six other luminaries, a combination of writers, actors, comics and, in the case of Robert Runcie, retired archbishops. Some guests were big international names (e.g. Steven Sondheim, Armistead Maupin, Peter Ustinov, Alan Bates). In the corner of the studio the musical acts sat behind their instruments, obediently waiting their turn.

Before we went on air Ned spluttered an alarming gullet-clearing cough, made brisk introductions, invited the assembled guests to laugh if they found his opening routine funny and always added, 'Don't worry about Arthur – he tends to cast a deadly gloom over the monologue.' It's true that I found laughing at gags, usually after an evening spent telling and listening to them, tiresome, especially so early. Besides, I felt my constituency lay among the listeners who might enjoy Ned's opening routine but wouldn't actually *laugh* at it. At ten o'clock the studio fell silent, as the news was piped through. 'We have to listen to this,' explained Ned, 'in case someone we have mocked in the monologue has died.' The continuity person announced: 'And now it's time for Ned Sherrin and *Loose Ends*.' A beat later Ned was off and running. 'Good morning. On today's *Loose Ends* we have a cornucopia of talent . . .' I came to enjoy the little *Loose Ends* rituals but, at first, the programme seemed like a formidable early-morning dinner party with no food or drink – though you could smoke – and a dinner party at which your every remark was broadcast live to a million people. But I soon discovered that I had a rapport with Ned, who treated me like a naughty bastard son, bred on the wrong side of the tracks. I, for my part, would heckle his terrible regional accents and take the rise out of his arcane knowledge of the performing arts.

Eventually I carried out the more conventional job of interviewing a guest in the studio, approaching this task with varying

degrees of rigour. On one embarrassing occasion I failed to ask
Honor Blackman any questions at all about her play and instead
persistently sang her virtually forgotten hit single, 'Everybody's
Talking About Kinky Boots'. My style was in calculating contrast
to Ned's fulsome sophistication – my segment introduced an air
of unpredictability appropriate to a good Saturday morning. That's
my story and I'm sticking to it. Staying up late and drinking heavily
the night before a show was something I *needed* to do to prepare
myself properly for my rôle. In this sense I was always well
prepared, though not as well as Roland Rivron, whose opening
question to an interviewee might be, 'Who are you?'

A *Loose Ends* contretemps occurred when I interviewed, or
rather didn't interview, Engelbert Humperdinck. I was suspicious
about Engelbert even before I met him, because Val Doonican,
whom I had taken to Copenhagen on a *Sentimental Journey*, (cf.
six chapters hence) – generous, self-effacing Val, a man full of
compliments for people he had worked with, revealed that the
only person in showbiz he could not stand was the stupidly named
singer. On arrival on the Saturday, I was told Engelbert was in a
bad mood. I don't know the exact reason but maybe he expected
to be interviewed by Mariella Frostrup and did not like the look
of me. I went over to speak to the saturnine crooner. His ludicrous dyed bouffant hair, a cut too far even for Melvyn Bragg,
was upstaged only by his open shirt, glittering gold medallions
and Las Vegas sunglasses. I offered him my hand and apologised
for any misunderstanding. He did not shake it, nor speak; he
turned and left the building, trailing his collection of anxious
sycophants in his wake. 'Please Release Me' indeed. Panic broke
out among the production staff. They could add some time to
the other items, but not enough to fill the gap left by the

Grumperdinck. I proposed we confess to the listeners that Engelbert had got the hump and, since I did not want to waste my many minutes of research, I would ask all my prepared questions to the brilliant young Geordie comic Ross Noble who was also on that day's show. And so, for six minutes only, Ross Noble was Engelbert Humperdinck and lo, it was funny. The next time I heard Mr H he was on *Desert Island Discs*, choosing *his own songs* for his island.

Loose Ends was dreamed up by 'nice Mr Gardhouse', as Ned called him, the man who had watched me at the rounders game in Edinburgh. Ian did not hand out instructions or diktats, but his flair for radio made you want to get better at it yourself. There were usually two bands in the studio, among them some major names. Over the years I have sat six feet from performances by a hatful of famous artistes. Let me pick four that I have especially enjoyed: Amy Winehouse, in all her shimmering extraordinariness; The Only Ones, who sang 'Another Girl, Another Planet' (which had become the anthem for my wild 1980s); 'Golden Brown' sung acoustically by Hugh Cornwell of the Stranglers; but, most thrillingly, I sat directly at the feet of Tony Bennett, one of the coolest dudes I ever met, while he crooned, 'I Left my Heart in San Francisco'.*

One of the programme's sparky elements derived from the interplay between Ned and whichever of the two 'regulars' was in the studio. There was a small pool of us on call, divided fashionably into East End boys and West End girls. Ned was the headmaster and we his naughty, clever pupils. He was a wonderful

---

* When I had seen Spike Milligan perform the song, he had changed the second line to 'I left my liver in Milton Keynes.'

sight to behold at the helm of *Loose Ends* as he whipped his way deftly through the topical opening monologue, the heavy- and lightweight interviews, the introductions, the quips, badinage and sauciness that made for a typical edition. Having presented it myself once or twice, I can testify that it is an extremely demanding job which requires a whole range of skills, but a job which somehow Ned made look easy. And hugely enjoyable.

After Ned's closing topical quip he rose from the table.

'Thank you, everyone. I am now going to the George pub round the corner. If anyone would like to join me I shall be buying the first round.' And so, at eleven a.m., we arrived for opening time at the pub, where Ned would buy his promised round, even if there were twenty members of a band supplementing the guests. Here hair was let down, anecdotes unsuitable for broadcast were told and, occasionally, a liaison was made. The latest I ever left the George was nine p.m. but the record was held by David Soul who, by staying for twelve hours, completed the full day's drinking session.

More usually, I would leave after a pint and unwind by walking through the West End. Great Portland Street to Oxford Street, where I duck away from the crowds down the avenue that takes you past the Palladium stage door, along Great Marlborough Street, right into Berwick Street with its sociable market stalls and Soho So High, a temple of femininity where for comedy purposes I sometimes buy funny costumes and copies of the *Cunt Colouring Book*.

Past the Raymond Revue Bar, left along London's premier gay thoroughfare Old Compton Street, to the Cambridge Theatre at Cambridge Circus and down alongside the National Portrait Gallery, siphoning off left before Trafalgar Square to Charing

Cross Station, where I take Villiers Street to the river and cross the Hungerford footbridge to Waterloo. On the skyline to my left Saint Paul's Cathedral, ahead the National Theatre, beneath me the murmuring grey waters of the Thames. To the right, if I could see through the railway, stand the London Eye, Big Ben and the Houses of Parliament. Every one of these names recalls stories and characters from my past. Oh London, multicoloured metropolis, the only world-city in Europe, the town that bred me, my London, look at the big old capital on a Saturday lunchtime, greeting all the world, relaxed, glamorous, glinting with promise, filled with a billion possibilities.

CHAPTER 18. HAD TO GO INTO PLAY WRITIN'

True football fans select a team, preferably their local one, when they are five years old and continue to support that team until they are carried out the front door in a coffin, draped in the club colours. Meeting such a creature I feel a charlatan if I proclaim my interest in the game, since I only attend a couple of matches a season and have, at one time or another, supported virtually every team in London. In Bermondsey I watched Millwall. In Kidbrooke I took my place with Dennis on the huge lonely windswept terraces of Charlton Athletic's ground, the Valley. At Merton Road, we sometimes went to Plough Lane to cheer for Wimbledon FC and I continued to follow the Dons for several winters after I moved to Balham and the team transferred to Selhurst Park at Crystal Palace. I went with Richard and his boys and we laughed and clapped at the exploits of 'the Crazy Gang', as the eccentric team were known.* I have always had a soft spot for West Ham because my brother Nick, and now his sons, are all ardent Hammers. On one shocking occasion, I even found myself shouting for Arsenal at the Parc des Princes where they were being roundly abused by the fans of Paris Saint-Germain.

* I once presented a late-night show on Channel 4 with Crazy Gang midfield destroyer turned hard-man actor Vinnie Jones. Vinnie left all script considerations to me which meant I was able to present him as an enthusiastic follower of contemporary dance and lover of twee poetry about flowers.

Nick Hancock, a comedian I met on the comedy circuit, was and still is a fanatical devotee of Stoke City and one of the funniest people I have met. A restless, impulsive figure, he had an eye for excess, encouraged no doubt by his belief that he would die young. These qualities made him a rip-roaring companion and for five successive years we journeyed to a different European capital every May to watch the European Cup (now Champions League) Final. He was in Mallorca that summer after my *Paramount City* debacle and so, it transpired, were several other friends, including Caroline. Sarah and I resolved to join them to swim, sunbathe, drink and watch the World Cup in company, a few hundred miles closer to Italy where the drama was set to unfold. Given the large amount of money I had just earned, Sarah and I treated ourselves to a flash hotel – the Son Vida Sheraton, lying luxuriously on a hill two miles out of the capital, Palma.*

Some sporting occasions and events have burned themselves into my memory such that I wonder if the last thing I remember will be Bob Beamon smashing the world long-jump record at the Olympic Games in 1968. I can still recall BBC commentator Ron Pickering's astounded reactions. 'On the runway now, the man they all fear, erratic but incredibly talented . . . and it's AN ENOR-MOUS ONE! It's an ENORMOUS one! My goodness me, he was up in the air for an age! It's an *ENORMOUS* one . . . Twenty-*NINE* feet, two and a half inches! It's the *GREATEST* jump by the *GREATEST* margin (pause) there has *EVER* been.

At thirteen, before thoughts of female contours began to preoccupy me, I was the perfect age for obsessing about sport.

---

* If it's still there – hello Son Vida, can I have a free weekend there for giving you this plug?

The Mexico Olympics thrilled me especially because the events were on TV live at peculiar times, because Mexico looked so infinitely far away, unfamiliar and hot, because I was fascinated by the Black Power salutes of the black American sprinters, and because Beamon's leap really *was* spectacular. Enormous, in fact. There are different reasons why the 1990 World Cup made a similar impression on me: relief at the end of the demoralising *Paramount City* episode, a joy in my friends and my Balearic surroundings, but a sadness too at the slow disengagement of Sarah and myself. Oh, and because England did really well. Italia 90 remains our best World Cup showing since 1966. At the end of the semi-final, when England had lost to Germany on penalties, our hotel room was a wreckage of bottles, cocktail glasses, fag-end spirals and dejected drunks. It had been a draining two hours.

Although I have become passionately involved in football games and been possessed by the desire to see my team win, I am never distraught for long if they don't. When Bill Shankly famously declared that football was more important than life or death, I thought it was the most ridiculous thing I'd ever heard. It is not a phrase one likes to use in public since it is a drab cliché but, in the end, it *is* only a game, so I was surprised to find the lingering despair that Hancock and his friend, comedy writer Chris England, seemed to be experiencing at our defeat by the Germans. I conjectured that football provides men with an opportunity to show emotion, weep, beat their tribal breasts and sulk without feeling embarrassed, tongue-tied or inadequate. Surrogate pain. Baudelaire's existential despair on the edge of the abyss was the same as Nick Hancock's misery at the potential relegation of Stoke City and they were both ways of expressing their feelings about lovers and partners (not that Baudelaire ever really had

231

any). Perhaps there was a play somewhere in this. I sketched out some characters in a scenario rather like the one in our hotel.

The play in hand, though, was *Trench Kiss*, about a couple, Sally and Jim, visiting the battle grounds, cemeteries and memorials of Belgium and France where Jim's grandad had died in the Great War. Ever after my bomb-site days I had read about the two World Wars and tried to estimate their influence on my own times.* Now that the Cold War was over and Fukuyama's phrase 'the end of history' was being bandied about, it struck me that the big repercussions of those earlier conflicts had been played out and that, given their immense significance, this was where future historians would end their chapters on the twentieth century.** It seemed an appropriate moment to cast a look back, before the new millennium began. At least this would mean that my books about the period were now tax-deductible.

Mercifully, I have not had to live through the kind of trauma experienced in war by my dad and grandad, but a small part of me (and what part might that be?) regrets never having been in such *extremis*. What could be more challenging than someone trying to kill you? No doubt I found theatrical triumph and disaster interesting but, even at Malcolm's Tunnel club, I had never been *shot* at. My life seemed frivolous and silly when set beside the catastrophic adventures of the two generations above me. What was it like to see your friends die around you in the course of a few deafening, insane minutes, as Syd had done? How did he

* A lot of middle-aged men, including Tony Soprano, are interested in the World Wars. I call the UK History Channel 'The Nazi Channel' and so did the American comedian I stole the joke from.
** Eric Hobsbawm nicked this analysis from me – though he added two years – in *The Short Twentieth Century 1914–1991*.

feel, crouched in a bomb crater in a desert, as the long silhouette of a panzer-tank gun barrel penetrated the sky above him, then slowly descended until it was trained directly on him? I thought about *his* dad, treading water in the Aegean Sea for eight hours, hoping that some boat, *any* boat, please God, would come by – how beautiful that vessel must have looked when, finally, it loomed up through the waves. I thought of the profundity of the emotion that Syd must have felt, aged twenty-two, squatting on the floor of the first aeroplane he had been in, when he looked down to see the white cliffs of Dover growing larger, approaching them after three years in prison abroad. He had sat on these cliffs as a teenager and looked up into the skies through which he now flew to watch the dogfights.* Syd had been reported 'missing in action' several months before his parents received word that he was alive. The telegram might have stated the opposite which made me wonder at the intensity of those seconds as they opened the envelope, of their titanic relief, of what a day that must have been for them. Whenever I cycled along New Park Road, where my father had lived, I liked to imagine the banner he saw strung across the road as he turned off Brixton Hill one day in 1945. 'Welcome Home Syd.'

Just as I reflected on what my grandad's generation had undergone, so I pondered on what they would make of now, of 1990 as now then was – a world of abundance, concrete, traffic jams, telephones, plastic, television, nudity and PR. Given Caroline's

---

* The word 'dogfight' here refers to a close combat between two fighter aircraft, not a canine dispute. A confusion between the two meanings once led to a very peculiar conversation with a young woman. 'I just don't understand why a dogfight would end with a man being killed and another parachuting into the sea.'

demand for a handsome young actor to work with in my next play, I started to write the character of Jasper, a First World War soldier.

An explosion brings Jasper together with Sally in a kind of time-warp limbo and thence to the present and her flat. At this point the whole thing turned into a strange triangular love story, returning finally to Sally, reunited with Jim back in Ypres, looking at gravestones with a renewed interest. An obvious outcome would have been the revelation that Jasper was Jim's grandad, and the biggest laugh of a sombre script came when I led the audience down that path only to crush the idea in one line. It felt too cheesy a finish but perhaps I *should have* gone for that narrative closure, because one of the problems with the play was its uncertain end. I copped out by borrowing Philip Larkin's poem 'MCMXIV' for Jasper to recite and by substituting easy one-liners for thoughtful conclusion.

The first performance of *Trench Kiss* took place in Bath (of course) in May, with Caroline as Sally and a young Ben Miller giving his Jasper. Temporarily overlooking my dislike of acting, and to save Rupert money, I cast myself as Jim. *Quite* well received, it was never much of a box-office draw and although amateur productions still surface from time to time around the country it did not have the impact that the other play I wrote (or rather co-wrote) had in the Edinburgh Festival Fringe in 1991. *Trench Kiss* ceded the limelight to its big brash brother, *An Evening with Gary Lineker.*

Having finished writing the war play I could not stop thinking about the football story. The success of the England team and their dramatic final fall had ignited a broader public interest in the game. The papers were clogged with articles about Gazza crying, while creamy-thighed Lineker could do no wrong – 'Gary Lineker, the Queen Mother of football,' as we wrote in the play, 'his farts smell of perfume.' Rupert must have been surprised and mildly appalled – 'mildly' is the only sort of appalled Rupert *could* be – when I asked if he would produce a second play with a set and five actors. Hardly a pause, though, before he agreed.

Rupert had a lot invested in my two plays and so did I. *Loose Ends* was a glittery perennial but it was poorly paid and occasional, while my stand-up career, following *Paramount City*, was afloat but in the doldrums. Filling in for someone one Saturday at the Comedy Store, I was introduced by Bob Mills with the words, 'Seems like the telly didn't work out for him, so here he is, back at the Store, Arthur Smith.'* Returning to the comedy circuit would be an admission of failure and my appetite for performance was, for the time being, diminished. I did the occasional low-key turn to keep my hand in; at one grim sixty-quid gig at a cricket-club dinner in a pub in Stockwell I realised afterwards, with a shudder, that it was a year to the day since the first *Paramount City* show.

If I was working, I was liable to be writing *Trench Kiss* and so, to alleviate the lonely hours when Sarah, now a celebrity booker on TV, was out at the office, I cast round for a collaborator for the other play. I asked Nick Hancock and Chris England. Nick declined but Chris agreed and I have no doubt that if he had not, the play would never have become the success that it did. Chris England is a man whose first impulse on waking is to seek out news of any developments in the progress of Oldham Athletic, a fan who has consumed Bovril in (nearly) every league ground,

* I bear no grudge, Bob. It was funny.

and who only supported the England 1990 team because, for once, it contained no Manchester United players. He was the chap to bring an undisputed authenticity to all the football references; he also thickened and tightened the plot and supplied some very fine jokes. We based a maverick character on Nick Hancock and persuaded him to play the part. Rupert gave us the title and received an assurance from Lineker's agent that he would not sue us which, given that the title seemed to promise a night of Gary's reminiscences, would have been easy money for his lawyers.

Chris and I created scenes separately before rewriting them together with some routine stand-offs along the way. After five months, we arrived at the denouement to find that the one we had agreed was tame and obvious. The end, get the end right. Several sessions were spent fruitlessly mulling, until one night we found ourselves yet again watching the video of the game. Sarah came in from work, put her bag down, glanced at the screen and sighed, 'Oh, if only we'd *won*.'

'Yes, yes,' I suddenly thought. *'We should make England win.'*

And we did. The characters arrive at their varying crisis points as they watch Stuart Pearce step up for England's fateful fourth penalty in the shoot-out. (When the play was running, an antici-patory groan always emanated from the audience at this point.) Hancock described the unfolding events in Rome: 'And who's this one? Pearce. He looks really nervous. And Pearce . . . *scores!* 4 – 3 to England!'* The next German penalty-taker in our new, enhanced version of the game misses (in reality Olaf Thon scored), Gary Lineker smashes home the last penalty ('Under the new rules he's

---

* When Stuart Pearce saw the play in Nottingham, I am told, he leapt out of his seat, punched the air and exclaimed, 'Yes!'

allowed to take up to three') and England are through to the Final of the World Cup! Mayhem breaks out, culminating in the arrival of the Pope sprinting onto the pitch to give Gazza absolution, thus cancelling his yellow card and permitting him to play in the Final. Having transformed the facts, we had licence to indulge a big showbiz finale – a soundtrack of Pavarotti singing 'Nessum Dorma' accompanies a Gary Lineker lookalike emerging heroically through flashing lights and dry ice, a *deus ex machina* for the football dreamer.

And there I am in the audience in the Technical College theatre in Bath on a June evening wearing football kit under my clothes, ready to be the first – and probably worst – Lineker lookalike to appear in the play. Most shows I have done in Edinburgh have had teething problems, tantrums and ropy first nights but *An Evening with Gary Lineker* didn't bother with any of that. From curtain up through till the ovation at the end, the audience laughed, clapped and were engrossed in the plot. In Edinburgh, and after at the Purcell Rooms on the South Bank in London, the play was like a confident child that neither sought nor needed nurturing or encouragement, smoothly hurdling all obstacles to arrive where it wished to be.*

That August in Edinburgh, Caroline Quentin walked off stage every night as the smallish crowd for *Trench Kiss* at the Pleasance filed out and, while Ben and I sat in our Portakabin dressing room and smoked, she changed hastily and took a cab straight to the Assembly Rooms where, twenty minutes later, she walked on stage for the start of *An Evening with Gary Lineker.* The play was a hit – in part because it had, without us realising, tapped into the

---

* Rather like my brother Richard.

zeitgeist – a popular word at that time. England's glorious failure in the tournament, the introduction of the Premier League, the new requirement for all-seater stadia and the publication of Nick Hornby's *Fever Pitch* made the game more appealing to women, the middle classes and the media. Football was suddenly more fashionable than kiwi fruit had been in the 1980s. TV, cash and marketing subsequently sustained and increased its popularity such that even polo-playing Tory MPs were obliged to confess an allegiance to a club in their constituency, but there didn't seem much precedent for fiction with a footballing theme, other than depictions of Nazi skinhead hooligans stabbing each other in pub car parks. The only stage play I could think of that showed football supporters was Peter Terson's *Zigger Zagger* (a production of which was mounted by every youth drama group in the 1970s). Why was this? Millions of people followed football and the high emotions generated by the game seemed an obvious area for drama.

After the play's success in Edinburgh, Rupert started talking to some London theatres and, a few days before Christmas 1991, *An Evening with Gary Lineker* opened at the Duchess Theatre in the heart of London's glittering . . . Oh, that's enough of that joke, at the Duchess Theatre in London. Chris and I did every interview we were offered and Rupert's PR team, aided by the renewed interest in football, ensured there were plenty. The first preview coincided with Caroline's marriage to Paul Merton, so Morwenna Banks took the role that night – though Caroline, the classic trouper, was back for press night. The audience beamed and laughed; the reviews, including Gary Lineker's on *Loose Ends*, were great. ('The funniest play in the universe' said the remarkably perceptive reviewer in the *Daily Express*.) Everything had gone so well that, inevitably, there followed a disastrous week of small houses, hardly bigger than you'd get at a gig in a pub.

Christmas was an anticlimax. In Bath, I received depressing reports of continued tiny numbers. In one of the clubs aimed at West End actors and techies, I met a member of the back-stage boys who revealed he was running a book on how long the show would run and that the longest anyone had given it was six weeks. On 30 December I walked down the Strand, my gloves on my hand, considering my diminished income and faltering career while fishing around for a brave face to put on in front of the weary cast. Turning off the Aldwych, I observed an unfa-miliar A-board outside the front of the theatre. As I approached, the words came gloriously into focus: HOUSE FULL. Good gracious. Rupert was standing gazing at it, sporting an uncharac-teristically broad smile; bookings had shot up – something to do with 2-for-1 and the price of kettles, according to Rupert. What a terrific surprise to end the year.

On New Year's Eve the cast came to Balham after another loud, sold-out show and 1992 was welcomed in with loud toasts, slaps on backs, actory kissings and unmanly hugs. The play ran, on and off, for another two years in the West End before cleaning up on tour. Chris and I adapted it for TV, versions turned up in Sydney and Johannesburg and it was nominated for an Olivier award. Even now, years later, I am still sometimes introduced on radio shows as 'the author of *An Evening with Gary Lineker*'. Of course I am *not* the sole author. The joke between Chris and me about how little he got credited for the play reached its perfect form when we received the great accolade of becoming a ques-tion on *University Challenge*: 'Which footballer,' asked Jeremy Paxman, 'was celebrated in a play by Arthur Smith and—?'

'Gary Lineker.' A student buzzed with the correct answer before Jeremy could finish the question.

Among the audience for the play one night was a party from the Old Roan Society, numbering old schoolfriends and, pleasingly, Alf Knott, my former English teacher, who had directed me in the school revue, taught me comic tricks and failed to make me walk like a woman. Thank you for all you showed me, Alf.

The income from *Lineker* and my separation from the comedy circuit gave me the freedom to follow my fat, reddening nose for a time, to pursue ideas purely because they interested or amused me. I organised a mystery weekend for Sarah which culminated in a surprise visit to Balham from Les McKeown, the lead singer of her childhood pin-up band the Bay City Rollers, with whom I had got drunk after a late-night TV panel show. I walked some more of the Cornish coastline, renewed my interest in Dadaism, watched cricket, wrote fan letters to novelists, did a turn at the start of a couple of Green Party sponsored cycle rides, went to Romania with Jo Brand on behalf of a charity and otherwise got up late and messed around at home.

Acting out whims can open up new directions, as when I struck up a relationship with *The Stage* newspaper. *The Stage and Television Today* is Britain's in-house showbiz journal, founded in 1880, when I'm guessing the title did not include the '*and Television*'. It is a publication that was much loved by my grandad Jim, who had once received a favourable notice within its pages, and I too had become a regular reader by the time I passed an hour writing to the letters page. It was a rather cruel critique, but in my defence I will record that Milton Johns had recently written in his column, entitled *Letter to A Young Actor*, that he subscribed to John Osborne's belief that 'whatever else, I have been blessed with

God's two greatest gifts – to be born English and heterosexual.'
Some of the *Stage* readers are not English and, unsurprisingly, a
few of them are not heterosexual either. It was a silly thing to
write but I chose to pick him up on another of his defects . . .

SIR – It is a sad fact that many young actors have to struggle
hard to make a mark in our profession. The end of rep and
cuts are undoubtedly factors in this but I believe there is
another, more insidious and telling reason.

Young actors often have to work in shoe shops and market
research in order to make ends meet. Consequently they
have to make the most of the time available to them to
improve their art and prepare for auditions. However, these
hours are severely depleted by the necessity of having to
read Milton Johns's interminable series of *Letters to A Young
Actor*. Is there no end to these excruciating epistles? Johns
has achieved the remarkable feat of making each one more
boring than its predecessor. Consequently it takes longer
and longer to plough through them.

In the early days, using the intense concentration I learned
at the feet of an Indian sadhu, I was able to complete one
in about four hours before falling into a deep sleep. Now I
have invariably lapsed into a coma after only one paragraph
of his dismal homilies and antiquated prose style.

Please do all young actors a favour and forward all his
future missives, unopened, to the *Journal of Insomnia*.

Arthur Smith
Balham High Road

The letter was published and I thought no more of it until I received a phone call from Peter Hepple, the editor of *The Stage*, saying Milton Johns had left and would I take over his monthly column? Peter, whom I had met in the audience of several obscure shows, was a classy old dude who, despite his jovial, unpretentious demeanour, knew even more than Ned about the theatrical scene and seemed to have seen every show that had been put on in Britain in the previous fifty years. In tribute to my predecessor, I called my new column *Letter to A Young Comedian*. One hundred and sixty-five essays later I am pleased to report that I have today filed my one hundred and sixty-sixth – a tribute to the great Ned Sherrin.

It was at Ned's request that I found myself one afternoon in front of an audience of twelve men, several of whom were convicted murderers. The venue was a room in the high-security section of Whitemoor Prison, my job to entertain the Lifers' Association, i.e. prisoners with life sentences. (Excluded from this were the sex-offender lifers who had to be segregated from the common or garden murderers and armed robbers.) At Peterborough station I was met by H, an education officer at the prison who told me that things were a bit tense as it was only a week or two since three IRA prisoners had escaped. H was upset about this, partly because the escapees had been her best students and were liable to do well in their exams. Now they had gone, her pass-rate percentage would fall. More seriously, she wondered if the 'students' – who had acquired a gun – would, if necessary, have shot their teacher. Blimey. As we reached the imposing entrance to the prison H told me about the Alan Ayckbourn play the prisoners were putting on, directed by the senior education officer who was, coincidentally, H's mum. In the absence of any other women, mother and daughter had taken the female roles and were fretting over a stage direction that demanded H's character should kiss one of her male cast members. The 'actor' in question was the infamous serial killer, Dennis Nielsen. I used to think *my* job was unusual until I met this remarkable woman.

After many unlockings, searches and lockings-behind, we reached the prison teachers' staffroom, where sensible people were preparing for afternoon classes. I wondered what their response was when schoolteacher friends complained that their pupils were difficult. In the bare room, the prisoners from the Lifers' Association lounged politely on plastic chairs in a semi-circle before me. They had no idea who I might be, but I was offering an easy hour in their endless incarceration. I tried a few jokes but they didn't go well, even though this was the ultimate captive audience. I was very far from emulating Johnny Cash in Saint Quentin. My popularity rocketed, however, when I produced a packet of cigarettes to distribute and they began to tell me their stories and talk about prison life. There was a long, lyrical debate about H's mum's breasts, which fazed H, sitting next to me, not one jot. Their tales of violence, drugs, regret and anger were at once fascinating and depressing. One of them said, 'The thing is, Arfur, anyone can be a murderer. Say some bloke is hassling your bird and you give him a slap and he falls wrong, cracks his head – bang! You're a murderer!'

The prisoner next to him looked at him quizzically and remarked, 'Yes, but in *your* case you glassed him in the face sixty-seven times!'

On the train back I reflected that it was the only gig I'd done where I sat back and the audience performed to *me*. I conceived a plan to return for the Ayckbourn play – but I never did, of course, and, unsurprisingly, the production never made it to London – although with Nielsen in the lead you have to think it would have received a ton of publicity.

Prison visitor, broadcaster, journalist – my next haphazard excursion entailed all these jobs and followed a phone call from my dear old dad.

CHAPTER 19. SYD'S RETURN TO COLDITZ

My parents each reacted differently to my showbiz career. Where Hazel was quietly supportive but undemonstrative, Syd could not disguise his delight at my public success. If I was with him among people we had just met, it was never long before he managed to sneak into the conversation a mention of some achievement of mine. He and Hazel once attended an amateur production of *An Evening with Gary Lineker* in Bath and before Hazel could stop him, Syd had blurted to the lady on the door, 'My son wrote this.' Years later, the director emailed me wondering if it really *was* my dad whom she had presented to the cast and to whom she had given a glass of wine. Discovering that the man had amused the actors and left the wine undrunk confirmed to me it was indeed Sydney Smith.*

Syd cycled off to the court every morning while my mother now worked part time as the 'lady who does' for a Landmark Trust house on the handsome old square in front of Bath Abbey. American guests frequently bracketed her with Jane Austen in the visitors' book. Hazel has certainly always chosen her words with wit and care. As a child I remember her relishing a phrase – 'A lorry has shed its load' – in the local news. 'Shed its load,' she repeated softly, 'poor old lorry. It must have been tired.'

---

* Syd shared his name with the eighteenth-century cleric and wit, although I have been unable to find any significance in this.

Sometimes, she told me, she hankered after the pungency of inner-city deprivation and the buzz of the capital's streets.

Hazel always felt herself a Londoner more than did Syd, who had spent his early years in Dover and relished the genteel Bathonian ambience. When he finally retired I felt concerned for Syd; he had worked all his life, been an active sportsman and a conscientious parent but he did not enjoy holidays – he associated them with arduous drives and unfamiliar regimes. He and his generation had had enough excitement during the War. They wanted a quiet life, no fuss – my mother's aspiration, above all others, was to be *ordinary*. Syd had no real hobbies beyond pretending to make a bookshelf while sneaking a fag in the garage. Would he get bored in the long afternoons? I certainly did.

But when I spoke to him he sounded like a man relaxing into a warm bath after a long day in the open air. He set up camp in his convertible armchair, which anticipated the dad's chair in the US sitcom *Frasier* (one of his favourite shows) and, from this stripy throne, he read the *Guardian* from beginning to end, watched all forms of sport on TV, conceived an unlikely crush on hearty broadcaster Clare Balding, played nightly games of Scrabble and went to bed after *Newsnight*. In excursions from base he bought the onions that formed the jewel in the crown of his range of pickles, ran errands in the car and meandered along the undulating Wiltshire and Somerset lanes and paths with Hazel. At weekends they entertained, fed and accommodated an eclectic bunch of friends, family and cast-members of my shows. Often, Syd was thrilled to see a comic actor who had stayed with them years before, receiving an award or fronting their own TV series. My parents were universally liked; Adam told me that an American lover he took round Britain nominated his favourite afternoon of the tour as the one he had spent having tea with my parents in Bath. It was as ideal as retirement can be, although Syd made fewer sorties after breaking his leg playing football with a ten-year-old Freddie.

Prompted by Richard, he also spent several months writing his 'memoirs' (he laughed at the prententiousness of the word) in his careful copperplate writing. His sentences, short and simple but full of interesting asides, were, in his own image, funny and warm. (Remember my second Chapter 1?) The account of his war years avoids introspection and relates concisely and movingly the arrival home that I had tried to imagine:

> We sat on the floor of the Dakota. We took off and it was hard to believe that we were on the way home. The plane rattled and vibrated. It was the first time I had flown and I prayed that it would make it because it sounded to me as if the engine was about clapped-out. We crossed the English Channel and there before our very eyes we saw the white cliffs of Dover. Men cried and we were all speechless with emotion. It was some time before we spoke. We embraced each other.

The fact that he was reminiscing spurred me to make a proposal: 1992 was the fiftieth anniversary of the battle of El Alamein at which Syd had been captured. I offered to return with him to North Africa where he had been so entranced by the Sahara – its empty, clean horizons, wild sandstorms and buzzing net of flies (he told me about the 'regimental fly-catcher') – that he had, ever after, read books about deserts. Come on, Syd, I urged him;

it will be great – you can visit Cairo again, return to Benghazi as a free man . . . but he declined, as I suspected he would. The next day, however, he rang to say he would be happy to go to Colditz while Hazel was in the States visiting her sister. During the rare times my parents were parted, Syd seemed touchingly lost and was always more liable to be available for outings.

Sarah, who mock-bickered with Syd to their mutual entertainment, said she would like to come too and Syd was persuaded that we should also visit the fortress of Konigstein, where he had been held before Colditz. At a dinner party with Simon and Olivia, mention of the forthcoming trip produced a gleam in Olivia's beautiful big-cheese-in-BBC-documentaries eye. A cobbled-up proposal earned a disconcertingly swift green light and soon a director, hastily assigned to 'Syd Goes Back to Colditz', wanted to meet the pair of us. Syd was anxious about all this: 'I wasn't an officer, I didn't escape, they won't be interested in me.' I assured him that he wouldn't be made to look a hero, but the prospect of the camera, the sound man, the rising blood pressure made him finally reject the idea. I wasn't too keen either. The TV doc, I knew from experience, would necessitate 'walking shots', retakes, set-ups and a whole grammar of proceeding which would agitate Syd and bore me. I wanted to be a son, not a TV presenter, although I *did* want to record my father's reactions in some way and felt it would make an interesting story which his descendants might one day want to hear. We settled for my recording our visit for a short Radio 5 documentary and writing an article for the *Guardian*.

One of the reasons why the media were interested in this story was the possibility of my father being traumatised by the return to these grim places. Memories of the pain, the hardship, the dead comrades would torment him, lead to breakdown and tears – 'the money shot'. This was not the reaction I anticipated, since Syd was never unforthcoming about his army days – though he preferred, as I did in stand-up, to stick to the familiar routines. He was bemused and a little embarrassed by the small fame that being a POW in Colditz had brought him. Rotary Clubs and Round Tables invited him to give after-dinner speeches about his war years and he accepted reluctantly because he didn't want to offend, but he used to dread their approach in the calendar. At weddings and family gatherings where he felt comfortable, Syd was eager to get up and rattle off a couple of his old jokes but in a formal setting, in front of the middle-class burghers of Wiltshire and Somerset, he felt intimidated and uncertain.

Colditz was not the grimmest experience he'd had. After his capture he was paraded through the streets of Palermo and sent to camps in mainland Italy, to a copper mine in Germany and then, via Konigstein Fortress near Dresden, to Colditz Castle from whose confines he was liberated by an American tank crew in April 1945. 'After the copper mines,' he said, 'Colditz was a holiday camp.' I sensed that what would upset him about going back to Germany was not the spectre of a lost youth, but the getting to the airport, the journey at the other end, the hotel, the food, the hassle, the *foreignness* of it all. My ambition was to get a snapshot of the young Syd in that extreme environment before he begat me. He had told me of how, while playing cards in Konigstein, he had become involved in a vicious fight with another British POW. I had found it hard to reconcile *that* Syd with the manifestly gentle Syd who was my father. Might I see this young person cooped up and punchy?

We flew to Leipzig and travelled to Colditz in a taxi with two air hostesses from the flight who were also keen to look round the castle. Naturally, they were impressed by Syd who, in turn, told them proudly: 'My son was on *Wogan* last week, you know. Yes, his real name is Brian.' Shut up, Syd. I was manipulating the tape recorder and trying to register his first reaction to seeing the famous place. 'That's it, there it is!' he exclaimed. I asked grandly: 'So how does it feel to see Colditz again after nearly fifty years?' 'Well, you know . . . it's interesting.' The stereotypical Colditz is a dark old courtyard full of handsome toffs in baggy trousers and cricket jumpers. Happily womanless, by day they perpetrate hilarious practical jokes on the dim-witted German guards; by night they plant one foot on a table, stick a pipe into the centre of a broad jaw and plan outlandish escapes. If the characters from *Brideshead Revisited* had reformed and gone to war, maybe this is where they would have ended up. Syd looked eagerly round the museum in the castle, pointing out from faded photographs prisoners he had known – some of whom wore baggy trousers and cricket jumpers. In addition to recidivist escapers, Colditz contained the *Prominente*, men who were famous or highly placed and therefore potential hostages. Syd was one of the orderlies, or batmans – batmen? – who 'looked after' the knobs and aristos, among whom he remembered Giles Romilly (Winston Churchill's nephew), Lord Lascelles (who had terrified Syd by asking him about the opera), the Earl of Hopetown and Earl Haig (son of the field marshal).

A young student called Hannah was our guide round the castle. As most Germans have never heard of Colditz (what German POW camps in Britain do you know?) our group was exclusively British and Hannah spoke in English. We started on the bridge leading up to the castle, where she sketched a brief outline of its history, then unexpectedly broke off to ask: 'Have you heard of August the Strong?' Her intonation suggested that *not* to have heard of him was an admission of gross ignorance. Syd, Sarah, me, the two air stewardesses and the eight off-duty British soldiers looked uncomfortably at each other, hoping that someone knew the answer. 'He was the greatest king of Saxony,' snapped Hannah. We nodded sagely. Of course he was. 'Do you know why he was called August the Strong?' After a terrifying silence, I ventured limply: 'Because he was very strong?' 'No,' said Hannah in triumph, 'because he was the father of three hundred and sixty children!' We laughed politely and followed her to the castle entrance, once the German guardhouse.

Syd was staring past Hannah as she told us about the Tory MP Airey Neave's escape in 1942* and when we finally entered the cobbled courtyard he pointed to a window on the ground floor and said rapturously: 'That was my room! That's where I was!' The squaddies exchanged looks; they'd guessed Syd had been here before. Hannah appeared oddly disconcerted, as though she feared we might gang up on her. She was certainly no longer the focus of the tour and while she stammered through her next chunk of facts, the soldiers were looking admiringly at Syd, who in turn was taking photographs of his cell. The courtyard, disappointingly small and shabby – although pleasingly claustrophobic – was now the outside area of a psychiatric hospital which a part of the castle had become. A patient, huddled on a bench, wailed intermittently as Hannah continued the tour. In the castle chaplaincy

---

* Airey Neave was killed by the IRA in 1979 in a car bomb incident. I recall the comedian Andy de la Tour's wince-causing line at the time: 'He got out of Colditz, but he couldn't get out of a car park in Westminster.'

she pointed to a display case containing some battered tins of food dating from the War. 'The Colditz villagers,' she declared, 'ate less well than the prisoners.'

'Well, I don't know about that,' came Syd's voice from the back. We looked round. I was surprised to hear Syd interrupting the guide; he was not one of life's hecklers. He explained to the group: 'After we'd peeled a turnip, we used to peel the peelings.' It was not the fear or the boredom of being a prisoner that Syd remembered, it was the never-ending hunger. When he was in a camp in Italy the POWs ate so little that they could only sit list-lessly through the hours and 'we had two bones for an arse'. A POW who had been a chef at the Dorchester would stand on a box and describe in detail how he would prepare a steak in the posh London hotel before the War, a painfully exquisite act with no laughs.

Syd told me he had eaten rats as a prisoner and when I asked him what rat tasted like, he replied with a phrase that I have discovered is funny enough to use on stage: 'a bit like dog.' In the copper mines Syd's weight dropped to six and a half stone (he was just under six feet tall). When asked about sex during those years, he had a stock response: 'If you had the choice between the most beautiful woman in the world and a cheese roll, you'd pick the cheese roll.' For the distribution of food they divided into groups of four and the man whose turn it was to have the last piece of bread divided it into quarters. In turn, the other three would examine a quarter from every angle before choosing which to take.

His remark in the chaplaincy was not meant to undermine Hannah, but it had that effect. She bristled: 'Perhaps it was different when you were here.' Back out in the courtyard Hannah indicated the roof where, incredibly, some prisoners had constructed a glider without the Germans noticing. Syd chipped in with a story about the liberating Americans wanting to buy it. Hannah related some of the schoolboy pranks the prisoners got up to and Syd added that sartorially, by comparison with the Poles and the Dutch, the British prisoners were 'a shambles'. He pointed out the room once occupied by the legless pilot Douglas Bader, played by Kenneth More in the film *Reach for the Sky*. 'Didn't they take his legs away to stop him escaping?' asked one of the squaddies. 'No, he had 'em back in here,' Syd responded authoritatively. Encouraged both by the soldiers and the air stewardesses, Syd was now reminiscing freely. 'We saw an American tank come over the bridge in the town and some German soldiers raised their hands to surrender. An American climbed out of the tank and one of the Germans picked up a gun and shot at him. So the Americans just shot the Germans. Fair enough, really.'

This new piece of information and Syd's casual delivery of it made me feel more sympathetic towards Hannah, who had been humourless but civil. Meanwhile Syd was becoming positively laddish. 'Top floor, third window from the right,' he said, 'that's where they kept the radio.' He turned to Hannah: 'Did you know there was a secret radio?'

'Oh yes, I knew something about this.'

'You never found it though, did you?'

Sarah and I found ourselves gaping in horror. Syd had become so carried away that he had unwittingly turned Hannah into a German guard from 1945. The rest of the group laughed. Syd didn't realise what he had implied but Hannah did, and blushed. 'That's the end of the tour,' she announced, 'I hope you enjoyed it.'

We nodded our thanks. 'Very interesting,' said Syd.

'Oh, I'm sorry you didn't find it interesting.' Hannah had misheard him. I chased after her and said: 'I just want to say thank you and—'

'You already have,' she said and strode on.

I wanted to catch hold of her and tell her that Syd didn't hate Germans, indeed he was intrigued by all foreigners. He and my mother had shown generous hospitality to all sorts of tourists encountered by their sons around the world. Syd had seen the continent nearly ripped apart by one country and believed in a 'united Europe'; expressing this later to our German driver in some clumsy but comprehensible mime. In the little square in Colditz town, Syd stopped at the spot where he had met a sixteen-year-old Polish girl in the brief period between liberation and the start of his journey home. He would have liked to have stayed with her a little longer and described her waving tearfully as the US army lorry pulled out of town. This sentimental little story raised the question: how, at a time when there were suddenly so many GIs and randy former prisoners, mostly officers, around, did Syd manage to cop off with one of the town's few available women?

In the café, with the tape recorder off, Syd told of two more of his old girlfriends. Before the War he had been engaged to Edna, who dutifully wrote to him while he was on the troopship which took the safe route to Port Said in Egypt via Cape Town. The letters grew less tender and then dried up, appropriately, when he reached the desert. But there were two letters from Edna in the first batch of correspondence he received after his capture. The first one revealed apologetically that she was seeing a Canadian soldier; the second, written a month later but read immediately after the first, announced that she had married him. Welcome to prison, Syd. This story, which sounded unbearably sad, Syd told as an amusing anecdote. He long ago forgave Edna whom he never saw again. 'I wouldn't have met Hazel otherwise.' The encounter with woman number two occurred on his return to England, when he was deemed too skinny for family viewing and was dispatched to a farm for a week to be fattened up. Naturally the farmer had a daughter and, inevitably, Syd and she had a fling – almost as though the farmer's daughter was part of the deal.

On the night of 14 February 1945, Syd had been appalled to hear from his bed in Colditz the devastation of Dresden. He, along with many others, had not seen the need for these revenge bombings and felt ashamed of them. When we arrived at Dresden station he didn't want me to ask for directions in case our English accents gave us away and caused offence. He was respectful of the ordinary people who had, like him, endured the hardships of the War. From Dresden a short train journey took us along the banks of the Elbe to Konigstein Fortress which broods darkly atop scarily high slopes, an enormous, imposing edifice that seems to grow straight out of the rocks that support it.

Before they were banged up in Colditz, Syd and four other POWs were marched up through thick woods by five German guards. They had no notion why they were being taken to Konigstein, but had heard rumours about the shooting there of a group of SAS men. We retraced his steps but more slowly – it was very steep and Syd was much older now than he'd been on his first visit. As we emerged breathlessly from the trees we were confronted by the massive thick walls within which Syd had been incarcerated. He seemed more affected by this sight than he had by the visit to Colditz.

This was a darker memory. Cooped up in a room all day, their food lowered down to them, the captives had no news of the War and empty hours to consider the possibility of an imminent and violent death. This was where Syd had the brawl. There were no Hannahs in Konigstein Fortress, no British soldiers, no familiar cinematic images. Dramatic though it is, for an Englishman the place lacks the romantic reverberations of Colditz. The plentiful tourists were all German and took no notice of the couple with the elderly man standing on the battlements. Later, he sent a postcard of the castle to my mother, marked with a big cross on a tiny castle window and the inscription: 'I was here in 1944.'

As we arrived at the white cliffs of Heathrow, I reflected that neither Syd nor Sarah nor I had experienced any startling revelations. I failed in my attempt to construct a Proustian theory about memory, history, ageing or imprisonment. Perhaps my relationship with my father had been coloured in a little more, but it was essentially the same. I had seen a small and affecting portrait of Syd in his early twenties but it was far away and unreachable. The lives of our parents before we are born are as unknowable as those of any other strangers. Syd was interested in it in the way we all are when we see again a house we lived in years ago. The fear and uncertainty of that time were untraceably mixed up with the influences from the rest of his life. In returning to these places we had done tourism; tourism with knobs on, but still tourism.

Back home we rang Hazel in America. Syd was most keen to tell her about the difficulties he'd had in the short-stay car park after he'd seen her off. He was brief about our visit to Germany. Before he rang off I heard him say: 'Looking forward to seeing you.' Then he added, 'I shan't be going abroad again.' And he never did.

CHAPTER 20. I DALLIED AND I DILLIED

Four weddings have seen me climb to my feet to make the best man's speech. Richard and Lin's was an informal affair in Helensburgh in the west of Scotland where my remarks were largely made up of the Max Miller-style jokes I had delivered at the previous year's Edinburgh Festival. The wedding photos really ought to be on display at the V and A as the perfect encapsulation of 1970s style which, until its next revival, continues to look like the decade where fashion went haywire (see photo page eleven). Richard, fittingly, looks the most ridiculous of all in his white flared suit and his bow tie of clownish dimensions. Like the other three at which I played my role, Richard and Lin's marriage survives so, if you're a bloke seeking to make a formal commitment to your partner and you have no friends, please get in touch with my agent.

Phil and Max's was a bigger do, with a five-tier entry, culminating in a wild party at Jongleurs. I remember nothing of my speech but I am persuaded it was acceptable – unlike my effort at the nuptials of Simon and Olivia, the proud new parents of Oscar, where I turned up in my shorts and trainers, having left my trousers and leather shoes in a plastic bag in a cab on the way to the event. I then proceeded to get drunk before mumbling some incoherent platitudes and making off early with their au pair girl. They have forgiven me now. The most pleasing effort of my four best-man speeches was the one I delivered at Gary and Bronwen's marriage. I found a copy of it the other day while muddling around in my archive and, with their permission, I now reproduce my tribute to my oldest friend and his wife.

'Gary Richard Ashcroft Rimmer has been my close friend for all bar ten years of my life. I first met him in March 1944 when we were both parachuted into occupied France. At the time Gary was in his early fifties and I knew him only by his French code-name – Gary. We have remained friends ever since despite his being tortured to death by the Gestapo on VE Day.

'This is the kind of bizarre scenario Gary and I created for ourselves every weekday morning for the seven years we used to walk to school together. I always wanted to walk across Blackheath, while Gary preferred the other route up the side of the motorway and past the girls school. Gary has always been an urban boy.

'When we were sixteen I was top in French, captain of the cross-country team, but I looked like Jimmy Sommerville with spots, glasses and an Afro haircut. I really used to envy Gary. He had done something I only dreamed about. He had *talked* to a girl. Not only that, he had persuaded some of them to snog him. He was the man who first taught me that the best way to appeal to a girl is not to whack her in the stomach with your satchel and run away. This is a lesson I am still digesting.

'Gary then seemed louche and dangerous and exciting and sometimes he still is. He used to get involved in fights quite often. His technique was to adopt a kung fu pose which would cause his opponent to run away in terror. He was, and is, naturally inquisitive and he was keen to experiment, becoming, variously, a rocker, a skinhead, a greaser, a Christian and a hippie – sometimes within the space of a single evening. He once announced to me that he'd decided to become a communist – but only after he had done his O levels.

'After college, for six years Gary and I shared a flat with a number of people who are here today and two or three hundred who aren't. Merton Road, South Wimbledon was a flat that will go down in history as one of the great shit-holes of our times. I'm sure Gary's mum and dad will remember the time they came round and their dog had a crap under the telly. It was finally cleared up a month later – by Mr and Mrs Rimmer.

'Gary has piles. Not medical ones. Not of money. Of magazines, of long-abandoned projects, of press cuttings, of film scripts, of ideas. If there's one thing I know about Gary, and Bronwen will find out, he likes a pile. I actually met Bronwen about thirty seconds before Gary did. I seem to recall I whacked her in the stomach with my satchel and ran away. Since their meeting I can honestly say Gary has been more content than I can remember.

'Everyone who knows him has a story about Gary; no doubt we'll hear some tonight, and probably one or two new ones will be created. Everyone has a soft spot for Gary, and now Bronwen has the softest spot of all. I'm sure your mutual soft spots will continue to flourish, and I'm sure we'll all continue to enjoy Gary and his wonderful theories, Gary and his piles of magazines everywhere, Gary and his notions, and his "whereupons", Gary and his sensitivity and his loyalty and his kindness and now, best of all, Gary and his Bronwen and Bronwen and her Gary.'

My own coupledom was ending. Sarah and I had grown so accustomed to each other and, apart from spats centring around my pathological messiness, so easy in our relationship that it had become, well, a trifle *dull* for both of us. Eventually she moved out although her new flat was close enough that we frequently ate and watched football on TV together. It was, as they say, amicable, and my regret and sadness at our inevitable parting was delayed while I eased myself out of domesticity and back into the haphazard underworld of life as a single man. My old man said follow the van and don't dilly dally on the way. Off went the van with me old home in it, I walked behind in me old cock linnet.

I dillied . . .

At a corporate gig in a London Hotel, I'd gone down well enough to seek compliments and drinks at the bar afterwards. Both arrived swiftly, delivered by a man with a needy look.

'You were very funny. Put your booze on my tab. I'm drowning my sorrows tonight . . .'

Uh-oh.

'Oh dear. Why?'

'Tell me, are you married?' He was itching to tell me his marital problems. Christ, I didn't want to be stuck with this bloke all night but, poor fellow, he so wanted me to be married.

'Yes.'

God, why did I say that? Make a joke out of it.

Indicating a woman I had never met who had just arrived at the bar next to me, 'I'm married to her.'

'How long?'

'Eleven years,' said the woman. Bobbed hair, red lips, enticing smile.

'We're still really happy,' I added.

The woman and I exchanged a glance of complicity as the

man embarked on an account of his failing marriage. I began to feel guilty that he was obviously distraught about his relationship whereas I, apparently, was in a long, happy love affair with a woman, a woman he did not realise I had only clapped eyes on five minutes earlier. I wanted to admit the lie, but my 'wife' and I were in too deep. By now we had two children and owned a small cottage in Suffolk. My other half had also described the magical evening on a mountain in the Pyrenees where I had proposed, it seemed, in some style.

'And do you still fancy each other?' asked the sad husband.

'Oh yes,' she said, and proceeded to elaborate on our sexual games and explosive mutual orgasms. Eventually the fellow had heard enough about this sickeningly successful liaison and he scuttled off forlornly. My wife – my grand passion, the mother of my children – and I were alone together for the first time in our eleven-year marriage. She introduced herself, we laughed, drank cocktails and later we repaired back to the hotel room I had been given but had not expected to use. In the morning she was gone and I was single once more. Best, I thought, to leave it a while to get hitched again. What was the point when my first marriage was so sublimely perfect – and all over in eight hours?

The French stripper, the RSC actress, a fuck on the centre-spot of Stamford Bridge, Chelsea's home ground, the human rights lawyer, the university lecturer, the single mum, the artist . . .

. . . I dallied . . .

At a party to celebrate the BAFTA won by *Whose Line Is It Anyway?*, on which I had appeared (not very successfully, once) I stole the award as I left, causing much unhappiness in the offices of Hat Trick TV. Dan Paterson, the programme's likeable inventor, probably does not agree but I felt it appropriate that a prize given for improvisation should itself be improvised away. Fortunately the taxi driver to whom I offered it on the way home that night did not accept my gift and the hard little perspex face stood on my kitchen table the next bleary morning with an accusatory expression that said, 'What now?'

Word reached me that Dan, now desperate, had called in the police and Tony Slattery was upset at being under suspicion – as well he might have been. This little stunt was getting out of hand. Having located a false moustache in my dressing-up box, I put the award in a plastic bag and deposited it at the offices of the *Guardian*, with a note saying that while walking my dog Pickles on Hackney Marshes I had found the enclosed. This reference to the episode of the stolen Jules Rimet trophy in 1966 earned the story a spot on the next day's front page underneath the headline, 'Whose Doggone Trophy Is It, Anyway?' The last sentence stated, 'Police are unlikely to pursue the case further.' I'm not sure if Dan ever knew it was me wot dunnit but, if he didn't, he does now. Sorry, Dan.

This incident occurred at the start of my Soho years when, on a couple of nights a week, after a trip to see the last scenes of *An Evening with Gary Lineker*, a gig, an art opening, a visit to the pictures or a heavy lunch, I would follow my nose round the delicious neon byways between Shaftesbury Avenue and Oxford Street. I did not seek membership of the Groucho Club since it felt like an insult to Groucho Marx's great line* but I could usually

* 'I do not wish to belong to any club that would accept me as a member.' As, I'm sure, you knew.

blag my way in there if I wished, or to Soho House, another nearby members-only media trough, or the Colony Room, the artists' bar of choice or, if I was suitably dressed and on form, to pretty well anywhere in London.

One night in a club in Frith Street I was excited to fall in with Damon Albarn from the immensely groovy Britpop band, Blur. Our chat was interrupted every few minutes by a succession of attractive young women, who interposed themselves between Damon and myself, stared at him, and made it clear that they did not want to talk about Radio 4, which, as it happened, Damon and I were doing. To one of them I said, 'You're not going to get his attention unless you've got a new angle on *Gardeners' Question Time*.' She glared at me indignantly, jealous that it was I, not she, who was sitting next to the heart-throb. Damon likes Radio 4 and, like all right-thinking people, was a fan of Ned's, which meant he had been thrilled to be invited on *Loose Ends*. His ambition, he told me while wafting away another panting girl, was to be on *Desert Island Discs*, and indeed he had already drawn up his list of songs. I told Damon that he was not the stuff of this sturdy middle-aged programme and recalled for him the outcry in the shires when the actress Wendy Richard had been chosen as a subject. If a young pop singer were on the programme, Sunday morning would be rent with the thump of posh matrons beating their breasts. Damon smiled politely, but was impatient with my argument; he was a bona fide rock star and had a huge following – his audience, he reasoned, was the type of listener Radio 4 wanted, and needed, to encourage. The upshot of all this was that we put a ten-quid bet on him not being on *Desert Island Discs* before the end of the millennium and, after more confidence-building booze, another tenner that *I* would be on *before* him.

Edinburgh, 1991

(*Facing page*) Some of my acting expressions.

Stand-up

(*Below left*) Giving my dame, Nurse Nelly Nightcap – notorious Danish prostitute.

(*Below right*) Phil and I in the double act, Fiasco Job Job. We were funnier than this photo suggests.

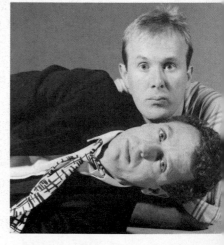

RUPERT GAVIN PRESENTS

ARTHUR SMITH & CAROLINE QUENTIN in LIVE BED SHOW

With Caroline Quentin in my first play.

Mary Grimer, aka Gary Rimmer,
my longest-standing friend.

Arthur Smith
Recycling old holiday
snaps for a better future
for our children

Looking slightly camp next to
Malcolm Bradbury in Bloomington,
Indiana University.

This was the photo which
accompanied my article about
taking Syd back to Colditz.
It was taken in Bath.

The Dusty Fleming International Hairstylists Cricket team and our traditional opponents,
England XI (Chris England's team). I shall name them all. Lounging at the front are Hu
Grant and Paul Mark Elliott. The rest are (l-to-r) Neil Mullarkey, Paul Simpkin, Bill Bai
Chris England, Gary Rimmer, Paul, Lee Simpson, Sarah Howell, Grub Smith, Me, Brot
Nick, Simon Humphreys, Andy Smart, Matthew Hardy, Jez, Dave Carpenter, Alan Davie
Andy Taylor, Keith Coughtrie, Nick Hancock, Jeff Green, Moray Hunter, Susan Englano

A funny costume guarantees you at least one laugh.

In the excellent company of Denis Healey
in the Bay of Naples.

With Corrie Corfield (passing Radio 4
announcer) and Barry Norman in
Johannesburg – all three of us childishly
amused by the name of the shop.

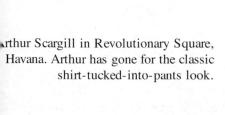

Arthur Scargill in Revolutionary Square,
Havana. Arthur has gone for the classic
shirt-tucked-into-pants look.

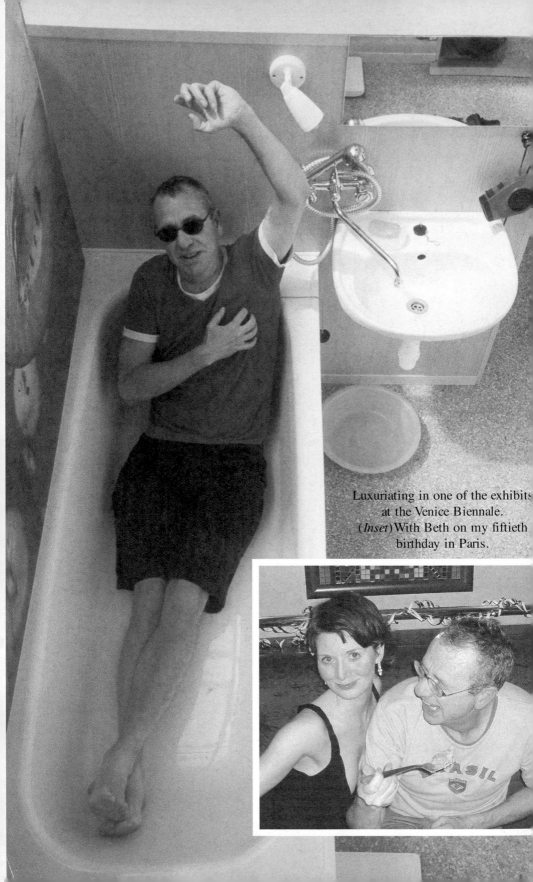

Luxuriating in one of the exhibits
at the Venice Biennale.
(*Inset*)With Beth on my fiftieth
birthday in Paris.

Damon from Blur strolled off into the neon night, trailed by the two remaining swaying fans. Three days later I bumped into a friend from Radio 4, who told me she was currently producing . . . *Desert Island Discs*. I persuaded her to send a fax to Damon, inviting him to be a guest on 2 January 2000, with a postscript: 'You will be on the week after Arthur Smith.' She thought better of this the next day and, as it happens, neither Damon nor I have been on the programme yet, so there's ten pounds still at stake.

During these frittering, dilly-dally times, I started the Arthur Cravan Society. The Society met, by invitation only, once every month or two, usually at mine and then in the Duke of Devonshire pub on Balham High Road. We started with some beers and, in my case, some performance-enhancing drugs, before a report from the treasurer (Gary) and twenty minutes of wrangling over constitutional issues. Since we could never agree on what the constitution of the society might be, nothing was ever resolved, although I believe my brother Nick still has some notes towards a 'mission statement' at home in a drawer.*

The main event, a talk by one or other of us on some aspect of Arthur Cravan, or matters related, was followed by a debate about the repercussions and quality of what we had just heard. Lindsay spoke about Jack Johnson, Mark Steel gave a lecture on Trotsky, whom Cravan had met on a boat to America – and

* Nick lived in Balham at this time and had done some stand-up comedy himself in a double act called The Natterjacks. As a solo comic, he won an episode of *Sky Search for a Star*. These days his natural talent for performance is given rein in his local amateur dramatic society. Tomorrow night I am going to see him in *Two Gentlemen of Verona* in the Pantiles in Tunbridge Wells. He is still the owner of a quiet dry wit that sneaks up on you unexpectedly.

I hope that, by now, you want to know who the hell Arthur Cravan was.

Cravan was a footnote in a book about Dada that I had read at university, in which he was identified as a 'beacon of black humour'. The nephew of Oscar Wilde, he was a 'poet-boxer' who, as an act of artistic bravado, fought the former world heavyweight boxing champion Jack Johnson in Barcelona in 1916, where he was knocked out as soon as Johnson tired of the charade. After outraging the artists of Paris with the abuse and would-be Wildean epigrams he heaped on them in his magazine *Maintenant*,* he scandalised the art buffs of New York by turning up to give a lecture too drunk to speak, but *not* too drunk to take his clothes off. He died young in mysterious circumstances, probably drowned in the Gulf of Mexico, but rumours persisted that he was still alive.

I had forgotten about Arthur Cravan until one idle afternoon in the ICA bookshop when I saw his name in the index of a book. Here I learned of his obsession with his uncle Oscar (whom he never met) and of his passionate romance with the poetess Mina Loy, who was pregnant with his child when he died. What a remarkable individual he was – a kind of Dadaist James Dean. I took to looking up his name in the back of books about Dada and surrealism. More ridiculous titbits about his life emerged, amusing me enough that I founded the Arthur Cravan Society, which was principally an excuse for a reunion of old friends, mostly veterans of Merton Road. We joined the small coterie of

---

* 'Rather than look at this painting I would choose to spend two minutes under water or go to bed with a member of the College de France.' Or, 'I have not seen this artist's work but I have got drunk with him once and beaten him up . . .'

Cravan lovers around the world and got drunk and belligerent in his honour. I even ended up corresponding with his seventy-four-year-old daughter in America.

An Evening with Gary Lineker, meanwhile, had transferred to the Vaudeville Theatre on the Strand and I began to consider my next Edinburgh show, not this time in terms of my career but as an opportunity to be experimental, recherché, ridiculous, self-indulgent. Hmm . . .

For every show I have ever done there have been several others which were strangled at birth and whose bones now lay in my bottom drawer. *Being,* for example, in which I would give an earnest lecture on the nature of consciousness. How does our understanding of the world differ from that of infants or animals? As I spoke, babies, ducks, goats, toddlers, penguins, junior-school choristers and finally a zebra would be ushered onto the stage and chaos would ensue. I, who thought I knew so much, am forced to learn the actors' hoary motto: 'Never work with children or animals.'

Or *In Vino Veritas*, a live chat show in which the host, the guests and everyone concerned is contractually obliged to be drunk. What are the chat shows that people remember? The ones where people were pissed, e.g. Oliver Reed, George Best, Tracey Emin, Oliver Reed again. Another alcoholic idea was *Arthur Smith Stands Up Pissed and Stoned*, whose content I would improvise while, as Lindsay likes to say, 'out of my box'. On the morning after my performance, an audience would be sneaked into my digs for my parallel show, *Hangover*, which would begin the moment I woke up.

One project that I actually tried to set in motion was called *Zzzzz*. which would surely have made it the last show listed in the Fringe programme. I could top and tail with 'Aaaaargh . . . it's Malcolm Hardee'. The audience arrives to soothing music and low lights, gentle people in dark clothes bring cups of cocoa, the punters relax, not on chairs, but in beds with soft duvets and goose-feather pillows. I tiptoe on and in my best soft late-night tones whisper a long-winded, hopelessly boring story. It's the only production in town to be pleased when the audience falls asleep near the beginning. Welcome to chill-out theatre for the end of the millennium. Alas, Rupert concluded from some brief research that acquiring twenty or more beds and finding a venue in which to place them was not practicable.

Poetry With Penetration, a proposal concocted over several drinks with comedy writer Jane Bussman, is a radio show which I recently pitched to the head of Radio 4 at the Christmas party, although I don't think he took me seriously – I certainly hope not. The *Radio Times* billing for *Poetry With Penetration* would run: 'Each week Arthur Smith has sex with a different well-known female while reciting her a poem from the English canon. This week Edwina Curry listens to "To My Coy Mistress" by Andrew Marvell.'

As *An Evening with Gary Lineker* was again extended, the Edinburgh Fringe brochure deadline arrived, as it does, earlier than I was ready for. What was I going to present? Any non-specific blether would do to describe the piece – more crucially for the deadline, what was it to be called? I finally plumped for a title that seemed to promise the grimmest conceivable evening of entertainment. *Arthur Smith Sings Andy Williams*. From there the only way was up.* I had no idea what the show might entail,

---

* I am reminded of Mark Twain's advice: 'Eat a live frog every morning and nothing worse will happen to you for the rest of the day.'

but perhaps I would enact the title and no more. In order to avoid a rip-off I would charge only 50p for my half-hour of bad crooning . . . but as August approached, I became fearful. I'm not a great singer and I didn't even particularly *like* Andy Williams whose voice made me think of evaporated milk. Tony Hawkes – comic, musician, tennis fanatic and soon-to-be adventurer – agreed to join me in Edinburgh to accompany me on piano and sing some of the high notes. But, like me, he grew apprehensive about deliberately creating a sure-fire loser.

Following an afternoon in Paris at an exhibition about Arthur Cravan, *'la belle Arthur'*, I approached the apex of my miniature obsession and felt compelled to discuss him in public – but where? Ah yes, of course! The show with a title but no content! Here's what to do – deliver a lecture about Arthur Cravan, punctuated, Dada style, by a series of Andy Williams's ballads. Tony was doubtful – so was I, but what the hell? We had nothing to lose except Rupert's money and he could take it from the *Lineker* profits. Apart from playing the piano, Tony would be my 'Huckleberry friend' and suffer the rudeness of my stern, pseudo-academic persona. At one point I told Tony to read out the list of his thoughts about the show and invited the audience to consider them as a description of Tony's own life.

'It appears to have no meaning. There is only one funny bit. There are long passages of incomprehensible tedium. Although it is very short, it is still far too long.'

We genuinely thought this might be the reaction of audiences to *Arthur Smith Sings Andy Williams* but since we were offering anyone who wished their 50p back, plus an additional quid, we suffered little fear. After the intensity of the previous year, when I had two plays opening, I felt a wonderful freedom about our little curio, this surreal indulgence. Tony and I egged each other on to ever sillier things. We took an interval after five minutes of the thirty-five-minute performance and nearly included the painfully long-winded saga of Tony's VAT registration. In the Andy Williams TV show that hung on the edge of my memory, Andy was interrupted once in every episode by the 'cookie bear', demanding American biscuits. I commissioned a bear suit and rang my old chum Carpenter. Dave had finally cut his hair and retired from the pub-rock circuit to become a successful businessman (though it was never clear to me what the business was) but he missed a little stage time. The bear could play electric guitar in the finale.

Entering the spirit of the event, Rupert listed the show not under Comedy but in the Latin Music section of the Fringe programme. To reduce losses we nominated one performance as 'Gala Night', for which we insisted the audience wear dinner jackets and pay fifty pounds a ticket. Two game TV execs on expenses came. This performance remains, despite Ricky Gervais, the most expensive individual gig ever mounted on the Edinburgh Fringe. For all the others the audience had the cheapest show in town.

After some warm-up from Tony offering money back, the lights went down in the auditorium and I strode on in cricket whites, a costume chosen at random.

– Knock knock.

– Who's there?

– Ike.

– Ike who?

– I claim only to live to the full the contradiction of my time, which may make irony the condition of truth.

Next I quoted my favourite line of Arnold Brown's: 'Anything you do not understand, please regard as significant.'

After three minutes of reading introductory remarks about Cravan and showing some slides I had taken in Paris, I unexpectedly broke off, and, as the lights turned blue and Tony played the opening bars, I began to croak-croon 'Moon River'. Throughout rehearsals I could hardly do this without laughing and these incongruous transitional moments were among the most enjoyable I have ever spent on stage. Our insouciance about the show seemed to be contagious and it became a small cult hit. William Cook, the *Guardian* comedy critic has, I read, named *Arthur Smith Sings Andy Williams* as the best Festival comedy show of all time. It was a fine fortnight for me and Tony; we roamed the streets of Edinburgh laughing at our adventure, making several bales of hay each while the sun shone. At nights we congregated with other comics and sundry locals in the bar at the Gilded Balloon. If conversation turned ugly you could pop into the theatre and see some stand-up, or at three a.m. dance to Ronnie Golden and the Rex.

Tony, Ronnie and I were in HUNX, a troupe of out-of-shape comedian strippers, also known at The Oven-ready Chippendales (long before *The Full Monty*). Caroline choreographed us, insofar as it was possible, while Paul Merton bought a cigar and became our manager. Paul promised that some big Hollywood agents would be in attendance at our debut performance in the Gilded Balloon and that a booking in Las Vegas was a cinch. The maiden performance of HUNX was accompanied by loud, ironic female screaming and was deemed to have gone well, but not so well that we could ever be bothered to do it again – especially since it turned out that, as a manager, Paul was all cigars and no trousers.

My tour of the Royal Mile in Edinburgh that year, a genre I now described as 'radical site-specific outdoor promenade performance art', was a riot, ending outside John Thompson's flat. John, a funny man and a mean impressionist, had that night collected his Perrier Award with Steve Coogan. He spoke from the shadows of the flat, convincing a number of my crowd that I was talking to Sean Connery. We dispersed minutes before several police vans full of coppers arrived. By now the tour began long after midnight; the most extreme starting time – four a.m. – is, surely, both the latest *and* earliest show to appear at the festival. The historical element of the event had been largely replaced by more muscular antics. I paid members of the crowd to climb onto an empty plinth, strip naked and sing 'Scotland the Brave'; offered the squaddies guarding the castle a joint to slowmarch (yes, they usually did); induced residents of the Royal Mile to open their windows and burst into song; staged kissing contests; introduced guest speakers such as Paul Merton, Hank Wangford, Mike MacShane and Big Bobbie the armpit-farter; I might hush the audience to sneak up on a drunk enjoying a solitary piss against a wall, or stop by a shop displaying mannequins in tweed suits, introducing them as The Oxford Revue; I led everyone onto the back of an empty lorry and once ended the show at the station where I got on the first train to Galashiels. Oh, we had some laughs.

A DVD of my 1990 tour turned up recently, and watching it alone in the sober light of a Monday morning I was appalled at how dangerous it now seems, how reckless I was, and how fortunate that no one was ever seriously injured or even killed. A fire breaks out, a pissed member of the Doug Anthony All Stars accepts twenty pounds to clamber up the scaffolding clinging to a building, a policeman appears in the background and then mounts the Portakabin on which Malcolm Hardee is standing in his traditional uniform of two socks. In the previous year's baccanal, I had turned up with an unruly mob of two hundred at a police lock-up round the back of the Royal Mile. It was while Nelson Mandela was in prison so I informed the throng that he was in this very jail. On cue everyone started singing, 'Free-ee Nelson Mand-e-la!' until a small old policeman appeared and barked, 'Will you please be quiet? You're keeping the poor prisoners awake.' Big laugh. Emboldened by my witty foe, I declared, 'We will go when you release Nelson Mandela,' to which the jailer responded, 'We'll be letting him out through the side door further up the road.' Everyone roared and clapped and we moved on. The funny copper, whoever he was, was a class act, a Scottish Syd, a man of style who defused a tricky moment with charm and humour.

Although I never did the daytime Royal Mile walks again after 1983, I have presented a couple of more elaborate and innocent promenade shows elsewhere in town. My eccentric take on *Swan Lake* unfolded unpredictably round the back of the Pleasance Theatre and featured a large cast of Fringe performers recruited in situ – youthful American drama students, eccentric street acts and, naturally, Ronnie Golden. We passed by the Dumbiedike council estate, where two beautiful sirens stood singing on a balcony. Their aria was interrupted by the estate gang, who leapt out to water-bomb the audience with an enthusiasm that grew incrementally with every performance. My belated apologies to that chap who got his glasses broken.

There was a small amount of ballet and a thin plot, but the biggest finish I ever created. Stopping with the audience facing Salisbury Crags, high behind me, I recited a poem of optimism and hope,* ending it with, 'and sometimes you will find that, far, far away up on a hill, there are six ballet dancers, dancing for *you*.' At this point, cued by text, the dancers placed up on the crags revealed themselves with a *pas de bourrée*. They were half a mile away and everyone, especially me, cooed in delight at such a stunt – especially when one 'dancer' (in fact a mannequin) tumbled down the steep slope. I should also like to claim this as yet another Fringe record; this must be the largest-scale joke ever seen in Edinburgh? For purposes of publicity or divertissement, I have traipsed small gatherings round other spots outside the mother ship of Edinburgh – in Montreal, Paris, Copenhagen and Nether Wallop (sic).** In Bath the tour was seen by gifted comic and street entertainer Noel Britten, who asked my permission to lead something similar on a more regular basis in the city. Now, under the name of Bizarre Bath, it has been running for over ten years.

I dallied and I dillied, I lost the van and don't know where to roam . . . my career was buoyant, my responsibilities minimal, my

---

* The author of the poem 'Sometimes' is so sick of its success that she has disowned it, so I will not give her name.

** I still laugh at some of the combinations on show at the 'Nether Wallop Festival'. Jenny Agutter was the vicar's magician's assistant, Wayne Sleep choreographing the Brownies, best of all, Stanley Unwin and Bill Wyman. For this footnote only I reintroduce *NdA* because the celebs doing a turn were Fry and Laurie, Rik Mayall, Professor A.J. Ayer, Rowan Atkinson, Brian Patten, Roger McGough and Michael Horden. I flipped coins with Mel Smith and Peter Cook for a tenner, causing me to have to hitch-hike home the next day. I nearly had a fight with Billy Connolly and he put me down with the withering remark: 'You. You're just a ten-second comedian.'

options multiple. I was due to roam some more – out of town, beyond the border to foreign lands. Pleasingly, most of these trips were paid for by the BBC, which is probably to say that *you* paid for me to swan round the world meeting interesting people. Thank you. There follows a report for your inspection.

CHAPTER 21. GONE TRAVELLING

Packing is not a skill I have ever fully understood. In the Scouts, as Patrol Leader of the Wallabies, I knew that however impressively I led my rank-and-file squad with my superior map-reading and hiking, I was sure to fall down in matters of kit inspection and tidiness. The first time I flew, aged nineteen, I waited at baggage reclaim until all the other passengers had collected their bags and gone. Finally a piece of off-white material was coughed onto the conveyor belt – a scrap of cloth that I was able to identify as a pair of my underpants. The pants were followed by the rest of my clothes strewn dismally along the carousel and, bringing up the rear, my large empty rucksack. I spent a lot of the 1990s packing badly and arriving in faraway places with nine pairs of socks but no pants, or a thin T-shirt as my only option for an interview with the French Ambassador – numerous are the fancy international restaurants and clubs in which I have dined dressed in an outfit selected from the concierge's back cupboard.

Most of my journeys were made for a Radio 4 show with a simple premise: each week I accompanied a well-known person on a trip back to a place, usually abroad, that held some significance for them. *Sentimental Journey* was the creation of Sara-Jane Hall, who had picked me as her presenter after seeing me compère the Comedy Store one night and concluding, she later told me, that I 'would not ask questions that I could predict.' She took quite a punt on booking me; I had done some comedy and still

turned out for *Loose Ends* on Radio 4 but mine was not a sufficiently well-known voice, lovely though it may be, for a prime
slot on Sunday morning and I had no track record in this kind
of programme. Indeed, until I had (recently) begun to do them
on *Loose Ends*, my only experience at interviewing had been in
The Time Out Chat Show, an episode in my career that had certainly
not marked me out as an incisive interrogator.

For *Sentimental Journey* I made sure to do my research and tried
to pitch the interviews somewhere between amicable enquiry and
serious probing – while also looking to ignite moments of humour.
I began drinking on behalf of the BBC because, as any journo
will tell you, getting drunk with your subject is liable to be helpful*
and I listened carefully to Sara-Jane, whose experienced ears were
attuned to anything that might help the feature and whose
recording equipment was always to hand. She taught me to be
alert to the physical context of an interview, to describe the
surroundings when required – nothing too fancy, you need to
give the listener some colouring-in to do. From a studio you hear
the unadorned voice, but on location the talk comes within a
mesh of sounds – footsteps, motorbikes, bird twitter, church
bells, trains rattling by in the distance, goats farting – and these
aural effluvia help form the ambience, the *texture* of a recording.

An unusual aspect of these shows was the amount of time
over which the guests were recorded. The two or three days
required for foreign trips allowed for a rapport to develop between
myself and the subject. Or not, of course. I didn't get on with
everyone: film director Ken Russell couldn't stand me while

---

* While I have been writing this chapter a man who got over-stimulated at a
newspaper interview confessed to a murder committed in his youth.

legendary foreign correspondent Robert Fisk, visiting the First World War battlefields of Northern France, as he had done as a child with his parents, seemed to me brusque, overbearing and tiring to be with. At Lords cricket ground the celebrated umpire Dickie Bird would not be diverted from the same spiel he had repeated in a dozen newspaper interviews so I asked him to resolve an umpiring dilemma that had troubled me since my cricket-obsessed summer of 1967. A batsman gets a thick edge on a ball which hits him on the chest, killing him instantly, before looping up into the hands of the wicket keeper. Is the batsman 'out' or 'retired dead'? This is, to a cricket lover, an important question since the answer would affect the dead man's final batting average. Dickie looked at me blankly and said, 'That's just stupid.'

In programme one I accompanied Denis Healey to Naples, where he had been stationed in 1944 before the Anzio landings further up the Italian coast. So taken was he by the area that after the War he returned with Edna, on their lemon-scented honeymoon. I was apprehensive about interviewing such a distinguished man but Denis was a tremendous hoot from our initial meeting at Gatwick to the moment, two and a half days later, when he dropped me off in his chauffeured motor outside my flat. Travelling with someone of elevated status (Denis did not, thank goodness, ask to be addressed as Lord Healey) is different from the dehumanising misery of ordinary air travel. We were greeted at the airport by two professionally charming people in important uniforms who whisked us past the scummy proletarians into a luxurious antechamber that outranked the executive lounge. Here our every need was attended to by batteries of attractive women before a shiny car took us direct to the plane.

On boarding, Denis drank wine and serenaded the crew with

Italian arias. They were, like everyone else we encountered on the trip, completely charmed by the old fellow (as he called himself). He peppered me with cracking stories about Churchill, Gandhi, Montgomery, Gorbachev, the Milan Opera House, Capri and his joy in discovering *vino rosso*. And *bianco*. He balanced two of my fags on each eyebrow, a trick I hope one day to emulate (I have managed one). If Sara-Jane and I left him for five minutes, by the time we returned he would invariably have acquired a curious audience of locals whom he quickly captivated – if need be by removing his false teeth. He was seventy-five, had lived through the War, been close to great events of the second half of the twentieth century, served as Defence Secretary and Chancellor, was known as 'the best Prime Minister we never had', and yet he retained a childlike appetite for life; his *brio*, his un-English *savoir vivre* was infectious and I joined him in singing, quoting Dante and living the days with Neopolitan gusto.

Programmes could be less riotous but equally affecting. I shall not forget the involuntary intake of breath that escaped John McVicar as he re-entered the cell in the Category A section of Leicester Prison that had been his home for eight years. Or, a moment to melt the heart of the most resolute sociopath, when Sara-Jane, Suggs (singer with the band Madness) and myself pitched up at the small Welsh primary school where Suggs had briefly been a pupil and were ushered straight into the school hall. A teacher struck up on the piano and forty tiny Welsh voices sang the Madness hit 'I've been driving in my car, it's not quite a *Jag-u-ar*...'

When the series was recommissioned I listened to the shows again and resolved to purge my speech of the clatter of 'you knows' and, worse, the irritating 'likes' which had infested young people's language and had begun to colonise mine. The grammar school boy within me found the slovenly speech and rising inflections of young people offensive and, in the case of a drunken young woman I fell in with one night, laughable ('The fing is, Arfur, basically, at the end of the day . . .' She paused to think. 'D'you know what I mean?') but the Marxist student of linguistics, the dustman, the trainee class-warrior that I had also been told me to *fuck off* with my pedantry and fear of split infinitives. We were all in agreement, however, that one of the pleasures of Radio 4 is the certainty that you can hear English spoken in full, fluent sentences.

It is not the done thing to say so in the Radio 4 showers, but I enjoyed the glamour of working for the BBC, especially in foreign countries where announcing we were with the esteemed corporation won us a respect I had not been afforded as a shambolic tourist. The reputation of the BBC and the trust that people have in it has been earned over seventy years and every time a politician or a media mogul calls for its dismantling I find another reason to defend it. How, given my career, could I not? The mini-adventures of *Sentimental Journey* continued and I took pleasure in refusing gigs by employing a double-whammy name-drop of person *and* place. 'No, I'm afraid I can't do that gig because I'm in Johannesburg with Barry Norman,' or, 'No, sorry, I'll be in Belarus with Miriam Margolies.' 'Alas, I'm away with Arthur Scargill to Havana.'

Scargill, who had visited Cuba several times as a delegate of the NUM, and had even contrived to meet Fidel Castro on one occasion, was an entertaining companion, reddening in the Caribbean sun – his shirt tucked neatly into his pants (see photo page fourteen). He was still impassioned about politics, vehement and plausible in his defence of his conduct during the miners' strike. As we toured the Museum of the Revolution, a remark of Arthur's was overheard and challenged by an American museum visitor; a political debate broke out between them. Later Arthur suggested that this man might have been with the CIA, possibly even keeping an eye on Arthur himself. This seemed to me preposterous until Scargill reminded me of the spooks' smear campaigns that he had had to endure. He was a stubborn man. When I picked him up on his misuse of 'literally' he would not concede – in fact, he would not concede anything. Scargill, like his nemesis Mrs Thatcher, never suffered any *doubt*. For those of us who inhabit a world of uncertainty and find moral complexity every where, this absolute manichaean self-belief can be both admirable and yet alarming.

My first encounter with Ian Hislop, you may recall from several chapters ago, occurred at early Edinburgh Festivals when we were both out on the street publicising our respective shows. He wore a lab coat, strummed on behalf of the Oxford Revue and, five years later, became the editor of *Private Eye*. Ian chose an eastern destination for his *Sentimental Journey* where he told the story of his childhood. As a boy he had attended a minor public school on the South Coast but during holidays he flew out with his sister to their parents' home in Hong Kong, where his father was responsible for building the first tunnel under the harbour. In a place that was then full of British expats*, he played with pals, went to the beach and basked in sunny weeks with his mum, dad and sister.

Ian's carefree days came to an abrupt end at the age of twelve

---

* There were still a fair few when we were there. I was told they were known as FILTH (Failed In London, Try Hong Kong. This is AFA – a failed acronym).

when he was called into his headmaster's cold English study one morning and informed that his father had died. His mother also passed away shortly afterwards so, for Ian, who had never returned until now, Hong Kong was a sentimental journey with a bitter-sweet flavour. Ian is not an outwardly emotional man but, as we climbed the hill overlooking Kowloon and he read innocent entries from his schoolboy diary, there was a momentary catch in his voice that spoke of his anguish then. I am not the first to observe that Ian's capacity for outrage and his air of the Victorian school-master may in part derive from his unusually early entry into adulthood. But what do I know? I *do* know that Ian is a useful middle-order batsman and an off-break bowler with a smooth classical action, and I'm sorry I gave him out LBW that time. It was missing leg stump, I think.

Ingrid Pitt had been a dolly-bird actress in horror films of the 1960s and 1970s, most famously *The Wicker Man*. We visited Buenos Aires, where she had lived with her racing-driver husband during the 1970s because 'Argentina was a wild frontier country ruled by a berserk military dictatorship at the time, it just suited my mood.' Ingrid was, even for an actress, something of a gusher, and I was permanently drenched in 'darlings' and 'wonderfuls', delivered in her throaty East European Zsa Zsa Gabor accent. Quite pleasant. Ingrid had led a picaresque life full of routinely extraordinary incident. As a child during the War, she had been in a concentration camp in her native Poland where, at one point, she had been ushered into a gas chamber. After searching all over Europe she finally located her father.

Moving to East Berlin, Ingrid became a member of the famous theatre company, the Berlin Ensemble, before escaping commu-nism and the *Volkspolizei* by swimming across the Rhine. In

Argentina she had evidently chummed up with the Peronistas and took us to a wealthy friend's ranch, an *estancia,* deep in the fertile green pampas. For someone who had been persecuted by the Germans, she was unconcerned that among the decorations at this sumptuous pad were fragments of Nazi memorabilia. Eva Peron, whose body Ingrid had apparently seen in the basement of a house in Madrid, was a kind of goddess to Ingrid. Such was her chutzpah that when we visited the presidential palace, the *Casa Rosada,* Ingrid managed to charm and bluster her way past the guard and onto the famous balcony from which Evita and, later, Madonna had done their stuff. It made for a dramatic final scene in the South American episode.

Exuberant and irascible, Ingrid maintained an upbeat enthusiasm for life that was commendable, given all she had been through. Ronnie Scott, whom Sara-Jane and I accompanied to New York City, was a more lugubrious prospect. We hung out on the jazz scene he had plunged into during his first visit to the city in 1947. Like Malcolm Bradbury, Ronnie had been dazzled by the American abundance and razzamatazz, but his most passionate memory was the beat of 52nd Street, where he stood in awe watching the musicians he had only heard on 78s. In the joints we visited Ronnie was greeted by jazzers of every stripe with an unforced warmth; playing his club in Frith Street, Soho must be a fine experience. He had not founded Ronnie Scott's to make money but to provide a room where he and fellow bebop aficionados could listen to the likes of Dizzy Gillespie, Count Basie, Sonny Rollins, Charlie Parker and Woody Herman. Ronnie was famous for his witty introductions to acts and we traded some lines from the compère's handbook:

RONNIE: The next act has played in front of the Duke of York . . . and a number of other well-known pubs.
ME: The next act is a member of the Royal Shakespeare Company . . . mailing list.
RONNIE: And now . . . she's a titled lady — she's the light-heavyweight champion of South London.
ME: And now an act who's been coming on in leaps and bounds . . . I said you can just *walk* on if you like . .

In *The Inferno* Dante wrote a line that has troubled me ever since I read it. 'There is no greater pain than to remember a happy time when one is in misery.'* I am unconvinced of the truth of this, or perhaps I am afraid of its implications about the end of life — is there no refuge to be had in the recollection of times past? As you fade away, can there be no consolation in the thought that you had some great adventures and loves? Despite, or perhaps — *pace* Dante — because of his colourful memories of post-war New York, Ronnie wore an air of melancholia throughout our visit. There were, I suspect, some private torments but Ronnie's despair also derived from the dental problems which meant he could no longer play the saxophone and, for all his success as an entrepreneur, when the lights went down and the audience fell silent, Ronnie Scott loved playing his saxophone above all else.

Nessun maggior dolore,
Che ricordarsi del tempo felice,
Nella Miseria
I quote the original for those who are interested but principally to endorse my own intellectual self-importance.

New York was the city to which I returned most frequently in those travelling years. Rupert got Tony and me a booking for *Arthur Smith Sings Andy Williams* at the Comic Strip on the Upper East Side in January 1994. Despite a good review in the *New York Post*, our show, in common with every other offering in town, failed to attract audiences. It was the coldest the city had ever been, *so* cold that on the local news people were officially advised *not to leave the house*. This, as you can imagine, is not the ideal local headline on the occasion of a first night. During the icy spell the murder rate in New York fell to its lowest for years and if it was too cold for homicide it was certainly too cold to watch a couple of English comics arsing about.

But Jesus, it was perishing; I had not, of course, catered for these arctic conditions and in the streets I was obliged to wear all of my clothes, all of the time. New Yorkers swaddled themselves and cloakrooms were swamped by excess demand. Every arrival in a building commenced with a lengthy divestment of garments to add to the vast piles clogging corners. Despite the shivering and the frozen toes, it was exhilarating to fight the punishing winds sweeping up Lexington Avenue and the shining ice in the streets. Even in this urban tundra the energy of the city crackled and crunched like the snow underfoot in Central Park.

Radio is the medium I find most congenial as a presenter, but on BBC 2's *Travel Show* I filed reports from Paris, Latvia, New Zealand, Antigua, Ibiza and, er, Wensleydale.* On each occasion

* Where's Wensleydale? Between Tuesleydale and Thursleydale. I am rather proud of this joke.

I was billeted in a first-class hotel, ate the best of the local cuisine and was whisked efficiently to and from a multiplicity of charming spots which, by and large, I was too knackered to enjoy. TV takes its time – or it did then. The camera was not interested in the guidebook clichés I was asked to regurgitate – it wished to record, as invitingly as possible, landscapes, buildings, market squares and sunsets. Travel shows exist principally to provide a passing fantasy for a winter night. As presenter, your job is subsidiary to the picture behind you. I became accustomed to skulking in city squares for two or three hours while the camera operator framed the shot and waited for the right light. It might have been as a result of the visible decline in my enthusiasm that I was eventually fired from the programme, but I choose to believe it was because I refused, finally, to work more than twelve hours a day.

One annoying aspect of TV holiday-show presenting is that you garner no sympathy from friends with complaints like, 'Oh God, it was tedious, I had to wait ages on this beach in the Indian Ocean.' Getting paid for writing about my travels was a better way of defraying their cost. As a freelance, you are master of your own itinerary and, if nothing particularly interesting happens, well, it doesn't matter, you can just *invent* it. A significant or amusing anecdote is, anyway, usually better imagined, or at least embroidered, than chased down. The downside of travel journalism is that, despite best intentions, you arrive home having written nothing. Then comes the task of recalling, or making up, your journey at length in prose. Homework: what I did in my summer holidays.

My initial meeting with former Labour Cabinet Minister Barbara Castle, the subject of a *Sentimental Journey* in its fourth series on

286

Radio 4, was a disaster.* Rebecca, the producer, and I had stopped off at the local museum en route to the rendezvous in Pontefract, in order to find a review of her performance in the school panto back in the 1920s. Locating it made us twenty minutes late and the small fiery lady, superbly coiffeured, was incandescent, delivering the biggest bollocking I had received since I had given a girlfriend crabs in 1978. Rebecca and I were a disgrace, the BBC was a shambles and she was seriously considering going back home to her house in the West Country without doing the interview. This diatribe reached an almost comical length and, in a rare pause from the hot blast of her invective, a mere pit stop to take on fuel for the continued onslaught, I took a chance and said, 'Barbara, you're right, my apologies are not enough. I am now going up to my hotel room to take my own life.'

For a second her eyes glared so intensely that I feared she was going to erupt into a new dimension of fury, but the explosion, when it came, was made of laughter. From then on, we enjoyed a splendid day – at her old school, in Pontefract Castle, and, for the first time in her long life, at the local racetrack, whose louche reputation had prohibited any visits when she'd been a girl. Her initial outburst demonstrated what a terrifying figure she must have been in the House of Commons: 'Dig your teeth in and don't let go' was her advice to stroppy backbenchers. Throughout the day she continued to refer to my tardiness, only partly in play, and it became an entertaining running joke in the final edited programme.

* I am aware that my list of guests so far would serve as an example of the left/liberal bias that right-wing commentators claim to detect at the BBC but I should record that a couple of subjects, including Norman Tebbit, fell through, while the Jeffrey Archer jaunt didn't happen because, I admit, I could not face chumming up with the self-aggrandising Lord of Mendacity.

Mooting guests was a good game. I regret not accompanying Twiggy to Japan, Gore Vidal to Ravello, or Julie Christie to anywhere at all. Sara-Jane felt similarly about Daniel Day Lewis. For one series it seemed there was a curse attached to *Sentimental Journey* as prospective subjects Lindsay Anderson, Anthony Burgess and Peter Cook all died, seemingly within minutes of signing the contact to come away with us. At the end of the last series, I was left with residual sentimental journeys of my own. Waiting at Heathrow for my bag, now firmly zipped if still incompetently filled, I told myself how lucky I had been and if I ever had to return to ratting or emptying bins, well, *tant pis*, it had been a gas. 'There is no greater pain than to remember . . .' Oh yes, these were dazzling days and they distracted me from the muddy boredom that was encroaching – but only for as long as it took to unpack which, given my technique, was but a handful of seconds. Perhaps my next play was written in reaction to my peripatetic regime. *Sod* was a drama whose central figure is a man buried in his back garden. The image was prophetic because, as I roistered toward forty, I began to sense a crisis closing in on me: a comedown, a falling-off . . .

CHAPTER 22. DEEP DOWN IN THE DUMPS

My fortieth birthday at home in sweet Balham. Big party, family and friends, music, dancing, presents, speeches – a warm river of goodwill flows over me. My health is good, my finances are in order, my profession is creative and glamorous and, within it, I am successful and respected. My flat, gaily decorated by Adam, the master of life-affirming campery, resounds with laughter and animated chatter.

It is one of the most miserable days of my life.

The party, co-ordinated by Gary, was supposed to be a surprise but, given my mood, I was told about it and asked if I would prefer to cancel. I gave it the go-ahead, not because I wanted to celebrate this dispiriting milestone, but because, with the advanced state of preparations, it was the easiest option. I made no attempt to disguise my depression on the night and my 'speech' was hardly more than a mumbled sentence. 'I'm sorry I'm so rubbish but thanks for coming.' I do not like to think of myself as a traditionalist but forty is the traditional age for the male midlife crisis and forty was when mine stepped out from the shadows.

It had first begun to stalk me in Edinburgh after the failure of *Sod,* the last full-length play I wrote, and the only one that was never published.* Aiming to be both poetic and comic, it

* Apart from a one-act play I wrote with John Dowie called *Walking Backwards to Brighton.* It had one outing. There may yet be more to come, who knows? I don't.

failed doubly and its audience left bored and disappointed. The words in *Sod* were all mine but the idea belonged to adman Nigel Cole (who has since directed feature films including *Calendar Girls*). Nigel asked me to flesh out this vision he had of a man buried in his own garden looking up at the sky through a tube. The actor playing Frank* lay beneath the stage and spoke his few lines into the bottom of the pipe. The perversity of a drama in which the main protagonist is never visible, where his image must be conjured up by other characters appealed to the Beckett fan in me. I read about Indian *sadhus* who buried themselves as an act of . . . an act of what? Why would anyone do such a thing? Why had Frank done it? Did he wish for immortality via the *Guinness Book of World Records*? Was it a charity stunt? Frank's wife, his son, a policeman, a reporter and the little girl next door puzzled over the question. Why had he entombed himself? His answer, boomed from the bottom of his hole, was the only line that got a laugh in the entire show: 'I need some space.'

Sod got buried and I mourned it. But it never occurred to me, until a therapist pointed it out months later, that the image of a man burying himself was a metaphor for my own malaise. Living alone, gadding around the world, loafing the London streets, unencumbered by the regular responsibilities of my age-group, I ignored my demons while I still could. Like Philip Larkin, I was 'unchilded and unwifed', but I preferred to characterise my position as 'wife-free, child-free'. Marriage, as far as I was concerned, meant performing an unpaid gig for my friends and family while making a series of promises I was not sure I could keep, to a council official who didn't know me. The company of children

---

* London's premier comedian/dentist Simon Godley.

was exhilarating in bursts but I felt no powerful biological urge to procreate nor, given the number of humans already in the world, any obligation to my species. There were plenty of children around to play with if I chose – and I was complacent in the position of 'best babysitter we have ever had' conferred on me by Freddie and James. I do not discount the possibility of providing them with another cousin but only recently have I felt any regret that it has not happened, and not much at that, so grant me no pity. My thoughts on reproduction were expressed in an extreme form in a speech by Cash in *Live Bed Show*.

CASH: Well, I don't know, having kids, it's like copping out. It's a way of fending off death. People don't have kids to keep the human race going, they do it as a long-odds bet on their own immortality. 'Yes,' they say, 'I may die but it's on the cards, but surely my child won't, well not before me anyway, so I'll never know.'

MARIA: It must be the saddest thing for your child to die before you do.

CASH: See, giving birth, it's unfair on the kid. You have a child and she, or he, becomes the most important thing in your life. It becomes more important than you. Yeah, you have to wake up in the middle of the night and wipe shit off the carpet and everything, but really the pressure's off. 'You have a go,' you tell the kid. 'You're more important than I am now. I'd die for you, really I would, but I've tried being alive and now it's your turn. I'll support you and, in the end, I'll live vicariously through you, when I'm alive and when I'm dead.' No child ever asked for that.

So, unrestrained and in denial, on free days it was back to Soho. I flitted through its alleyways in search of stimulation. Restlessness. 'Teach us to sit still,' wrote T. S. Eliot – but I preferred Thom Gunn's line: 'One is always closer, by not keeping still.' Even as a boy I had run everywhere. Why be buried in your back garden? Why keep still? There might be something amazing round the corner, up the road, in the club, along the street.

One of my West End stations of the cross would probably be the Atlantic Bar beneath the Regent Hotel near Piccadilly Circus – plush, dark red, where beautiful, dim women in shimmering dresses on barstools slurped cocktails invitingly. Or perhaps the robust atmosphere of Soho's venue for the pub intellectual, the Coach and Horses in Greek Street. The Coach was the setting for Keith Waterhouse's play *Jeffrey Bernard is Unwell* about the notorious low-life boozer and writer, a drinking show directed by Ned which, irritatingly, ended just after closing time. Once or twice I saw Jeffrey Bernard in the pub he made famous, looking as glum as a horse. On to one of the actors' clubs, where West End techies and chorus girls gathered and gaggled after work. Then Jerry's Bar, which I could never locate when sober, but never needed to. If it got very late but I was still prowling, I would seek out a subterranean unlicensed den round the back of a video shop – tap twice and ask for Omar. Sometimes, as I emerged from these places, dawn had broken. Nearly always I returned home alone.

For comedy purposes, I fabricated a diary entry of a typical degenerate day, a routine that enlarged on the truth but was still anchored in reality.

10 a.m. Wake up. Have piss. Go back to bed.

11 a.m. Wake up. Have piss, get dressed. Decide not to go swimming. Go back to bed.

1 p.m. Can't sleep. Get up.

1.29. Turn on telly.

8.03. Turn off telly.

8.17. Go to pub.

8.23–9.27. Feel fantastic. World is my oyster. Meet my old friend Geoff. Rejoice in the infinite variety of the human personality.

9.39. Geoff is a wanker. He persistently jabs his finger in my face and says, 'Mark my words.' Eventually I say: 'I *have* marked your words, Geoff, and you got three out of ten so shut the fuck up.' He punches me in the face and leaves.

10.06. Middle-aged woman on neighbouring table does not wish to go to bed with me.

10.10. Nor does her mother.

10.18. Purchase cocaine from shifty-looking dude by fag machine.

10.21–11.17. Tremendous session in toilet confirms my suspicion that I have paid fifty quid for powdered laxative.

11.18. No toilet paper. Remove socks.

11.23. Middle-aged woman's mum now up for it. Before we can get to car park her care worker drags her off.

11.30. Fall into black depression. Life has no meaning. Resolve to give up alcohol and go swimming every day.

11.35. Back home. Drink bottle of turnip schnapps purchased at Reykjavik airport three years ago.

12.30. Arrive at club in West End. Fail to gain entry. Notice

Geoff inside. He is laughing and joking with shifty man.
Get cab home.

1.17. Start work on novel.

1.18. Stop work on novel.

1.19. Ring ex-girlfriend. Put phone down after one ring.

1.20. Ring ex-girlfriend. Put phone down after two rings.

1.22. Decide to check email.

1.23. Realise I don't own a computer.

1.25. Phone rings! Answer eagerly. It is boyfriend of ex-
girlfriend. He is coming round to cut me.

1.35. Lock door. Go to bed.

5.30. Wake up. Drink seven pints of water. Remove clothes.
Go back to bed.

10 a.m. Wake up. Have piss. Go back to bed.

11 a.m. Wake up. Have piss. Get dressed. Decide not to go
swimming. Go back to bed.

Syd spoke to me about my drinking on several occasions over the
years but I ignored his warnings. I could not be called a binge drinker,
but only because the phrase had yet to be coined. Alcohol supplied
the excitement before a fine oblivion. Ah drink, it makes the shy
bold and the repressed randy; it enables you to talk to a man at a
wedding about his membership of the Roundheads Re-enactment
Society, it permits you to participate willingly in a karaoke evening
and it is your certain friend for the night, if not the morning.
Drink makes you feel the way you should *without* drink, and after
that it makes you feel like shit. My intake of alcohol was not much
more than it had always been, but then it had always been too much.

And then, oh fucking hell, here we go again, another soul-
pumelling, fucked-up love affair whose disastrous course proved

to be the cue for the crisis to step out in front of me. The 'relationship' lasted hardly more than six months but rendered me bewildered and brittle. Get out of my head, woman. But I could not get her out of my head, however much I got out of my head. I was grieving, not just for that affair, but for Sarah, for my failed play, for my disappeared youth – for the bright-eyed, clean-living schoolboy I had once been and the aimless, debauched, middle-aged man I had become.

The centre cannot hold. Something in me collapsed.

Suddenly unable to concentrate, the weather in my head turned grey and nothing could illuminate it. Finding no reason to get up, I lay in bed or on my settee for a week, enveloped in a fog of unenthusiastic self-hatred, until every hour was lasting a month. I tried reading some of the novels I'd always meant to, but the only two genres of prose I could face were sports biographies and self-help manuals, the buying of which gave me a plausible motive for leaving the house. The biographies had predictable plots, little reflection, no sex and lots of sport; the blander they were, the more I liked them. The self-help guides furnished accounts from other depressives and offered remedies that ranged from the sensible to the laughable – and, thankfully, I *could* still manage to laugh, albeit in an inward, mirthless way. 'I bought a book about addiction,' I joked later, 'and liked it so much I bought another one.' The self-help books in my library eventually became so numerous that I had to get help categorising them.

Eventually I prised myself out of bed and trudged to the doctor who put me on the fashionable new anti-depressant, Prozac, as I had hoped she would. I started therapy but abandoned it after six weeks when a new torment in my life had become the prospect of seeing the therapist. The sessions were an ordeal, a boring, self-indulgent exchange that took me nowhere. I laughed heartily at the *Simpsons* episode in which Homer goes to therapy and upon saying the line 'I realise now I hate my mom and dad' a bell goes off and he is pronounced cured. The doctors, the therapists and the self-help books – even the silly ones which proposed you wear quartz underpants and listen to whale music – were all agreed on two things: coping with depression required moderation and regular exercise. Although I had always gone running and swimming, I tried to be more sporty, to eat more healthily and to smoke less, but the only time I could find any sanctuary from my black dog was in sleep, and sleep was now a stranger to me. At five a.m. one morning I cabbed it to A and E at Saint George's Hospital to ask for a sleeping pill and when I told the doctor how awful I felt, he studied my face, 'Wasn't that you on *Have I Got News For You* last week?'

Friends, usually women, visited me or offered a bed for the night if I wished not to be alone. I confided in them and in my family. In fact I confided in *everyone*. If asked 'How are you?' I replied in dire detail, even though it might only be in the newsagents. 'So, yeah, I'm pretty low . . . and a Mars Bar, please.' Depression, I realised, and so did anyone who met me, makes you a self-obsessed, heavy-duty bore. Syd and Hazel listened sympathetically and Syd recalled a period of depression he had suffered at a similar age, when he would lock himself in the toilet at work and fret. 'Drinking's not good for you,' he said, his big generous face frowning in concern. I tried giving up drinking completely, consuming not a drop at that dismal fortieth birthday party but, sober or stoned, I was capable only of a monotone despair. During these anguished months I never contemplated suicide and, though I established that I was 'clinically depressed',

I was not liable to be chronically so, and I felt it likely I would resurface at some point. The books suggested that the centre of the storm usually lasts around three months. From further reading, I also finally learned the truth about an event from my past. Botham *had* deliberately run out Boycott in the 1978 Test against Pakistan.

As spring bloomed, time and the Prozac softened the edges of my pain. I began to participate in the world again. The writer's consolation is that he, or she, can mine the rough days as raw material; I steeled myself to present a show in Edinburgh, in which I would air some neuroses in the company of a genius and act out the ultimate, clichéd, tears-of-a-clown comedian's ambition – I would play Hamlet.

CHAPTER 23. YES, I AM PRINCE HAMLET

Hamlet is the heftiest part in English drama, but not the way I did it. My interpretation, lasting forty-five minutes, was subtitled 'the Artist formerly known as Hamlet, Prince of Danes', and focused on Hamlet as literature's first – and best – depressive. A rich area for laughs, I'm sure you'll agree. There were only ten minutes' worth of Shakespearen verse in my rendition of the play, including two soliloquies muttered into the microphone in the bleak monotone of the melancholic, the same dull contours of my own recent speech.

My misery bottomed out as I raided my small store of energy to prepare the show. Unwilling to go through with it on my own, I cast Sally Phillips, a young comedy actress and writer, as my Ophelia, giving her carte blanche in the mad scene to do whatever she wished, providing it sprang from something that genuinely impassioned her. Sally and I spent a few afternoons swimming in Tooting Lido, sharing talk of our respective regrets and her imaginary boyfriend 'Steve', who turned out to be a right bastard, thus reinforcing the opinion she had formed of men since her split with her comedian boyfriend. I mention this only because Sally was determined that her mad scene would contain a ferocious slagging-off of her ex. Having myself no bone to pick with him, I tried to discourage Sally, but the intensity of her desire won me over. My insistence that she use a pseudonym was pointless given the one she chose. No doubt the ex-boyfriend realised, along with everyone else, that *he* was the inspiration for 'Dick Kipper'.

At our one preview show in Bath – the 'world première', I suppose – several members of the audience, quite reasonably, asked for their money back and I was jolted into frantic reworkings of the script and a throbbing apprehension about its next crucial outing.

Sally required such a heavy dose of reassurance herself, however, that I had little opportunity for my doubts to solidify into a crisis of confidence before the first Edinburgh performance of *Hamlet*. Good. Sally was to make her screaming entrance from the audience, so when she left backstage to take her place among them I peeped through the door at the auditorium to see that the gathering crowd included Caroline (now a TV star on *Men Behaving Badly*), a coterie of fellow comics, several suitfuls of TV executives and agents, plus three men I knew to be critics.

An Evening with Gary Lineker had finally closed in London, *Sod* had been a failure; it was three years since my last success in Edinburgh and within the pre-show buzz I detected the scratchings of hungry vultures. No one knew anything about this *Hamlet* of mine and whatever the word of mouth about it was going to be would, given the high proportion of comedy insiders in attendance, be established on this first night. Jesus, if I went down the pan, would I ever come to Edinburgh again? Even veterans can't endure for ever. And if I died on my arse now, might the hard core of my depression return? As the house lights went down and I walked the few paces through the dark to the microphone at centre stage in the Pleasance Cabaret Bar, I was gripped by a panicky suspicion that this was going to be a defining performance for Arthur Smith. Another thought followed hard upon: 'Do I care?' It seemed that I did.

The audience fell silent. You cannot see out of a spotlight but I imagined, sitting among them, Raymond and all the scruffy boys of the bomb-site gang, gazing up expectantly at me on the dustbin-shed roof. Come on, Smiffy. Jump. Later it occurred to me that it would take a dedicated method actor to be as mentally prepared as I was to deliver Hamlet's exquisite and painful opening soliloquy, in which he contemplates the idea of suicide. Took a deep breath: 'O that this too, too sullied flesh would melt, thaw, and resolve itself into a dew . . .' This speech contains the line that most eloquently describes the internal landscape of the depressive: 'How weary, stale, flat, and unprofitable seem to me all the uses of this world.' Shakespeare – Jesus Christ, how was he possible? At the end of these poetic lines I added gravely, 'I'm going to take Prozac.' Lights, and I was away . . .

– Good evening and welcome to *Hamlet*, in which I intend to do to the play what Hamlet himself longed to do to his mother.

– I have seen every production of Shakespeare's masterpiece since the Gielgud at the Old Vic in 1946 and have witnessed the great male actors of the late twentieth century attempting the part. Laurence Olivier, Paul Schofield, Kenneth Branagh, Jonathan Pryce, Daniel Day Lewis, Fiona Shaw, Ian Charleson, Trevor McDonald and Ralph Fiennes.

– They were all shit.

– The reason they were all shit is that they are not me. Yes, they have experienced pain – so have you, no doubt – but clearly it is not as painful as *my* pain. Only *I*, with my unique insight into the human condition, can truly understand the enigma that is ... ARTHUR HAMLET, PRINCE OF DANES.

An ominous drumbeat.

– Hamlet is Shakespeare's longest play, running, in the uncut version, to an unendurable four and a half hours – unless Richard Briers is Hamlet, in which case it's about an hour and a quarter. In Elizabethan times it would have been dark before it ended. Hamlet himself ...

Breaking off from this stern lecture ...

– Oh God, what am I talking about? This is utter bollocks. I can't play Hamlet. I'm too old. I can't act. I'm rubbish at sword-fighting. What am I doing here – some clapped-out comic pissing about with Shakespeare? I can't learn all those lines. I just liked the title. Please go home. It's embarrassing. My career's over. My girlfriend's left me. I'm going to kill myself. This is crap. My life has no meaning.

Regaining composure ...

– Interestingly, Shakespeare himself never ate a potato.

The audience were rapt, but uncertain. I went to a lectern stage right and read from the works of East End gangster 'Mad' Frankie Fraser.

Until he became an author, singer and raconteur, Frankie Fraser's job was beating people up. Or stabbing them, chopping them up with an axe or – Fraser's signature dish – pulling their teeth out with a pair of pliers. Hanging and shooting also featured on his menu of torture with some light armed robbery served on the side. These activities necessitated lengthy spells in prison, during which time Frankie kept in trim by beating up prison warders and, wherever possible, the prison governor. I had, unaccountably, come to own a copy of his book, *Memoirs of a Life in Crime*, a relentless litany of violent assault showing no concession to plot, characterisation, description, reflection or grammar. As in life, there was the odd grim glimmer of humour among the beatings.

> After I finished me seven I got later for slashing Spot, Sambridge had his leg blown off in London and everyone thought it was me – and they was quite right.

The absence of remorse or subtlety in Fraser's memoir led me to propose Mad Frankie as the antithesis of the Prince of Denmark. In the time Hamlet spends dithering about, mooning introspectively, trying to will himself to revenge, Frankie would have maimed most of the cast and have been halfway through a two-year stretch. Hamlet had an overdeveloped conscience, Fraser has none. On a whim, I rang Fraser's publisher and, in an alarmingly short time, I had arranged to have lunch with the ex-con. Sally came too and we must have made a curious trio in the Italian restaurant on Upper Street in Islington. From this encounter came an exchange that produced my biggest laugh of 1995.

'Frankie, I'm doing Hamlet.'

'Don't worry, Arthur, *I'll* do him for you if you like.'

After the Mad Frankie interlude I recounted the Mrs-Logan-shorts-out-the-window story (cf. page 35) and sang a weird, nearly tuneless drinking song apparently called, 'I've Seen Your Arse in the Water', which I had heard an old duffer sing in a pub. The turtle story at the start of Stephen Hawking's *Brief History of Time* formed another fragment in my *Hamlet*, although in shorter form:

A prominent cosmologist gives a talk about the universe. At the end an old lady puts her hand up. 'This is all very well but I believe the world is resting on the back of a giant turtle.' Stifled titters. The cosmologist smiles indulgently: 'Ah, but what is the turtle resting on?'

'You're a very clever young man,' she says, 'but I'm afraid it's turtles *all the way down.*'*

Quackish accessories in the self-help section included 'relaxation' tapes. In my parody of these, the soft comforting transatlantic voice turned nasty – from benign clichés about a walk by the sea, the tone abruptly changed and the voice screamed 'He killed your dad, Hamlet, and he fucked your mother!' My visits to the therapist prompted me to deliver one of the great soliloquies as a duologue between myself and Sally:

* Hawking's story changed the word from 'tortoise' to 'turtle' halfway through – a basic error in anecdotage which made me doubt the veracity of his thesis, or it would have done if I had understood it.

THERAPIST: Why have you come to see me?

HAMLET: I have of late, but wherefore I know not, lost all my mirth, forgone all custom of exercise and indeed it goes so heavily with my disposition, that this goodly frame, the earth, seems to me a sterile promontory . . .

THERAPIST: Uh-huh.

HAMLET: . . . this most excellent canopy the air, look you, this brave o'erhanging firmament, this majestical roof fretted with golden fire, why, it appears no other thing to me than a foul and pestilent congregation of vapours.

THERAPIST: Go on.

HAMLET: What a piece of work is a man, how noble in reason, how infinite in faculties, in form and moving, how express and admirable, in action, how like an angel, in apprehension, how like a god. The beauty of the world, the paragon of animals and yet – to me – what is this quintessence of dust?

THERAPIST: What do you mean by 'quintessence of dust'?

Carpenter was in town and since I still had the bear costume there was another brief and meaningless ursine entry. Despite the show's apparently random form, I was, obliquely, monitoring my own journey through depression. Towards the end, I renounced Prozac after reading the warning on the side of the packet.

'Side effects may include: headache, nervousness, sleeplessness, muscle tremor, anxiety, nausea, diarrhoea, sweating, itching, poor sexual performance.'

– Fucking hell, I've got all that lot already. They might as well put: PROZAC is used to defeat depression: side effects include . . . depression.*

In the press release for my *Hamlet* I described my approach to the play as 'cubist' – although after the Bath debacle 'slap-dash' would have been more accurate. For the penultimate scene I had persuaded Rupert to book an opera-singing Gertrude, who boomed forth 'I've Seen Your Arse' as a full-blown aria before falling dead between the corpses of Ophelia and the bear. The bodies lay draped at my feet as I brandished my toy plastic épée and spoke my last speech, as Arthur Fortinbras, back in the spotlight, dressed now in black tights and a lacy codpiece. My device to tie these strange ends together had fallen apart in Bath in a confusion of forgotten lines, but here, in its first proper run-out in front of my peers, as I began the incantation of 'becauses', the audience was listening intently. The show had passed for me in a blur of concentration, but at last I relaxed. I knew these lines well now and my heart sang as I recited them.

Albert Camus said that in answering the question 'Why should I not commit suicide?' we answer the fundamental questions of philosophy. Knowing that Camus, more or less, committed suicide, I offer the following reasons to stay alive:

Because there's nothing good or bad but thinking makes it so.

*This joke is not strictly fair since you could do the same gag with most drugs.

Because, despite everything, Frankie Fraser is *not* the ruler of the world.

Because the unexamined life is not worth living.

Because, even though Robbie has left Take That, we still have his music.

Because, somehow, Sally *will* get over her Dick Kipper sadness.

Because somewhere, someone fancies you and I've seen your arse in the water.

Because, if you're a comedian and you want to be Hamlet, then fuck it, you *can*.

Because, boys throw your shorts out the window!

Because it's turtles all the way down.

And because in 1599 a man wrote something that can still bowl you over with its beauty.

And the rest, of course . . .

(blackout)

is silence.

A deep second of thoughtfulness, the end beat of communal appreciation that every play seeks, before the audience erupted into loud applause with a suggestion of cheering. Emerging into the sunlight at the back of the venue, I had, for the first time in months, an unfamiliar feeling of, of satisfaction, of . . . yes, of pleasure, fuck it, of *elation*. I had gone the whole show without once thinking about her, or about my stupid boring mid-life thingy. The courtyard here was empty and, like a footballer after he has scored a goal, I threw my arms in the air and looked up at the sky in triumphant satisfaction.

And then I was sprawling on the ground; I had done that thing that never happens except in old comedy films – I had actually *slipped on a banana skin*. And I laughed, like I hadn't laughed for an age.

Arthur Smith's Hamlet, thank goodness, was popular. Back again in Edinburgh – I'd spent the previous festival sulking in Cornwall – I rejoiced in my success and allowed myself to drink in the drama – and in the pubs – of the city. The stultifying greyness that had engulfed me lifted, although it was many months before I regained an equilibrium. Sally and I did *Hamlet*, as half of a 'Best of the Fest' bill, at Her Majesty's Theatre in London and played a limited season after the main show at the Duke of York's ('with new added gravedigger scene'). This was where I had appeared in *Hamalonga Yorick* all those bathfuls of beer ago. Each performance took me closer to normality. The heartbreak wore off, as it does, and I found myself *looking forward* to my trip to Southern India where I was to record a *Sentimental Journey* with the actress Stephanie Cole, "er off of *Tenko*.' Given my recent despond, it was a programme that had reverberations for me as well as for her.

Ten years earlier, after she hit fifty and her husband left her, Stephanie had gone to Tamil Nadu on a journey of 'spiritual self-discovery' in order to 'find' herself. You may detect from my inverted commas that I was sceptical about this sort of enterprise but my whole being had been shaken by my depression and if so many people before me had taken the route east in search of enlightenment, I wondered if something might be revealed to me too in India. Stephanie's crisis had been like an enlarged version of my own, and given the good humour and apparent competence in coping with life that she displayed on our journey,

307

I guess she did indeed find something there, an end to her turbulence, some peace of mind.

We visited first an extraordinary place where Stephanie had worked called Auroville, a largely self-governing community of around two thousand whose aim was to 'realise human unity in diversity', 'a New Age metropolis conceived as an alternative exercise in ecological and spiritual living.' Locals mixed with people from dozens of different countries and the place was visited daily by hundreds of tourists. At its centre stood the *matramandir*, a golden dome for meditation. The villages which radiated from here made up Auroville and – I seem to remember, but have failed to confirm – had names like 'Hope' and 'Optimism', so that instructions for navigating the town might be 'Turn left at Love, past Trust and you'll find Happiness just beyond Redemption.' There was no village called Laughter and, as ever in these environments, I felt that the humorist was an outsider. Auroville contained some pleasant people but it was not my cup of sweet milky Indian tea and, anyway, I was disqualified from a full understanding of the place since, in order to live here, 'one must be the willing servitor of the divine consciousness.'

I was even more doubtful about our next destination, an ashram in Pattaparthi. The word 'ashram' comes from the Sanskrit for 'hermitage' – although the place was teeming with pilgrims and residents. It had been created by, and for, Sai Baba, a guru with millions of followers in India and abroad who treat him as the deity he claims to be. He has performed numerous miracles, the greatest of which, in my opinion, is to persuade so many people that he is God on Earth. Thousands of people in white robes gathered in the hot sun for his daily appearances at the large outdoor auditorium in the centre of the ashram. We attended this afternoon of worship, during which the great man, who resembled Gary Glitter in a billowing orange frock, produced some sweeties from behind a child's ear, the same sort of trick I had seen performed by countless magicians on stages round Britain. In five years' time he had promised to fly across the sky on the eve of the new millennium, and I see that in 2003 he advertised an appearance on the moon. Bold stuff. I'm not sure what happened to Sai Baba's maiden flight (which, one of his followers told me, would involve Bill Clinton) but it seems only the cloudy skies prevented his disciples from clocking the avatar's lunar visit.

The word 'spiritual' was scattered throughout the literature here, as it had been in the pages of my self-help manuals, but its meaning remained elusive to me. When people announce 'I'm a very spiritual person' I assume they are liable to be thick and to have pots of snake oil stored at home. The phrase also implies that the person who is not 'spiritual' is not privy to the deep feelings of those who are. For the unbeliever like myself the escape from the quotidian, the entry into something more profound, is mediated not through an imagined deity, but through art and – I have to concede – often through art whose motivation is religious. Who could not be moved by the Sistine Chapel, or the soaring towers of Chartres cathedral?

A secularist challenge, I suppose, is to create monuments of this magnitude. Shakespeare had done it. And he had done it for me, because it was not in the brick temples of the world but in Shakespeare's phenomenal chronicle of the human heart that I had found catharsis. And may I apologise to the followers of Sai Baba, of whom I know nothing really. I do not seek to belittle the beliefs of millions of people, beliefs held more tenaciously than my own – mine hang in a humanistic fog of doubt and uncertainty, after all. There are more things in heaven and earth than are dreamt of in your philosophy, Arthur Smith.

CHAPTER 24. MY SUMMER WITH DES

Being a writer, which sometimes I am, can entail long periods of waiting followed by humiliation at the hands of some squirt in a jacket, rejection and finally bitterness. To those among you who are writers in search of a sponsor for your beloved idea, I beseech you to understand, when you read my next sentence, that it only happened like this for me once and it surely never will again. One Thursday a man at the *Independent on Sunday* asked me to write a short story for that week's paper and the day after publication another man offered me a commission to write it up as a full-length one-off drama on BBC 2. Er, yes, all right then. The success of *An Evening with Gary Lineker* had been noted.

England had been knocked out of Euro '96 as had happened in Italia '90 – on penalties in a semi-final against Germany. In the newspaper I recounted a fairy-tale love affair between an England fan and an erotic angel, a romance that unfolds to the rhythm of the tournament. When the BBC pencilled it in as a curtain-raiser to their coverage of the 1998 World Cup in France, the narrative was framed by scenes set in Paris two years after the main story and introduced an all-seeing muse in the form of the charming and raffish sports presenter Des Lynam. The lead parts of Martin and Rosie were given to Neil Morrissey, a crowd-pulling name since his performances in *Men Behaving Badly* and the less well-known Rachel Weiss whom I had come across in Bath when she turned up, tousled and beautiful, already looking like a movie star, in an old Mini (car and skirt) to see her boyfriend Ben in *Trench Kiss*. We had met again in Edinburgh where she and her friend Sasha put on strange, intense shows, one of which required them to climb up, then jump off, a stepladder, over and painfully over again, for fifty minutes.

Martin is a chain-smoking piss-artist, out of a job, broken-hearted and in denial for as long as he can manage. Eat, drink and be merry because tomorrow the football ends. Into his life, like a lubricious fairy godmother, flutters Rosie, a magical creature who seduces and bewitches Martin before disappearing at the instant that Southgate misses the crucial penalty. The Paris scenes make it clear that she left him in a condition from which he has rescued his life. Oh, and Des Lynam was God, or her dad, or something. The screenplay was punctuated by footage of Euro '96 and moments from the BBC studio coverage that were relevant, or just funny. When Martin and Rosie have their first hungry copulation, in a Portakabin down Wembley Way, Martin prevents himself from coming too soon by picturing Jimmy Hill in his England-colours bow tie. I wrote more gnomic remarks for Des Lynam to complement those he had actually delivered during the tournament, added a colourful finale to the rousing football anthem 'Three Lions on a Shirt' and they all lived happily ever after.

That I was obviously playing out my own dilemmas was not lost on the costume designer. When I saw Neil's outfit of shabby shorts, launderette-grey T-shirt and scuffed sandals, I found him just a little *too* 'care in the community' but then I looked down at what I was wearing that day . . . Some thought had gone into Rachel's wardrobe, too, but none of it was mine. Rosie was my own fantasy figure, the female equivalent of a knight in shining armour, so, like any right-thinking heterosexual man, insofar as I had considered her wardrobe at all I had envisioned a selection of outfits ranging from tarty to slutty; my costume ideas were ignored, thank God.

The eye of my depression had moved on but had left disgruntlement in its wake. During the making of *My Summer with Des* I was a cantankerous sod, grumbling ceaselessly about the casting, the costumes, the script compromises and the long Tube journey into Television Centre. Once filming started, I showed up for a token afternoon and eschewed the small part I had written for myself in favour of a trip to Barbados to watch the cricket. My previous encounters with TV had left me with a cynicism about the medium and a reluctance to believe this drama would ever really happen. Something would intervene. The pessimism was most toxic during my many hungover hours. *Hamlet* might have restored me to a fuctioning normalcy, but the problems which had presented themselves were still in place and the most damaging of these was my drinking. My negativity about my own script was, I now see, derived from a peculiar jealousy of the character I had created, who was, to all intents and purposes, me – except that the fictional me is redeemed and the me who wrote that fiction was adrift on a cloud of booze, creative uncertainty, loneliness and cheap sex.

It is a mistake, commonly made by people who are floundering in their lives, to believe that a new environment, a new city, or even a new continent will reveal a path out of their turmoil. Alas, the problems you seek to leave behind always find their way to your refuge. Emotional baggage never gets lost in transit. Unheeding of this, two months before *My Summer with Des* was broadcast, I decamped to New York for a month with the aim of starting another play, finding a better end for *Trench Kiss* and hunting sensation in the culture and flesh of Manhattan. In my rare bouts of optimism, I envisaged doing stand-up with such swift success that I would get a booking on the *David Letterman Show* and an HBO special straight after.

That's what you're meant to do, isn't it, in show business? You're supposed to win acclaim at home and then crack America? I had seen stand-ups like Lee Evans, Steve Coogan, Eddie Izzard – all acts I had introduced dozens of times (Eddie Izzard, indeed, had been my warm-up man on *Paramount City*) – become names in the States and, no doubt, much richer as a result. That would be exciting, wouldn't it? That would lift me out of my torpor, surely? But in my heart, I knew I did not possess the requisite ambition, the orthodontic work, nor, probably, the talent, to book myself a designer lounger by the pool at the Chateau Marmite among the bland unwalked, eternally sunny boulevards of LA. To attain that outstanding status I would, long before, have acquired a manager, an unbending determination and a proper professional attitude – i.e. I would have to have been someone else.

My weeks in New York were restless, wet and fruitless. I couldn't even be arsed to arrange a booking in a comedy club. As I sat in my room in the Beekman Tower Hotel, my writing pad in front of me, trying to resist an early bourbon from the minibar, I gazed down listlessly on the endless procession of angular yellow taxis streaming down First Avenue, feeling completely separated from the city I was in. Karen O, a New Yorker whom I had met while doing *Arthur Smith Sings Andy Williams* at the Comic Strip four years earlier, was my guide round town, but I made no other friends, and the fabled single female New Yorkers I had been led to believe would be suckers for a sweet-talking Englishman turned out to want men who were richer, younger, better-dressed and better-looking than I could manage.

It didn't help my romantic ambitions that the New Yorkers often failed to understand my London accent and when they did, my civil, euphemistic English – standard currency in Britain – sounded ludicrous in a city where I spotted a restaurant with the typically upfront, upbeat name 'EAT HERE NOW!' In a doughnut shop I found myself murmuring politely to the waiter, 'I don't suppose you have an apple doughnut by any chance, do you?'

He glared at me in contempt: 'This is a goddam *doughnut* shop, baby, we got fuckin' *crocodile* doughnuts!'

Intimidated by the sky scrapers and the city's indifference to me, I became a shy speck blowing round Times Square. A line that Arthur Cravan had written in a letter to his wife played persistently in my head: 'Still you have not written and I drag the sadness of fifty cities in my soul.' Unlike Arthur, I was not expecting a letter but I sure as hell would have liked to receive one. After three weeks I flew home.

My income, if not my morale, continued to rise, largely due to a spate of adverts I voice-overed. Doing adverts is frowned on if you wish to be a state-registered left-wing comic; Bill Hicks, the brilliant, uncompromising American comedian, who died tragically young and was an inspiration to dozens of young comics in Britain, took a very hard line indeed:

'You do an ad and you have sold your soul to the devil. You are off the artistic roll-call. You can never go on stage again and have an opinion without it being compromised. You will rot in hell.'

John Dowie had said something similar but I assuaged my guilt by remembering the large number of benefits I had done and all the grimy, ill-paid – or *un*paid – pub gigs that had led me to this cushy number. At least I had managed to turn down McDonald's and the Conservative Party, even if my endorsement of Tesco's was an embarrassment to my socialist friends.* Entertainment and capitalism are closely intertwined and, besides, even if Ben Elton didn't do ads Alexei Sayle did. In truth, I had been in them long before I heard Bill Hicks's words. My first, in the 1980s, for Tennent's lager, was filmed over a week in a sexy Spanish resort, involved dancing girls, helicopters, cranes and dozens of extras. At the swanky chrome hotel bar one night, I overheard the director, an authentic 1980s adman, telling the writer that his – the director's – jacket was worth more than the writer's car and his car more than the hack's house.

Auditioning to appear on screen in a telly ad comes as quite a shock the first time you do it. The lucre is so filthy and fellow actors so desperate to get their hands on it that if, say, you are auditioning for the role of a castaway, you will find ten or twelve people sitting in the waiting area wearing shredded clothes and sporting false beards. I know one actor who, in an effort to get the role of Captain Hook in a fish-finger advert, actually sawed his own leg off below the knee.** By the back end of the 1990s I was too old and ugly to appear in most ads and too unhealthy-looking for the role of bank manager. Never mind, there were still voice-overs.

* That was before they gained the reputation as an empire but coincidentally I have today been asked to do another Tesco's VO. Given what I've just written, I'd better say no.
** No, of course I don't.

Doing VOs is significantly less demanding than any other form of employment. You are picked up in a car (if you wish – I go by Tube) and taken to Soho where all sound studios are, by law, located. You sit on a plumply upholstered chaise longue for a couple of minutes while the receptionist alerts the agency bods and you can check your emails, eat some fruit or chocolate, make a phone call, read a glossy magazine or just luxuriate and watch MTV on the plasma screen. Around you, pretty young women called Annabel work quietly. A polite, camp young man brings you a caffé latte, then ushers you through to the studio where you are introduced to five or six people who may have spent long weeks pitching, writing and tweaking the short script with which you are presented. After some gentle badinage you proceed into the soundproof booth – in the grander studios it is the size of a three-bedroom bungalow – through the window of which the clients and ad agency people observe you as you earn your money. Now comes the tough endurance test that is reading out loud for a few minutes. Sometimes they make you do it twice and you have to struggle your way through an exhausting quarter of an hour. Bastards.

Job done, you make peremptory farewells and emerge smugly into the streets of Soho where people are working who will certainly earn less in the day than you just did in one twenty-fifth of it. Now is when you allow yourself to be coaxed into signing a standing order for a charity by a woman in a yellow bib – 'chuggers', I believe these preternaturally perky creatures are called. Shorn of a little guilt, you go to a shop and buy an expensive pair of trousers that you only wear once. Heading home, you spot a couple of 'voice-over artists' hanging round the coffee shops and members' clubs – roaming Soho waiting for a call.

They are probably rich but unfulfilled, the source of envy but little respect. Like investment bankers.

On the eve of the opening game of the World Cup, I watched *My Summer With Des* alone in my front room and was oddly disappointed that it was quite good. It won decent viewing figures and when it ended several friends left congratulatory answerphone messages but I took little pleasure in its minor success – it had come too easily, it had been buggered about but, worse, it said to me, 'Brian, you are not happy.'

Yet the story was to prove prescient and, it transpired, a crucial catalyst in a future more contented than this present, because three hundred miles from Balham, up on the north-east coast of England, in Sunderland, a beautiful young woman had been touched by the poetry in *My Summer With Des* . . .

CHAPTER 25. LEONARD COHEN, THE LEITH POLICE AND BILL CLINTON

'That for which we find words is already something dead in our hearts. There is always a kind of contempt in the act of speaking' – Nietzsche

1999, more commonly a price tag, had now become a year, precipitating the release into the atmosphere of tons of millennial bullshit. The big scare that computers were too stupid to change their calendars so the world was going to end did not scare *me* since I had met a woman at a gig who was off with her cult in a huge space ship on New Year's Eve and was offering me a spare ticket. As a determined rationalist, I knew it was just a date, an arbitrary number, but as the New Year approached, I was unable to stop myself indulging in some millennial taking of stock.

Me, I was bored.

It was fifteen years since I had become a professional performer, comic, warm-up man, broadcaster, bloke-on-panel-games, playwright, journalist and international male escort – longer since I had first taken my subsiding Afro to the Edinburgh Festival of sixteen chapters ago. I was, I supposed, 'established' and at the Edinburgh Fringe I was described as 'an institution'. Like the Bank of England. Or Belmarsh Prison. It was hard for me now to summon a clear memory of the motivating hatred I had felt for the brutish alarm clock, or of the soul-puncturing prospect of another day doing market research in a call centre. Similarly, the ecstatic thrill at hearing my name read out on the radio, the sexual charge of my early stand-up successes, the raggedy joy of the Revue days, felt like songs I'd once loved but whose reverberations I no longer felt.

Well off, slightly famous – the best sort of famous to be* – a kind of *Zelig* of the comedy scene, I still liked to think of myself as *marginal*, as Lindsay had instructed me in Paris when I was twenty – not a young but a middle-aged Turk, still cranking out a whiff of the rebel; Radio 4's bit of rough; a reliable maverick – never entirely in fashion, I had never, therefore, been entirely out of fashion. But here, in 1999, I noticed that all my work required me only to react to other people's endeavours: my weekly columns in the arts page of the *Guardian* were made up of whimsical musings about events and performances I had attended – and some that I hadn't. ('I never see a show before reviewing it – I find it prejudices one so.') On Radio 4 I was presenting a Saturday-morning show called *Excess Baggage* in which a procession of hardy travellers appeared before me with tales of outlandish exploits in far-off places, but the task of staying engaged with them was becoming increasingly arduous. Once you've met *one* bloke who's trekked across a thousand miles of jungle, fighting off tigers and sucking the blood of crocodiles for sustenance . . .

Offers of work glissandoed into the inbox of my new computer

* Thankfully, tabloid newspapers had not shown much interest in me, which meant I earned less than I probably could have but, equally, did not suffer the kind of scrutiny I had seen poor Caroline and Paul endure after the breakup of their marriage.

but I had no appetite for any of them. Abandoning two commissioned TV scripts, I wrote in my diary:

> For years I would have been amazed and pleased to be offered a free hand to write for TV. Now it seems a chore and I don't really need the money.

It was nearly a decade since I had done the comedy circuit in the three-gigs-a-week way that plugs you into the supportive solidarity of the jobbing stand-up – although most London comedy bills still featured at least one comic I knew. My performances were sporadic and my material creaky.

> As a stand-up and performer at live gigs I feel more and more like yesterday's man.

In demand, but creatively stalled, I found myself adopting a public tone of weary cynicism that swerved into complacency and smugness. If I died tomorrow (and this seemed more likely for me than for most), well, I'd done OK, exceeded expectations, I'd briefly illuminated one tiny crevice in the cave. A woman told me she thought I was in love with the idea of myself as a jaded romantic poet, heroically drinking myself into oblivion in defiance of the meaninglessness of life. Or something. My life among the metropolitan chattering classes was ostensibly glamorous and crowded with interesting characters, but I was bored, bored, *bored* of my tired old tunes. I had hoped that my diary, resumed after a gap of several years, might become a repository of sparkling aperçus that could generate some inspirational energy, but an early entry stated my dilemma.

It seems all I am interested in is my apparent lack of interest in anything. And I'm not that interested in that.

Bertrand Russell, I discovered, had said: 'Boredom is a vital problem for the moralist since half the sins of mankind are caused by fear of it.' I took to asking people if they got bored. The best response came from Clive Anderson: 'Not till now.'

27 April 1999. Alison said she was never bored. I said that I was always bored. Boredom, unless you are struggling for your life, is the natural state. I'm amazed when people want more hours in the day. I think there are far too many. The most brilliant moments of a life are just that – moments – but every life contains billions of moments that measure out merely the dull drudge of mundanity.

When I was depressed it felt like a kind of boredom *in extremis*, a boredom on the edge of panic. In some ways I have chosen boredom. You can assuage it or ignore it more easily by having busy jobs, children, cooking, sports, etc. I have/do none of these things. I have, without really planning it, arrived at a life with few responsibilities, enough money and free days. Free days to nurse a hangover, get up late, go for a walk, make a few calls, smoke, read, watch TV, take drugs, be bored. Think too much, get gloomy, cynical – yes, I can go and do stuff, but what's the point?

The thought was perversely liberating. The subject which did not bore me was boredom itself and the paradox of trying to be entertaining about tedium was a challenge that appealed. And that was the germ which grew into *Arthur Smith Sings Leonard Cohen*.

The year before at the Fringe I had mounted a big outdoor show on a putting green in Inverleith Park, with trumpeters, a princess, men jumping into ponds, the bear suit – filled now by Michael Dolan, Carpenter's successor – and a big finish in front of a Victorian statue, which bore the legend: '*So passes life, alas how swift.*' Ronnie played guitar and led the cast in singing this mournful motto before a firework display that did not please the Park's department. Back to battling with the Parkies. Following this, I had constructed in my mind – for no real reason – the possibility of performing a trilogy of trilogies at the Edinburgh Fringe: three alfresco shows, three shows based on classical works (I'd already done *Hamlet*) and three *Arthur Smith Sings* ... After *Andy Williams*, which name to complete the title? *Arthur Smith Sings Serge Gainsbourg? Arthur Smith Sings The Supremes? Shirley Bassey?* I toyed with these and others but, given my new interest in the boredom of being, Leonard Cohen was clearly the best candidate for part two of this third of the trilogy.

'I first came across Leonard Cohen when I was at school and my brother brought his records home from university. I always had a problem with my brother. He was a straight As man – he seemed to find life so easy, but when we listened to Leonard Cohen together I felt close to him for the first time. I never felt close to him again because two weeks later he was killed in a car crash.

'This show is dedicated to the memory of Richard Sydney William Smith.'

So ran the alarming opening lines of *Arthur Smith Sings Leonard Cohen*, enunciated gravely after I had groaned my way through half of 'Suzanne', Leonard's best-known number. The audience looked suitably appalled at the prospect of an hour of a maudlin, laugh-free eulogy to someone they had never heard of, until I added. And that's how I *would* have started this show if my brother *had* been killed in a car crash.' This was the longest I had ever gone at the start of a show without a joke (2 mins 40 seconds); when it finally arrived, there was palpable relief mixed in with the laughter.

Another concept I toyed with was silence, which people imagine to be a cousin of boredom. It had struck me that as mobiles became ubiquitous, TV and radio channels proliferated, new glossy 'celebrity' magazines shouted for attention, train announcements tripled in frequency, whirring TV cameras sprouted from lamp-posts and the internet began its job of eating the world, there was such a clamour building up that silence was making an increasingly small contribution to the world. George Steiner had talked about being in the nerve centre of a large American broadcasting company and seeing the lists of the programmes on all their twenty-four-hour-a-day channels in the forthcoming year. 'Why don't you have *nothing* on for an hour, sometime?' he asked. To a TV executive, of course, this question is so left-field as to be meaningless, but Steiner said he realised at that point just how much time, energy and talent there was invested in there *not* being silence. Silently, I jotted down some notes on silence.

– The carol 'Silent Night' – beautiful but self-denying.
– 4' 37".
Track by John Cage of recording of nothing. NB listen to it.
– Chalkie White and my last school lesson.
– We come from a long silence and we go to another. For

a Buddhist, nirvana is silent. All religions seem to revere it
– who is more holy than the hermit?
NB day of hermitage at Barney's in Norwich.

Some cursory research revealed that Leonard Cohen had spent
long periods in a monastery in California as a humble monk,
taking the name *Jikan*, which means 'the silent one'.
Silence.
My whole career, I concluded, had been a war against silence.
For a stand-up comic, silence is merely the substance from which
he sculpts his material. He chips away at the silence between
words until his timing is right; any *more* silence than that and he
is in trouble. He must stop the quiet; if his audience is silent,
he has failed. He must make his noise, however pointless. Six
months after the death of Princess Diana I had been asked to
take part in a radio chat show discussing the proposition that it
was time to stop the endless outpourings about her. 'Do you
not see the absurd paradox at the heart of your programme?' I
said to the producer. 'You're asking me to turn up to talk about
why I shouldn't be talking about *what* I'm talking about. I'll do it
for seventy-five quid.' The Leonard Cohen gig should feature a
long silence.
Me singing Leonard Cohen, a discourse about boredom and
a long silence – I seemed to have hit on a recipe for the most
tremendously boring evening of entertainment imaginable.
Excellent. My accomplices for the show were stalwart guitarist-
savant and Samuel Beckett lookalike Ronnie Golden, John
Dowie, whose wit, gloom and cynicism exceeded my own, and
Ali Duncan who bravely volunteered to stage-manage this trio

of curmudgeonly old bastards. John directed and we wrote it together, holing up in odd hotels for several days. We tried it first, as ever, in Bath* for two nights, where it went down, as tradition dictated, quite badly. We were not helped by an additional performer to whom I had given a walk-on, or rather a waddle-on part. Here is my account of the evening in *The Stage*:

> . . . another disconcerting moment concerned George, a member of my cast who got very nervous and failed to play his part. This was particularly galling because George was earning substantially more than me and Ronnie.
>
> I should explain that George is a duck. Obviously any tribute to Leonard Cohen could not proceed without a live duck ('Bird on the Wire', etc.) and I had forked out a considerable amount to ensure that the creature in question conformed to all regulations concerning poultry on stage. In short, George was a professional duck and also a member of Duck Equity.
>
> Yet, when it was time for George's entrance, George got into a flap. Literally. One could sense discomfort in him and consequently in the audience. From being a reasonable fellow who had cracked a couple of gags and crooned in a misguided but charming way, I was transformed into a heartless animal-torturer. Liz, the duck handler, fired George and, on the second night, cast a new duck called Al. Al performed with great aplomb, and the audience were

---

* I didn't know it then but it was the last time I was to play Bath.

comfortable with his presence. However, when Al appeared, he drew all the attention (despite having no material to speak of) and nobody listened to me.

George and Al may have been fired before the Fringe (and roasted in orange sauce) but they provided an excellent anecdote for the duck section of the Leonard Cohen show in Edinburgh and a PR story for when it transferred for a run in the Ambassadors Theatre in London. The fact that, at Equity minimum rates, you could hire four human actors for the price of one duck tickled news editors everywhere and the story even made its way across the Atlantic to the *New York Post*. ('Duck bill too big.')

It was a full, fat, hard-drinking festival for me in 2000, with a suitably dramatic finale which contained the words, 'I am arresting you for breach of the peace and possession of a megaphone.'

I was in an Edinburgh police station at five a.m. when a police officer spoke this sentence to me. How did this unfortunate situation come about?

The story starts in the small hours of Sunday, 27 August, m'lud. A large crowd is gathered opposite the Tron church watching a man standing on a wall talking through a megaphone. His underpants are on display and he seems somewhat the worse for wear. It is myself and I am declaring an end to my tour; what remains of my audience are drifting off home. A couple of policemen arrive on the scene. Unsurprisingly, there is some light jeering from the remaining tourists. But now there are five police cars, a van and an armoured Black Maria. A couple of revellers hustle me round a corner where I put my trousers on and return in time to see post-renaissance comedian Simon Munnery being handcuffed and bundled into one of the cars.

At the time Simon had just taken the sacred megaphone from me, which he was perfectly entitled to do, since he had taken hilarious part in the improvised promenade, having reprised the role of Heinrich, the deranged Nietzschean German tourist. Now a new part was thrust upon him – arrested man sitting in a cell feeling very pissed-off indeed. I felt guilty that it had been Simon and not me whom the police had nabbed, so I led a few stragglers, whose outrage briefly outranked their tiredness, to the police station to await his release. It was a long, strange night. At around five a.m. Rich Hall came by, fresh from collecting the Perrier Award, and joined our vigil for as long as his eyes were able to remain open. Not long after he left I was taken into a room, charged and immediately released. Later, when I was less angry, I was able to laugh at an imaginary conversation between the coppers.

PC: This Arthur Smith is obviously the Mr Big, sarge.
SARGE: Aye, we'd better arrest him.
PC: I wonder where he could be?
SARGE: Let's try the waiting room.

They seek him here, they seek him there . . .

At eight a.m. Simon was released from custody. I decided to stay up since my last Leonard Cohen show was at lunchtime and it felt like Simon and I should top the night off together. We repaired to my nearby digs and an unlikely bottle of Asti Spumanti. Sipping it, smoking, dazed at the chaos that had led us there, I grimaced at the realisation that I would have to tell Syd about this one. And then I laughed at the thought that I was forty-five years old. It was a sumptuous sunny late-summer morning. 'Goodness me,' I thought, 'if this is what I have to do to avoid being bored, it's pretty damn exhausting.'

'One must have chaos in one to give birth to a dancing star' – Nietzsche

Arthur Smith Sings Leonard Cohen took Ronnie and me on several memorable jaunts before it had its last performance in, appropriately, Montreal, Len's home town. Most notable of these was our night at the Hay Literary Festival, where I had appeared in earlier summers with the *Andy Williams* show and in a discussion about football and literature At a *Sunday Times* party there one year, drunk on free champagne, I had capered naked across the moonlit lawn in protest against Rupert Murdoch.

It would take the sort of writer who attends the festival to describe Hay-on-Wye without using the word 'nestles' (perhaps it is not coincidental that Nestlé have been sponsors of the event) but I'm going to try. Nestling in the hills of the Brecon Beacons, an interminable car-ride or a tricky train route from London, Hay-on-Wye is a tiny town which sits prettily astride the green border of England and Wales and houses a disproportionate number of second-hand bookshops. The size and panache of the annual literary festival is in sharp contrast to the modest rural community who live there the year round. At the end of every May Nobel Prize-winners jostle with sheep farmers to get a last pint in before closing time. It is not only because I should like to bag a booking there when this book is published that I declare Peter Florence, the eternally youthful sophisticate who runs the festival, to be a class act.

The 2001 Hay Festival featured the usual collection of world-famous authors, top musicians and comedy shows, but no one was talking about them after Bill Clinton was booked. Clinton was giving a talk directly before my show in the same venue and, in the weeks leading up to the day, I did not tire of boasting to my friends that my warm-up act was none other than the President of the United States. Even the locals who resented the festival could not disguise their excitement at the prospect of seeing Bill Clinton limousine-ing along Hay High Street. I arrived the day before he was due, to find that the fires of anticipation were being stoked by the appearance in town of a breed new to Hay – tall, fit men in their thirties, sharp of suit and short of hair, with earpieces and dark glasses. They blended in with the populace like a camel in the Crufts trot-round. Rumours abounded; there were snipers on the roof of the primary school; Clinton was planning on a pint in a pub before his speech; he couldn't stay in Hay because his entourage needed five interconnecting rooms – a facility unavailable in the local bed-and-breakfasts.

Come the night, not come the President. Hay residents and earnest readers lined the streets behind unfamiliar crash barriers and muttered, 'Where is he?' In true rock-star fashion he arrived an hour late meaning my show too would have to go up late. At the end of his speech, he began glad-handing everyone in the front row. The rest of the audience filed regretfully out, and I looked at my watch. From the edge of this crowd of admirers I shouted, 'Come on, Clinton – I'm on next! I've got to do a soundcheck!' This produced a nervous laugh from the syco-phants but there was a nanosecond of panic in Clinton's eyes.

One of his advisers, with whom I got drunk later, told me that at that point I was moments away from being smothered and arrested by jumpy secret servicemen.

When the Silvery One left the big tent that was our venue, I am proud and embarrassed to report that a small section of my long-suffering audience queuing in the rainy street was chanting my name. The ex-President heard this on his way to the billion-pound-a-ticket dinner at which he continued to exercise his pathological bonhomie. Although my show was delayed, the audience was understanding and laughed at my reference to the American comedian on before me. Afterwards, despite my best intentions, I allowed my friend, the radio producer, to bully me into infiltrating Clinton's glitzy supper, a feat which, given the posses of security toughs, we managed with surprising ease. And, sure enough, I found myself in conversation with the man.

'Hello, I was on after you tonight.' 'Oh, *you're* Arthur Smith. Yes, you were singing Leonard Cohen. I was your warm-up act.' Appropriately for a man whose lecture had been entitled 'Conflict Resolution' he apologised and, since I had seen the speech, I forgave him. I asked if sometimes he didn't just want to go back home after a show, have a quiet drink and stare at the wall. He didn't. Feeling a need to make him laugh, I said, 'It's all right, I've finished talking to you now. You can move on.' He did laugh and, perversely persisting in his engagement with me, he then recited the first line of Leonard's most famous number, 'Suzanne'; naturally I responded with the second line and we finished it off together. I wanted to make some sort of angry political point, but I knew I wouldn't because I'm too polite and he was too charismatic. And, anyway, none came to mind.

'Are you staying in the youth hostel?' I asked lamely. But by now Clinton had noticed my producer's recording machine; he seemed less concerned by the microphone than by her crestfallen expression as she explained that she had failed to record our epic dialogue because she had low batteries. To which he replied, 'Arthur doesn't seem like a *low batteries* kind of a guy.' He turned his attention to her. Bill and I have not spoken since – we are both pretty busy.

CHAPTER 26. SPRINTING AT A BRICK WALL

The festival hubbub of the Pleasance courtyard on an August night finds me standing, swaying, clutching a pint, fingering a fag, wearing no doubt the grimace that possesses my face when I am thinking, a rictus-grin hangover from the bent-framed, slip-down-the-nose glasses of my childhood. People I haven't noticed often imagine that I am smiling at them.

Whatever is in my mind is deleted the moment that a woman walks past me: slim, high cheekbones, short dark hair, pencil skirt; she glances at me and – did she? – she pouts. I am a man; I follow her into the bar where I see another woman who looks strikingly similar. It is, I discover, Emma, her twin sister.

'What are my chances of getting off with your sister, Emma?'

'You'd better ask her yourself.'

I see her outside: 'Who are you?'

'I am a diamond smuggler, I am a single mother. I am a computer programmer based in Vienna, I am a dangerous virgin, I live in the pagoda in Battersea Park.'

Good gracious. This is the same answer Rachel Weiss gives in *My Summer With Des*. This woman was quoting back to me words I had written four years ago.

And that is how I met Elizabeth Ann Kilcoyne, also known as Beth. Despite some keen sleuthing, it was a year before I saw her again.

*　　*　　*

In the new millennium I had yet again become a single man. (Whatever happened to the bachelor? Only Cliff Richard left.) Resigned to this status after so many defeats and false starts, in some ways I wallowed in it. Not for me the constrictions and tears of love, or the humdrummery of domestic life. Celebrating women, trying to impress them, entertain them, amaze them was a *raison d'être*; the complex rituals of seduction were like a hobby that obsessed me. Experience taught me to back away from commitment, to promise nothing beyond some shared fun – an attitude which made me the sort of cad who is demonised by agony aunts. The man who pursues women exists in a nomenclature of disapproval; *Don Juan* has a raffish air but is to be avoided, *Lothario* suggests a grubby creature, while the worst noun of all is *womaniser*, a word with no French equivalent which recalls 'liquidiser' and therefore sounds like a machine for mashing up women.

Whilst I was what is now called 'a player', I made no false declarations and often there was no sex, more a kind of tantric anticipation. I hope, and believe, that there are not too many females out there who hold a grudge. When I run into old lovers (who have often become, it seems, heads of TV departments, respected comics or award-winning journalists) there is usually a sly exchanged smile of complicity or a snatched reminiscence about some mad night in the pissed, roaring days. But, despite my pleas, my reputation as a philanderer (another pejorative word) and a heavy drinker was not without substance – and some of the time nor was I.

Girlfriends came and went and sometimes didn't come and went. One or two came and wouldn't go, until finally I had to ask them to. Living alone gave me the unfettered freedom to live

334

like a bear with furniture.* On nights when I wasn't abroad, or in Soho, I might do a tour of the pubs and bars of Balham from where, if the wind was right and I was on form, I would arrive home with a large bag of booze and an entourage of new friends. Or, after a gig, I might invite my fellow acts and their hangers-on – and, once, the whole audience – back to mine for a spontaneous party. There can be relatively few comedians from that era who did not, at some point, leave my house at four o'clock in the morning. I was as popular with the local minicab firm as I was unpopular with the night porters in Du Cane Court. The hangovers could be debilitating, but being debilitated was what I needed some evenings so that I might eat a proper meal, stay off the alcohol and watch anodyne television. I would not have conceded this then, but at times I was lonely. I took on Ralph, a young member of my cricket team, as my 'butler', to carry my bags to gigs, type up scripts, tidy up, buy stuff and run errands around town. Ralph played the part with such commitment that he would wear tails to the off-licence to which he was too frequently dispatched.

Oh yes, I drank too much: my friends knew it, my family knew it, the people I worked with knew it and so did I. The boredom of which I had sung, the romanticised ennui, was caused, as well as soothed, by alcohol. In my feeble way I tried to keep it under control – in my diary the letters ND appear once or twice a week, signalling a day spent with 'No Drink'. Frequently the ND days were devoted to recovering from the previous night's buccaneering around town or in wee-small-hours rendezvous in Balham's sumptuously seedy, secret, late, late bar. D-days might see me hanging

---

* This metaphor is stolen from American stand-up Rita Rudner.

out with the little coterie that surrounded the journalists John Diamond and Nigella Lawson, as John, suffering from throat cancer, died high on the hog. We rampaged around Nigella's kitchen table, dyed our hair blond and went to Saint Petersburg.

My determined line was that I was a *good* drunk who did not conduct himself like a dribbling dipsomaniac: I always got home at the end of the evening, cleaned my teeth and got my clothes off before getting into bed; I was not aggressive or maudlin but loud and amiable, liable to take fellow barflies on adventures, a pied piper of fun, if not for my neighbours then for whatever retinue I had acquired. If I vomited during the festivities I was merely paying homage to the Roman emperor at his dinner party. Like many decadents with a literary bent I was fond of recalling Blake's line: 'The road of excess leads to the palace of wisdom.' And Nietzsche: 'The secret of reaping the greatest fruitfulness and the greatest enjoyment from life is to *live dangerously.*' Forgetting that he died paralysed and impoverished at forty-six, I also quoted Baudelaire, hero of my Paris days: '*Il faut toujours être ivre.*' ('One must always be drunk.') It was in drink that I introduced several couples who are now married, and many others who just paired off for the night. Oh me, I was a marvellous bacchanalian figure. I was, wasn't I?

Someone at Radio 4 must have agreed that I was a respectable and entertaining boozer when they commissioned a series from Sara-Jane, *I'm Still Standing*, for which I drank local tipples in the famous establishments of six different foreign cities – bellinis in Harry's Bar in Venice, Guinness in the Grafton Hotel in Dublin, Martinis in the 21 Club in New York, daiquiris in the Floridita in Havana and, for the last trip, beer and vodka in Berlin and Helsinki. A punishing regime of all-night drinking, followed by early-morning interviews with the sober contributors left Rebecca Moore, the producer, and myself in testy conflict. After six days of bars we were fed up with each other so, having completed the last interview in the joint where Trotsky first met Lenin, Rebecca (now a sound friend) scuttled back to the hotel, leaving me to consider my solitary end-of-recording wrap party. Ordering a bottle of champagne, I sat disconsolately at the bar failing to write a poem. Looking round I noticed a table of women. Live dangerously. To one of them I sent over a glass of champagne with an anonymous lyrical note praising her beauty.

But not very dangerously. This was not the first time I had played this game; experience told me that the lady would be thrilled and intrigued when the waiter delivered her gift and on a few occasions, following my cheeky *billet-doux*, I had shared drinks with a party of female celebrants. A couple of times I had done it and left the café before the message arrived so that I might imagine the amusement of a bunch of girls I would never see again. This time I stuck around and, as the only single man/lounge lizard in the joint, I knew I would be rumbled straight away. I did not necessarily expect any reaction beyond a friendly wave but I did not anticipate what followed.

She marched over, clutching the glass. Her English was fluent.

'Did you send me this note?'

'Yes, I confess I did.'

'How dare you! You think you can interrupt my evening with my friends?'

Oh dear.

'I'm sorry, please forgive me.' She went on berating me for my sexism, all the while drinking the champagne I had bought. I continued to apologise until we had drunk the bottle between us.

'Well,' I announced, 'I'm sorry for my intrusion. I hope you have a great evening with your friends. I'm going back to my hotel.' And then – you never know – 'Do you want to come with me?' This suggestion fuelled another invective but, as she delivered it, she retrieved her coat, waved goodbye to her pals and joined me outside. She continued to act the hapless victimised woman even as she removed her underwear and joined me in bed. In the morning she demanded I give her the money for a cab and left. That afternoon, back home, I savoured the thought of my best-ever end-of-term do.

It had been a sensational encounter, the sort of night that I had spent hundreds of hours in foreign bars waiting to happen. All those times I had stumbled back alone to a hotel were worth it for this, my finest hour as a wild rover – the perfect casual fuck, unexpected, passionate and then vanished, except in the memory. Alas, the memory slowly evaporates. I know the woman was half-Finnish, half-Ethiopian and as beautiful as you might imagine that combination could be, but I do not recall her face, or voice, or anything about the sex, except the fact of our mutual satisfaction. Why did I find her combination of aggression and compliance so exciting? I don't know but it had certainly been a turn-on to be consistently encouraged at the very moment when I was about to retire from the engagement.

When the series started going out, friends fulminated at my luck. Protestations that it had been a tough assignment were shouted down. On the Radio 4 comedy *Dead Ringers* there was a joke about 'Arthur Smith spending the entire BBC budget on tequila and Mexican prostitutes.'

You, who have, perhaps, read my fourth Chapter 1, may have

been wondering when my medical crisis arrives. I, who wrote it, can tell you that it is after this next paragraph.

At the time I ignored the persistent diarrhoea and stomach pains but I was conscious that I could not carry on for much longer like this; that I was sprinting towards a brick wall. Sarah, now living in her beloved Cornwall, stayed with me on visits to London and found a note from me one morning: '6.15 a.m. – why is it so late and pointless?' It was my own fault; my medical adviser was Malcolm Hardee, whose prescription was 'Fuck it' and with whom I had a bet as to which of us would die first. In Edinburgh, August 2001, my first port of call was the magist-rates court where I was fined a hundred quid as a result of the previous year's arrest. Thence to my outdoor tour of Edinburgh film locations, paid for by Channel 4, during which a drunk pushed me off a bench and a nurse in the crowd suggested a trip to A and E. This meant, I boasted in a bar later that night, that I had been admonished by the law, and bandaged by the medics – in court *and* hospital – before I had even *got the keys* for my Edinburgh flat. If God was considering striking me down, perhaps his final motivation was my decision to lend Malcolm two thousand pounds for his new floating comedy pub.

When it came it was sudden, at just before twelve midnight on the twelfth day of the twelfth month 2001, my own private armistice. That pain, Gary, the taxi, how much do you drink? Agony. I would rather die then endure much more of this . . . Ceilings start to roll across my eyes. Then a lift and more ceiling, before I come to rest in a room bathed in a serious, almost reli-gious, hush. I am attached to more machines, administered more, but not enough, pethidine . . . a mad rodent inside me . . . is that Richard here? It is. I tell him that I've had the baby now, by which

I mean the super-pain has subsided, but it must have sounded to my older brother like raving, and probably was. This is the first night I have spent in hospital since my birth but I have started at the top. I have joined the sad congregation in the Intensive Care Unit of Saint George's Hospital, Tooting. I've arrived at Chapter 1.

Late on the morning of the thirteenth, after some hours of confused, skithery dreaming, I come round enough to see that a large semicircle of people has formed around my bed: my mother and father, both my brothers, and several of my closest friends. My father, Syd, is trying not to cry, but failing. 'This, then,' I think, 'is my deathbed scene.'

CHAPTER 27. HOSPITAL DAYS

That was not the day that I died but I began to understand how serious my situation was when I saw it written on the faces of my family and friends. The condition I had is not normally fatal unless, as in my case, the word 'necrotising' is inserted between the two words 'acute' and 'pancreatitis'. In acute necrotising pancreatitis the pancreas is so sodden and confused about its job that it begins to digest *itself*. As I lay sweating, gasping, whacked-out on painkillers, I was not aware that it was more likely that I would die than live, but I sure as hell knew this was a Big Thing. Jesus, twelve hours earlier I had been sharing a drink with Gary – but that was already another epoch. Come on, Smiffy. The medics were gearing up for the likelihood that my inflamed pancreas would lash out, causing my body's collapse. In an attempt to avoid this, various organs were given time off; tubes and wires were drilled into me and an oxygen mask was clamped onto my face. There was talk of putting me on a ventilator and, at night, a nurse sat at the end of the bed monitoring me at what looked like an enormous Hammond organ.

I had never visited an intensive care unit before, let alone been a resident in one. The atmosphere was muted, reverential even, like some strict antechamber. The lights were permanently dimmed and around me my fellow-patients lay in silence like the corpses that some of them would soon, no doubt, become. My ability to speak out loud made me the closest there was to a life and soul of the unit. A doctor told me that the NHS budget for a spell here was £1,500 per person per night which must make it, by some distance, the most expensive bed to be had in Tooting and, at the same time, the one you'd least like to find yourself in.

How I survived this attack when so many don't I cannot know; perhaps it was the exercise that I had always taken in tandem with my unhealthy pursuits, or maybe it was the sustaining waves of love that washed over me from the outside world. I was showered by bouquets of flowers, scores of cards and letters – including many from people I had not seen for years, knew only slightly or, in one case, not at all. I still have that card discreetly affixed to a wall: 'Hope you're feeling fine and dandy and back writing for *The Stage* soon, Clare Creasey. PS and no, you don't know me . . .' At the BBC Radio Light Entertainment Christmas party, at which I had been disreputable in years gone by, an announcement was made and Dave Cohen toured the room collecting messages from the guests who knew me. Delicious Dilly Keane, the plush chanteuse with whom I had dallied during the early days of the comedy circuit, wrote a glowing obituary of me in *The Stage*. I was humbled and touched by the concern that so many people showed for my well-being and looked forward to the post each morning in a way I had not done since my first lonely days in Paris twenty-five years before.

Once off the critical list, I was relocated to a 'high dependency' unit and then to a general ward – demoted to the ranks. As the pain diminished, so did the number of tubes invading me. I began to feel a little stronger and my attention turned to *getting out* of this miserable place. Like the soldiers of 1914, I longed to be home by Christmas. Many are the drugs available to ameliorate one's physical state but there can be few that are as effective as the thought that, if you make progress, you can leave hospital and *go home*. I did not yet seek long explanations of my condition or prognoses about my future. Ignorance is a good friend of optimism and, as the pain continued to lessen, my overwhelming desire was to proceed as swiftly as possible to the moment where I could step out of the hospital and breathe the sweet outdoor air of South London. I was impatient not to be an in-patient.

The doctors were unconvinced: 'You're not out of the woods yet.' Eventually my catheter was removed and I was attached to nothing except a fierce desire to escape the drab food and petty indignities of life on the ward, to put behind me those marathon nights, known to all hospital patients, when you can't sleep because you've been lying, dozing all day – except you aren't really dozing, you're just wishing the hours away and fretting that you might be due a relapse. And even if you *do* sleep a while, you are liable to be woken by groaning, retching or tumultuous snoring in the beds around you. At three a.m. one night I was alarmed to see the elegant old gentleman opposite standing fully dressed, announcing he was going into Bromley to do some shopping. The nurse on duty wearily coaxed him back into bed.

One afternoon towards the end of my second week, as I was failing to sleep, an expensive bow tie appeared at the end of my bed. Above it stood the perky bearded head of a consultant who, pulling the curtains round my little world, sat down and said, 'You will have to give up alcohol.'

'Yes, I'm going to.'

He looked at me.

'I have.'

*   *   *

343

It was a more essential liquid than alcohol that brought me a glorious moment in hospital. In intensive care I had been – in that odd, sinister phrase 'nil by mouth' – not permitted to eat or drink, sustained by a drip and an uncomfortable tube up my nose. Food held no interest for me but the drip did not prevent me developing a craving for water. Not allowed. Sorry, not yet. Finally, after I had asked a tiresome number of times, the doctors capitulated and, goodness me, when it arrived, that little paper tumbler of humble Thames tap water tasted more beautiful than any drink I had ever consumed.

Waiting out the front of the hospital was a further exhilaration like stepping out the back of the theatre after my maiden Hamlet. Syd, Hazel and I sat in my flat sharing a cup of tea and, like my father when he had arrived by my bed, I could not stop my eyes from filling with tears. Had I died I could not have complained (no dead people can) but how awful it would have been for my parents to endure that worst sadness, to bury their own child (even when the child was 47). How did Paddy Moxom's mum and dad cope? When Syd and Hazel returned to Bath I sat quietly for several hours, delighted that no one in the near future was coming to prick, prod or manhandle me, that my timetable was my own and that, fuck it, Malcolm, I could if I wished, and I did, have a fag.

For the next few weeks, as I perambulated around Balham, I experienced that shining wonder at the world described by those who have recently, and narrowly, survived death. The icy green and blue shades of Wandsworth Common, the unexpected peal of a child's laughter, the friendly, familiar face of Georgina the lady in the shop opposite, every ordinary, un-hospitalised detail was charged and vibrant. Family, friends, succour and havens were available whenever I wished but, after all that, solitude was desirable too. I needed to process the experience and adjust to a new *modus vivendi*.

Abstaining from alcohol was not difficult. White wine, which I had begun to knock back as though it were light ale, now smelled to me of pain, while beer looked like a headache in a glass. 'How have you managed it?' is a question that was frequently asked of me by people evidently worried about their own drinking habits. Just as I could not really explain why I consumed so much, so I did not really understand how I had stopped with such ease. Somewhere during those gut-burning hours at the start of my ordeal a switch had been thrown in my head and my love affair with alcohol ended. As an insurance against any future lapse, I told myself that if I had even *one* drink then *that* pain, that dreadful, ripping agony that had afflicted me before Christmas would revisit me like some brutal torturer come to administer the *coup de grâce*. Alcohol had not quite ruined my life but it had very nearly ended it and it was time to tell it to leave. In my thank-you letters I enclosed a change-of-address card: 'Brian (Arthur) Smith has moved from "Boozed Up", 2 Arseholed Street, Pissex to "No Booze", 4 The Rest of my Life, Tee-Totalshire, Soberland.' In an article in the *Guardian* I declared:

I have bid farewell to Arthur the drinker, delivered a speech, put him on the boat made of beer-mats and sent him off down the river. Now I wake every morning to a soppy mantra in my head: I'm alive. I haven't got a hangover. Fantastic.

This secular prayer did not come to mind on the mornings I woke drenched in sweat, with my stomach gurgling and gasping like the plumbing in a cheap hotel. But as those days grew rarer I began to resume my professional life. In early March, I assured Sara-Jane that I was well enough to go to the Vosges for a Radio 4 show that she had commissioned about the different regions of France. It was a project I had been looking forward to, but from the moment we touched down in France I knew I was ill again. Stomach cramps crushed my appetite, I felt enfeebled and my urine was the colour of a full-bodied Rioja.

Our visits to the former residences of Rousseau and Voltaire were an endurance test for me. I took no pleasure in the mountains or the lakes and nearly vomited during the section about the strong local cheese but I was determined to make it through the recording. I made frantic phone calls to Richard in search of medical advice. The three days became an ordeal – for Sara-Jane as much as for me. Having your presenter die on duty abroad would look bad when she next had to fill in a risk-assessment form. She is my friend; she fretted. I was now considering the possibility that I might be dead very soon – possibly even the next day. On the last night I sat in the hotel in Geneva writhing and writing,* trying to stave off the inevitable collapse until I had flown home. This clearly was the sequel to the pancreatitis I had been warned might occur and like all sequels – except *The Godfather*, of course – it was worse than the original.

I wasn't out of the woods yet. I was near their dangerous centre.

* What I wrote is lost and I now recall nothing of it.

346

The pain was not, as it turned out, as shocking as the first time round, but it lingered longer and dark prognoses hung in the sterile hospital air. If people ask me for advice on how to cope with a stay in hospital, I say: make sure that your brother is the editor of the *British Medical Journal*. Richard kept an eye on my condition, interpreting the doctors' pronouncements to me and to all who asked. Admitted just before Easter, I was returned to the care of my old friend 'nil by mouth' – attached to a drip, with dinner again coming in the form of brown sludge through the nose. The tube dropped out on the first night and, since it was a complicated business to reinsert it, and the relevant department was closed over the Easter holiday, I had the prospect of three days with no food. The next morning, when Richard realised that I had also not eaten for three days *before* being admitted, he pointed out that that would make *seven days* without food. Having no appetite, it had not occurred to me that here, in hospital, I was starving to death. Richard's instant transformation from quiet visitor into formidable and commanding professor soon had doctors, who had previously wafted by like Roman emperors, kowtowing to my brother and fetching me a cup of tea and a sandwich.

For the next month I was in and out of St George's, but mostly in. There were tests, scans, injections and painkillers (hoorah for morphine), but there was no 'intervention'. My treatment was described, embarrassingly, as 'conservative management'. Numerous friends came by to join me in my spaced-out conservative glumness and to help me bathe, a complex operation when you have to manipulate a catheter. We didn't discuss too many details of my illness – partly because no one knows what the pancreas is, or does. The noun 'pancreatitis' has a certain humorous dimension since it sounds a bit like St Pancras Station and contains the word 'tit', but it is a condition that most people have never heard of. If I'd had a more conventional drinker's malady, like cirrhosis of the liver, my visitors might still have had trouble spelling it, but at least they would have some notion of what it was.

My most frequent and, it seemed, most welcome bedside companion was Beth, whom I had eventually tracked down by shamelessly advertising for her in my *Stage* article.* There had been some vicissitudes – especially regarding the sundry other women I had been seeing when we met up – but she was becoming precious to me. Clever, beautiful, funny and unpredictable, I was never bored with her and I never have been. It was not long before I had to tell her to call me Brian rather than Arthur.

Life on the ward was not how it is portrayed in TV shows and *Carry On* films. None of the doctors resembled George Clooney and I never spied a nurse wearing a short skirt and suspenders. Hospitals are not in the least sexy and nor was I. One afternoon the staff nurse came in and announced: 'I thought all you old gentlemen would like to know that the Queen Mother has died.' Nick Revell's joke, first heard at the Comedy Store two decades earlier, came back to me and I called out a politer version: 'What a shame – I used to go out with her!' This was not the

---

* 'My search continues for Beth, the gifted Geordie writer who possibly only exists during the Edinburgh Festival. Who is the mysterious sprite? Is she benign or malignant? Should her name be prefixed by Lady Mac? I am offering a reward of a million pounds to anyone who can point me in her direction.' What followed is an entire story in itself but Beth tells it far better than I. Perhaps one day she will.

only occasion when my humour went unappreciated in hospital. During the course of a conversation with a doctor I was seeking elucidation:

– So, are you suggesting, doctor, that I might need to have a colostomy bag?

– No, not at all.

– Well . . . could I have one anyway?

He looked at me askance, wondering perhaps if he should reduce the strength of the painkillers I was taking.

Hospitals are 'total institutions', like public schools, prisons, the army or the BBC. My days were regimented and dull, until a world beyond my bed became accessible. When my condition improved sufficiently I was kitted out with a kind of coat-stand on wheels. My drip and the piss-bag of my catheter – now more *rosé* than Rioja – hung elegantly from its metal branches. As I pushed it slowly along in my hospital gown, I felt like a kind of demented pope wheeling his staff. My first journey took me to a place of fable and legend; it seems incredible now, but at the end of my ward and left past the lifts lay a small *smoking room*! Within its yellow walls I found a low table, an overflowing ashtray, harsh lighting, a stained linoleum floor and four tatty chairs of different shapes – one of them bleeding dirty yellow foam – all clearly past their sit-on-by dates. This was a place that only a hardened nicotine addict, such as myself, would willingly enter.

Two or three times a day I made my way up to the smoking room. Here, in the poisonous atmosphere of stale fags and roll-ups, slippered patients sat in their baggy gowns and saggy bodies grumbling, bewailing their treatment and smoking. Everyone present was an amateur doctor and a full-time philosopher. Most were people I would not normally encounter in my comfortable, rarefied milieu: Barry, a wizened homeless old bloke – who was in fact thirty-nine – seemed to have every disease available to man and had been in St George's for nearly five months, admitted initially to have a bullet removed from his leg. During one shared smoking session he unscrewed a tumbler to show me the phlegm he had accumulated during that day. It was bright green. Some of the stories I heard were frankly unbelievable: a very fat woman reported that if she ate just *one* piece of toast she put on three stone; an old Irishman related that his friend had got cancer from twisting his ankle. Barry told me about the doctors' conspiracy to kill all the patients and produced a bottle of vodka one day. No, thanks, Barry. The smoking room was a tiny riot in the earnest hospital world, a gathering place for the out-there in-patients, the sort who dared commit the transgressive act of smoking a fag in the house of the sick.

One night, after lights out, I got up and went to the pub round the corner from the hospital. They didn't seem to mind, in the dark little bar, when I walked in in my pyjamas pushing my catheter-coat-stand. I ordered a pint of bitter and a vodka chaser, in the old style. Chatting to a French girl, it became apparent that she was hot to trot: 'I have nowhere to stay tonight,' she whispered. 'Oh Jesus,' I thought, 'I *can't* invite her back to stay in my hospital bed . . . or can I?' My dilemma was resolved by my waking up.

The dream shocked me with its dangerous, seductive invitations and stark final question. There was a time, perhaps, when I *might* have taken a girl back to my hospital bed but if so it was long ago and it would have to have been a very peculiar girl, even by French standards. Other than in dreams, there was no

escaping to dark bars round the corner any more, not for me –
I'd drunk enough for at least one lifetime. There were further
tribulations to come – but not that one again. Done my drinking
now.

CHAPTER 28. *COME WHAT COME MAY*

In my mind, recovering from serious illness was conducted in tranquillity, huddled in a bath chair on a windswept English seaside front or, if you were in a novel or a play, in a spa in Switzerland, or a hotel on the Côte d'Azur. Convalescence was, like the word itself, long and sensuous, with walk-on roles for beautiful nurses and monocled doctors. Nowadays, no doubt, if you pay enough, you can do your convalescence, like your rehab, during your lunch hour, but after my second spell in hospital I plumped for the more traditional approach. I did not want to rush back to work and, conveniently, there wasn't much work to rush back *to*, especially since I (was) retired from *Excess Baggage*. *Sentimental Journey* had finished for the time being, and I was not doing gigs. My career seemed as battered as my pancreas.

A lot of bad TV passed before my eyes as I sat on my sofa. I took afternoon naps, read the *Guardian* assiduously, ate simply and regularly – just like Syd in Bath. For a few days after I was fired from my *Guardian* column, I switched to reading the *Independent* but I couldn't sustain my petulance as well as I once could. Sarah, the sister I didn't have, came to stay in the spare room and oversee my recovery, earning herself the nickname 'Matron'. I turned in early and read some of the novels I had missed when drunk, marvelling especially at the prose of Philip Roth whose long sentences rolled deliciously across the page. For a few months I found myself among the early risers, relishing the dawns I had previously only seen *before* going to bed.

When Matron left to resume her complicated relations with men called Neil, I emerged tentatively into the world. On weekends I noticed, as I never had before, the shrieking sirens, speeding toward some disaster that, marvellously, wasn't mine. The sirens – these days surprisingly camp – punctuated the yelping and booming of revellers in the street. I ventured out on little strolls to look in wonder at the midnight parade as it weaved and vomited its way along the boulevards of Balham. The drunks looked so *peculiar* to me now, like injured beasts – wretched creatures with no reason; if you came from a culture with no alcohol you would think that these people, scarcely able to walk or talk, needed to go straight to hospital. Yet, every Friday and Saturday, people *chose* to end their night in this condition. Why didn't they stop at the point at which they were convivial but sensible? Why hadn't I?*

Alcohol had nearly killed me and I could be angry at its power, snapping at drunks who collared me: 'I don't want to talk to you because you're pissed and boring.' I learnt that no drunk will ever concede these demonstrable facts. Given my own history, though, I tried not to linger on the moral high ground – uplands where I am never happy for long. Alcohol, after all, had provided me with some astonishing nights and was responsible for my ridiculous profession; the first dramas were rituals in praise of Dionysus, the god of wine. Stand-up comedy needs drink like opera needs ears. Is there a teetotal comedy night in the West? If it exists you can be sure the audience will be a tough crowd to please.

*Dave Cohen had a line: 'Got a terrible hangover today. I *would* have been all right, if it hadn't been for that last . . . four pints.'

Six months after I left hospital I put my thoughts on drink and sobriety into *Arthur Smith's Last Hangover*, a half-hour show with Caroline Quentin on Radio 4. Just as I had returned to *Hamlet* so I gnawed again at Dante, when I did a live version of 'my booze hell' in *Dante's Inferno* in Edinburgh and beyond. It was a relief to find that I could perform without feeling the need for a beer beforehand and several after, and it was not really a surprise that I was sharper as a result. Syd and Hazel came up to watch the recording of the hangover show and all we Smiths and off-spring went for a lunch at the restaurant in Battersea where Freddie was making his name as a chef. We toasted (elderflower pressé for me) Syd's eightieth birthday, Nick and Sue's new baby, Jack, Richard's CBE and sundry other family achievements – but mainly we rejoiced that we were all together and alive.

It was a reconfigured world without drink. I sought out my oldest and closest friends and let go some more recent ones, especially those that were bonded to me in booze. Going out now happened less often than staying in – and especially staying in with Beth – while pubs and bars became places that could not hold me long. When I did go out, it was to walk the amiable contours of the South Downs with Adam, Simon, Lindsay and our old gang of roué ramblers, or alongside Richard and his old Edinburgh chums with whom I did the Coast-to-Coast walk across the top of England, from Saint Bees to Robin Hood Bay. A youthful love of running has become a late middle-age passion for walking. My secular bible is a walking guide. It is for me a quintessential pleasure to descend from the hills after a day's hike with the prospect of a warm bath, a decent supper and a welcoming bed.

During a gentle stay in my first teetotal Edinburgh, where Beth had written a show with her sister Emma, I spent afternoons ambling around venues and some of what now felt like 'my old haunts'. Everywhere I found a touching, if tiring, solicitousness and concern. 'You've lost weight!' they all exclaimed. I learned to perform a resumé of my condition that headed off further enquiries at the pass. In truth, my robust rambling energy had diminished of late and my health was uncertain, with new worries like an infernal itchiness and a renewed loss of interest in food – but this was too much information for all but my intimates. The scans and tests continued and I began to struggle through the days until my weight loss, thirstiness and blurred vision took me back to hospital, where I heard the sentence:

'You have diabetes and you will have to inject yourself every day for the rest of your life.'

Oh Gawd, now this.

Oddly, it was a relief to hear the diagnosis, because at least now I had an explanation for my symptoms that did not indicate my imminent death, and a way of reversing them. Of all the popular chronic life-threatening syndromes, diabetes ranks among the least nasty since, if you can get your blood-sugar levels close to normal, its more sinister complications can be avoided, or at least delayed. The disease has been recognised since Roman times but diabetes type-1 only stopped being a death sentence in the 1920s, thanks to Sir Frederick Banting and his team. I doff my cap to you, Sir Fred. Beth supplied a Tupperware box in which to keep my syringes, needles, and blood-testing kit and I was soon seconded into the ranks of 'celebrity diabetics', supreme leaders: Olympic rower Steve Redgrave and old-time comic Jimmy Tarbuck. If ever you find yourself in a doctor's waiting room with nothing to read, have a look at a copy of *Balance* – the quarterly magazine of Diabetes UK. Located on the inside back page is 'Arthur's armchair view'. I wanted my byline to be 'Arthur Smith on the lighter side of diabetes', but you will see that the editor preferred 'Arthur Smith brings his off-the-wall perspective to all things diabetic'. I would not advise you to contract diabetes but I do offer three upsides to the condition:

1. Suddenly discovering that you have left your insulin, or pills, at home is the perfect excuse for leaving any function, at any point.
2. When your blood sugar levels are lower than is possible for non-diabetic mortals, food becomes so profoundly desirable that I have finally understood Syd's ravenous wartime preference for a cheese roll over a naked Gina Lollobrigida.
3. It is enjoyably rock 'n roll to shoot up in the toilets of restaurants before you eat.

On diagnosis I spent another five days in hospital before passing once again through the unfortunately named 'Patients' Discharge Lounge'. Once sustained by insulin, my recovery was rapid: I put on some pounds and felt more vital than I had for years. Beth and I had alcohol- and drug-free low-sugar outings to visit her wonderfully hospitable parents, Brenda and John, in Sunderland – our visits often coinciding with those of Emma and her ebullient partner Colin. We went to Venice, where Richard was writing a book; to Tonbridge to play football and 'go on patrol' with my brother Nick and Sue's lads, to Barcelona, to see our friend Rachel in a wild and entertaining *Hamlet*, to Swindon to take part in the literary festival, to Bath, of course, and then, unsated by each other's company, Beth and I returned to what became *our* home in Balham.

My years of living alone were a blast for a long while, but now it felt, it feels, warmer, sexier and safer sharing with Beth. I found an intimacy that had eluded me for too long. The delights, rather than the torments, of domesticity are rarely portrayed in fiction, but they are subtle, various and the most common pleasures in the world: eating together, discussing your day, apple crumble (made with sweetener), TV, reading in bed, the little silly games couples play. As my life became calmer, quieter and more ordered, so my boredom at the world, my impotence within it, my anger, my depression, my fatalism, my self-destructiveness, these anxieties which might ripple through my cheery stability, which had cursed me, inspired me, and, in part, defined me, began to fade and become less urgent.

At the end of my forties, through advancing age, long weeks lying in hospital and alcoholic abstinence, I had grown calmer. I even overheard a friend reporting that I had become 'nicer', which was ironic now that I was becoming a celebrated grouch. Cantankerousness was still well within my range, as it had been as a twelve-year-old diarist and a thirty-five-year-old dramatist.* I worked up some bile for a TV interview in which I was invited to rail indiscriminately against anything I fancied. Outside a pub near Oxford Circus one afternoon, I started whingeing gently but, as I went on, I gathered momentum and a surge of

---

* This is a speech from *Live Bed Show*: 'This country is shit. The food is shit, the government is shit, the weather is shit, the transport system is shit, education is shit, the health service is shit, the music is shit, my job in TV is shit, life is shit, death is shit, I am shit.'

indignation began to swell forth from deep in my bowels; I complained zealously about the distressing business of being alive and middle-aged at the start of the third millennium. I blazed away for an hour, raging about call centres, mobile phones, computers, cars, trains, young people, etc., etc., until I nearly orgasmed on my own negativity. After a cigarette, I immediately forgot about my diatribe, assuming that the programme, whatever it was called, would be transmitted in some obscure slot on a new BBC channel that no one yet watched. But no, it turned out to be a whole *series* on prime-time BBC 2, voice-overed masterfully by Geoffrey Palmer, arriving to fanfares, and soon meeting with approval from audiences, reviewers and BBC management alike. I was, officially, a Grumpy Old Man – life is a dismal conspiracy of meddling bastards. I'm mad as hell and I'm not going to take it any more.

In the previous twenty years I had been on hundreds of TV shows, but none had the impact of *Grumpy Old Men* which raised me several notches in the public consciousness and means that I am still approached by men proclaiming their own disaffection with the modern world. 'I'm a grumpy old man too!' 'In that case,' I say, 'you'll understand when I invite you to *piss off and leave me alone*!' No, I don't. It would be churlish, rather than grumpy, to disdain the blokes (and women) whose enthusiasm for the shows means I can now raise decent audiences for my one-man show in provincial theatres and, I expect, it increased, or even created, the advance that I received for this book.

I note, as have several fellow TV grumpies, how ridiculous it is that a couple of hours of casual, unconsidered interviews can turn out to be the thing for which you are best known, but one should be aware how arbitrary the world can be. Consider King

Alfred, who beat off the Vikings, encouraged education and reformed the judiciary. King Alfred *the Great* is remembered now for burning cakes. *Grumpy Old Men*, the creation of TV maestro Stuart Prebble, touched a nerve among viewers and flourished in numerous series, soon branching out into *Grumpy Old Women*, *Grumpy Old Holidays*, two books and even a *Grumpy Old Man* cuddly bear, modelled after the cadaverous Will Self, who was for me the star of the show. (I have always felt that Self might have made a phenomenal stand-up comic.) My appearances on the shows were good for 'my profile' and I was thankful for this, but I declined to join in a live version with Rory McGrath and Rick Wakeman, and meetings about a *Grumpy Old Big Brother* foundered, I presume, because no self-respecting GOM would volunteer for such a torture. In the end I was able to say I was just *too grumpy* to do *Grumpy Old Men*.

'Come what come may, time and the hour runs through the roughest day'

These words, spoken by Macbeth, are an antidote to the wallowing negativity which is the boring end of full-on grumpiness. The quote is chiselled into a rock in the little ornamental garden in the grounds of Saint George's Hospital. Except that it is not quite right. Somewhere, between conception and chipping, the second 'come' has been lost, which doesn't change the meaning but disturbs the rhythm of the line. When I had become 'independent' in hospital, and the smoking room was too asphyxiating even for an Olympian snout-hound like myself, I would sit in this garden – situated unpeacefully on the roundabout outside the main hospital entrance – and conjecture about the loss of the second 'come'. At what point in the chain of command was it eliminated? Did an accountant choose to dispense with it as an unnecessary extra expense? ('We charge by the letter, sir.') There was a lot of time to fill in those fraught hospital stays. Shakespeare's observation, even abbreviated, proved a comforting thought that had kept me clear of panic and self-pity on the long bad mornings in hospital when I awaited test results or geared up for the next scan. 'Days are what we live in,' wrote Larkin. One way or another, this day will end and another will succeed it, and eventually you will not be in the day but it will continue anyway and give way to the next day . . .

Beth had first met my parents at my bedside in Saint George's. Syd's opening line was magnificent, 'Are you from up north? They're all thick up there, aren't they?' Hazel and I were appalled, but Beth laughed out loud as Syd flashed his mischievous grin. He knew, of course, that she had a classy degree and a sense of humour; he would never have been so provocative with a slower, less playful woman. Beth accompanied me on a late-summer weekend to Bath, when Syd proudly showed off his towering sunflowers, resplendent in their dazzling maturity. Stooped and frail now, he walked into Bath less often but still derived a child-like pleasure from rooting out bargains in the charity shops; Syd believed that anything you might get in your posh designer shops was available in the Cancer Research shop at a fiftieth of the price and, in essence, I agree with him. He never forgot the hunger of his war years ('I ate a raw onion and then twelve bananas when the troop ship docked in Cape Town.') He hated throwing food away and if an item was approaching its sell-by date, however much he disliked it, he would be sure to gulp it down. Frugality, to Syd and to many of his generation, was a necessity that evolved into a pleasure. Every night he relished the cheapest ice cream on sale in Sainsbury's.

But by Christmas 2003 he was in low spirits, tired and concerned about his weight loss, just as I had fretted about mine before the diabetes diagnosis. Hazel was breezy and cheerful, but later told me that she knew that Syd was ill then and had already begun to face up to his death. He had spent a lot of his time ferrying people around in his car but that Christmas, the last of his life, his ruddy face and unique hooter did not appear at Bath station. Since being bashed into by a boy joy-rider, his confidence as a driver had diminished until he was pulled over by a copper and ticked off for driving too slowly. He stowed his car in the garage for the last time.

One evening, early in the New Year, Hazel rang to say that Syd had coughed up blood and had been admitted to the Royal Free Hospital in Bath.

The next day, Beth and I joined my mother at the hospital in the old high-ceilinged ward in which my father lay in his blue pyjamas. Opposite, a tall thin window threw a beam of sunlight onto him through the hospital gloom so that he looked as though he were the central figure of a Rembrandt painting. On the wall a needlessly large clock stared down at him, a harbinger. Shortly after our arrival, a nurse and two doctors placed a screen around Syd and spoke to him while we went outside. On our return we learned that an X-ray had shown a shadow on his lung. Hazel left with Beth to weep her way home while I sat with my father in the quiet of the afternoon.

'She's been a wonderful wife,' he finally said, 'You'll look after her, won't you?

'Of course.'

After further tests and consultations he was diagnosed with renal cancer, which had spread to his lungs. The next time I visited him in hospital, he told me, 'I just want to go home, have a fag and let it all go.' When he did return home, he fell into a sleepless despair; one morning, stumbling my way to a five a.m. piss, I found him sitting in his battered old adjustable armchair, staring out the window.

'I'm desperate,' he whispered to me. From this moment, I was in the almost unendurable position of wishing that my father would die as quickly as possible. Mercifully, he had no pain as sleep, at last, began to envelop him and he seemed to enter a kind of limbo, a detachment from the world and from the people in it. His brother drove up to Bath from Dartmouth and they spoke for a few minutes until my father indicated that he needed to sleep. Arthur stood up and Syd too rose unsteadily to his feet.

– Goodbye, Arthur.

– Goodbye, Syd.

Men of their age and generation do not hug each other. They shook hands. Arthur turned and left. The two brothers knew they would never see each other again. Witnessing this scene gave me something else to sob about in Kingsmead Park up the road from my parents' home. I spent a lot of time in Kingsmead Park that winter.

A few afternoons later, as I sat at his bedside, Syd woke up and said, 'I've been thinking about reweyan.'

'About what?' His feebleness and exhaustion and the absence of his dentures made it difficult to understand him.

'Rewiyin . . . re . . . oh . . . never mind.' He went back to sleep.

Downstairs, a few minutes later, I realised he had said, 'I've been thinking about *religion*.'

What did he mean by that? He had never been religious nor had, as far as I knew, any belief in an afterlife, but I returned to his bedroom where he was still asleep and found myself making a little speech: 'I don't know about God, or what happens to us in the end, but maybe, Syd, maybe it's summer and you're cycling off to Devon with Maurice again and you'll be young and strong and some time Hazel will join you, and we'll all come by in the end . . .'

'Religion,' wrote Phillip Larkin, 'that vast moth-eaten musical brocade created to pretend we never die.' Yes, but *in extremis* fantasy, denial and pretence can be the narratives you need, just as you need to suspend your disbelief for a play or a film. Sydney Smith dreamed on . . . and then . . . did I? Did I detect a tiny smile on his sleeping face? I choose to believe so.

Much later that night Beth and I were woken by Hazel.

'I think there's something wrong.'

His hand was closed tight but he looked comfortable, peaceful and impossibly still. No pulse, no breathing. I unclenched his fist, kissed his still-warm brow and stood in the dead silence of this room. My darling dad, gone now. Hazel told me that his eyes had flickered open before she woke me, which provides me with the consoling thought that the last image he saw in life was the face of his beloved wife. Downstairs I embraced my mother and Beth before I made the phone calls.

My heart broke for Hazel as she bravely entered widowhood. She had never lived by herself and, given that she had shared a bed with her sister until the day of her wedding, and had rarely spent nights apart from Syd, she had only seldom *slept* alone. She busied herself as she had always done. Among Syd's papers she discovered several *billets-doux* he had written her during his dying days, as well as his police record in which he was described as an 'exemplary' copper. To me he was an exemplary dad too. When people who knew him have said to me that I am like Syd, then, although I know I lack some of his best qualities, I am pleased and flattered. Big nose, a bit of a laugh, a love of tea, I am, as best I can be, my father's son.

'Come what come may, time and the hour runs through the roughest day'

There had been a lot of rough days for me in the previous fifteen months – the pancreatitis, intensive care, the return to hospital, diabetes and now the death of my father. In Edinburgh that summer I took part in the least interesting show on the Fringe, a changing bill of old comics doing a gig that you could have seen in 1986 – but you probably wouldn't have bothered to go then, so there was no reason to do so now. After my short sentence, I returned to London and considered the forthcoming months. My birthday, I noted, fell on a Saturday. I was born on a Saturday too.* I recalled the celebrations I had organised around my birthdays as a student – in the launderette, up the Eiffel Tower, the big lie-in on campus – and my thirtieth with Richard outside the Tivoli Gardens in Copenhagen.

But the last attempt at a big birthday jolly, when I hit forty, had been such a grim evening for me, stuck as I was in the cold

---

* 'Saturday's child works hard for a living.' Hmmm.

deep-winter of my depression, that I had never since made any birthday plans. The year before I had been too worried about the symptoms of my as yet undiagnosed diabetes to register 27 November. Now, however, I felt that I had, after all these trials, found my way if not out of the woods, then closer to their edge, at least for a while. Like Gloria Gaynor, I had survived. Go on, have a party, Mister Smith and MAKE IT A BIG ONE. You're not dead yet – and this is a significant day in everyone's life. Beth and I drew up some lists and made the arrangements to return to the city that had furnished a crucial experience in my life, the crucible where I had turned twenty-one and lived out my poetic fantasies. I sent out the invitations for my fiftieth birthday party – to be held in Paris.

CHAPTER 29. TWO DEATHS, A PROPOSAL AND A BIRTHDAY

If, in some future time, the River Thames is drained, there will be a rich and fascinating haul of items revealed on the river bed. Among the Roman coins, medieval weapons, unexploded bombs, bones and punctured yogurt pots, there will be a large pair of thick black-rimmed glasses. Whoever finds them will not know that they once clung to the ears of Malcolm Hardee, who toppled into the river early one drunken, frozen morning and was pulled out thirty-six hours later by police frogmen still clutching his final bottle of beer. It seemed that our bet as to which of us would die first had been won. No doubt the cheque is in the post.

When the news broke that Malcolm had drowned, comedians and citizens of Greenwich immediately began to congregate at the last venue he ran, the aptly named Wibbley Wobbley, the pub/boat moored at Surrey Quays in which I had invested before, astonishingly, Malcolm paid me back (no profit, obviously). People stood around in shocked clumps although, given his reckless nature and his known penchant for messing about on the river, no one could really be surprised at what had happened. Most of those present had spent an afternoon or two drinking heavily with him on his boat as it spluttered and chuntered uncertainly downriver to the Thames Barrier at

Woolwich (useless, according to Malcolm). I had put in my time on board this vessel, which seemed to me hardly more than a motorised bath tub although, following the benefit he had conned me into, it had been upgraded to motorised kitchen. Malcolm's longest affair was with the river and his extinction in its murky green arms was tragic but entirely appropriate. His father had been a Thames lighterman who, Malcolm had boasted proudly, had towed the *Cutty Sark* into dry dock. Malcolm lived on a boat across from the Wibbley Wobbley and had fallen in while rowing between the two – standing up as he rowed because that was what men of the river did. It was not the first time he had tumbled into the water, though it was, of course and alas, the last.

Mister Hardee, as he liked to call himself, had been at the Comedy Store at the beginning and in the Tunnel Palladium he founded, and personified, a club that was the most distinctive of all the early London comedy venues. He booked, managed and slept with acts that others wouldn't, was a stalwart of the Glastonbury and Edinburgh festivals as well as a consistent disappointment to the police, the Inland Revenue and the big-money agencies who had moved into comedy. He represented the anarchic, ramshackle early days of the circuit when there was little cash but a wealth of vitality, creativity and laughable experimentation. Erica Jong remarked recently that the backlash against feminism has lasted far longer than feminism itself and I feel the same about alternative comedy, whatever it was. The scene now is slicker, more professional and less politicised – you can see material which would have been deemed reprehensible in the mid-1980s but is accepted because it comes in a sharp suit and hides behind a half-baked notion of irony.* This has ushered in a revival of misogyny masquerading as experimentation among male comedians that disappoints we old lefties. Och, look at me on my prehistoric high horse.

It was twenty-five years since the birth of 'alternative cabaret' and, while the name was long gone, the circuit it gave birth to thrives all over Britain and in numerous foreign outposts. You can now study 'the theory and practice of stand-up comedy' as part of your drama degree at the University of Kent.** It is, arguably, London, not New York or LA, that is the funniest city in the English-speaking world although the big money is over there. Comedians in Britain have infiltrated all aspects of the media – as actors, TV presenters, radio stars, political activists (cf. Mark Thomas) novelists, playwrights, film-makers and internet-ticklers, while some – like Dave Gorman and double act Noble and Silver – are closer to conceptual art than they are to comedy.

Malcolm, who had lived his life as an undeclared work of conceptual art, provided, as his final scenario, the conditions for the perfect funeral and Alex, his younger brother, paid him the compliment of creating it. Alex works in the popular music business now but I had come across him when he put on some comedy gigs in Edinburgh one year. At the show I played, in a boozer for the depraved and degraded, a man poured a pint of his urine over me during my set – which was a sort of inversion

---

* Here is a line of Jimmy Carr's: 'The male gypsy moth can smell the female gypsy moth at up to seven miles. And that's still true if you remove the word "moth".'
** A course taught by Oliver Double – and rightly so.

of Alex's brother's trick. The 'heckler' explained to me that he had done it because he liked my routine, which made me wonder how he would have reacted if he had hated it.

In keeping with the grandeur of the church to which it was heading, Malcolm's funeral cortège was formed of a sumptuous line of shiny old black cars and, in keeping with the body it was transporting, the flowers bedecking the hearse spelt out 'Oy Oy', 'Knob out' and 'Fuck it'. This novelty vehicle led the procession slowly past the Wibbley Wobbley, the *Cutty Sark* (soon to go up in flames itself), past Up The Creek – where the pavement was lined with respectful locals – and round the corner to Saint Alfege's Church, where hundreds more mourners were waiting. He was never famous himself, but Malcolm was known to many who are. Among the congregation joining his family in Saint Alfege's were enough well-known comics that if a bomb had exploded, all TV panel games and talking heads/clip shows would have been postponed for months to come. And there were young comics, ex-comics, failed comics, soon-to-be comics, strippers, musicians, techies, betting-shop boys, a range of Malcolm's lovers and the assembled *demi-monde* of all Greenwich, overflowing from the church into the courtyard outside. People who had not met for years shook hands and embraced. The atmosphere in the stern dome was charged with emotion and anticipation of whatever was about to happen – maybe, in his greatest stunt yet, the lid would fall from the coffin and Malcolm would sit up, adjust his glasses and say, 'Oy oy! What's all the fuss about?'

Ever alert to the increased comic possibilities offered by a formal setting, Malcolm had married the redoubtable and fabulous Jane at Saint Alfege's on April Fool's Day ten years earlier. He had asked me to read something from the Bible.

369

'All right, which bit?'

'Oh, you choose – anything as long as it's from the Bible.'

I had selected a fire-and-brimstone passage from the Old Testament raging against the misuse of one's rod, an invocation I suspect he ignored. That ceremony was recalled now as his funeral got under way and Martin Soan, his old partner in the Greatest Show on Legs, recited Malcolm's traditional opening line, tailored to whichever venue he was playing, and blatantly stolen from Ian MacPherson: 'They say you only play Saint Alfege's twice in your life. Once on the way up and once on the way down. Great to be back.'

The coffin, an L-plate fixed to its front, was carried in by six soberly attired pall-bearers, to the accompaniment of the cheesy balloon-dance cha-cha-cha, and placed gently on a platform in front of the altar. The vicar leading the service introduced the sweetly naive hymn 'All things bright and beautiful' – 'because Malcolm *was* bright and he *was* beautiful.' The organ struck up and the singing was plangent. As co-host, the secular compère, I stepped up alongside the coffin:

'The Lord God, if you do exist, you did indeed make the little flowers that open, you did make the little birds that sing . . . and then you had a couple of pints and you made *Malcolm Hardee*.

'Everything about Malcolm, apart from his stand-up material, was original. He was the one-off's one-off.

'But before we start, let's release a little tension and give a big round of applause to one of the most remarkable people any of us . . .' But I didn't finish the sentence because everyone had already started clapping.

Other than in the artificial glare of industry dos, comedians very rarely come together in large numbers but here, in this sublimely incongruous setting, audibly united in our goodbye to one man, there was a feeling of communality, a shared comprehension of the deprivations and glories of the stand-up life and this most colourful of its exponents. All those who could rose to their feet, cheering and whistling in a heart-stopping ovation. The first among us to die – and what a death. He was a stand-up comic. I am a stand-up comic. And so are you, my friend. Who would not wish to be such a creature?

Eventually the applause subsided and the funniest and most moving gig I ever attended or ever played continued with brilliant speeches, poignant musical interludes and outrageous spontaneities until, finally, the coffin was borne from the church by the pall-bearers, trying hard not to laugh as Elvis Presley's 'Return to Sender' played Malcolm Hardee out of the church and on to the crematorium.

Beth, who supported me most beautifully that day, observed that I had been born to feature in this funeral. Malcolm and I were of a similar age and had been around comedy for the same amount of time. Like him, I was a South London grammar-school boy who had spent too many nights marauding around the pubs and streets of Greenwich; I had performed at most of the sundry venues Malcolm opened, written a short story ('The Man With Two Penises') in the book he had compiled called *Sit-Down Comedy*, and he and I had frequently participated in each other's Fringe escapades – it was only when his autobiography was published that I had learned he had, as a matter of course, rung and complained to the police at the start of all my tours of the Royal Mile. Malcolm was the supreme Mister Greenwich but his funeral cortège had passed several milestones in my own early life. Surrey Quays is where the insurmountable fences (even by Raymond) of

Surrey Docks once stood – I had grown up next to them, fighting in the bomb-site wars. A few years later, as a gauche carbuncular schoolboy, I sat in Saint Alfege's church looking in awe at the girls across the aisle and, as a young man, I had made my first, failed bid for stardom at the *Cutty Sark* boat with Gary, Dennis and hot Miriâme from France. It was all a long time ago. Or a blink of the eye. So passes life, alas how swift. It's a game and a half where you are, Ron; it's a game and a half where we all are, Brian.

That it was the end of an era in comedy, or at least in the lives of a bunch of comics, seemed to be confirmed by another death a year after Malcolm's epic departure. Brilliant, radical, erudite, principled and less starry than it is possible to imagine a gifted, famous person could be, Linda Smith's premature death at forty-eight was more shocking than Malcolm's – which had been on the cards ever since he had dangled from a railway bridge, aged nine. Where Malcolm was an example of what Tom Elsasser had called me at UEA, an 'eventist', Linda was a sculptress in hilarious words and a radical thinker who had started her career playing Miners' Welfare Clubs during the strike of 1984–85. I had met her many times on the comedy circuit, laughed with her on sundry radio shows, introduced her in the Hackney Empire New Act of the Year competition and on TV in *First Exposure*. As a political female stand-up there was no one to compare with her – and there still isn't.

'If God had wanted us to believe in him,' Linda used to explain, 'he would have existed.' When she died she was the President of the Humanist Society and at a gathering in her honour soon after, a speaker from the society started with a yelp, 'Gosh! Look at all the famous faces! Oh my God . . . well, not God obviously . . .'

It intrigued me, as the sad ceremony proceeded, that even the most hardline atheist felt the need to use a 'and-if-Linda-is-listening-now' formula in order to express their regret and sorrow. Why is 'Oh my God' the most popular exclamation even among rationalists? 'I've been thinking about reweyan.' Fantasy, denial and pretence can be the narratives you need. 'I don't believe in God,' wrote Julian Barnes, 'but I miss him.'

There has been a surfeit of illness and death in the closing pages of this book, yet I am a man whose job it is to generate laughter. I have no highfalutin song to sing; I am a humble comic – a clown – and this book must, therefore, be a comedy. All tragedies are finished by a death, all comedies are ended by a marriage and so I am happy to report that one classical Mediterranean afternoon at the tip of Cap Ferrat in the South of France, I proposed to Elizabeth Ann Kilcoyne. Elizabeth Ann Kilcoyne said yes. Hurrah. And if my autobiography were more important to me than my life, then we would marry immediately so that the story could conclude with a heart-warming account of the wedding. Or, even better for sales, I should drop dead as I type the final sentence, thus providing a profitably tragic dimension to the story.*

In Paris, at my fiftieth birthday, I was surrounded by many of the people whose names are recorded in this book. On the Saturday afternoon before the evening event, I pulled on my fluffy yellow duck jacket, purchased the entire stock of an ecstatic balloon vendor and strolled with a party of celebrants down the Champs Elysées to the Place de la Concorde. As my fellow

*Paul, my estimable editor, suggests that, as regards sales, November 2008 might be the best time to die. If this has happened when you read this then please call the police.

boulevardiers arrived, I was standing on the spot where I had waited, waited for *La Lapine* in the days when I taught English to the son of the President of France. Ah, Monsieur Smeez and his misplaced certainty about the modishness of the donkey jacket. What would he have made of the person he was going to become?

There were many friends from the world of comedy among the party-goers, including the incomparably upscale Rupert and Ellen; the Empress and King of the Hackney Empire, Clare and Roland Muldoon; Jo Brand – who came to Paris for a girl's day out with Betty, her mate; owlish, out-there brainbox Simon Munnery and, cackling ferociously, Karen Koren from the Gilded Balloon Theatre in Edinburgh. When we arrived in the gardens of the *Théatre Marigny*, Ronnie Golden and his guitar stood on a bench and sang – as they always will if you ask nicely. Ronnie was one of various guests with whom I had collaborated over the years; others were Phil, my double-act partner; Tony Hawkes who had helped me murder Andy Williams songs; Chris England, co-author of *An Evening with Gary Lineker*; Caroline and Audrey, veterans of miscellaneous theatrical ventures. Sara-Jane led a collection of Radio 4 producers and there, with his recording equipment, was loyal comedy aficionado Andy Foster who has produced umpteen series of the *Smith Lectures* on Radio 2. (Oh, did I not mention that?)

At eight o'clock the party began. My brothers, their wives and their children were all present and correct, although Harry and Jack were hardly more than toddlers and Tom had, so far, failed to be born. The Nat Rev Co – Adam, Babs, Max, Phil (and me) – reprised some old songs; John Hegley did a poem; Hawkes, now a best-selling author, observed that the event resembled a funeral with the dead subject present. But I wasn't dead after all!

374

I laughed with my oldest friends from school, from UEA and from Merton Road – Gary, Dennis, Lindsay, Simon. Matron came (with a Neil, of course), Sol, the Queen of Balham Towers, displayed her remarkable hair, Harry, my accountant, wore his dress-down Friday jeans and we all talked, drank or moaned into the microphone in the Leonard Cohen karaoke room. Beth's high-flying Cambridge friends glittered glamorously onto the dance floor, and Beth, gamine and chic in her slinky dress, really *did* look like Audrey Hepburn. And, because this chapter ends before it begins, I am able to report that Malcolm, with his six weeks left to live, dribbled with glorious predictability into his mouth organ and that, when the party was over and the lights came on, the last person on the dance floor was Linda Smith.

The only notable absentee at my birthday celebration in the Hotel du Nord was my mother, whose dislike of big bashes is exceeded only by her determination to stay as close to home as possible. She hasn't renewed her passport; she won't be going abroad again. After Syd died, she moved to Tonbridge, round the corner from Nick and Sue and their lads, in a neat little house on a hill – just as the homes she shared with Syd in Bath stood high up overlooking the city. I visit her with Beth, and the three of us sit on the bench in her garden and gaze across the weald of Kent towards the North Downs on the horizon.

Life does not, as I had imagined when I stared up the river to Tower Bridge aged six, become more comprehensible when you enter adulthood; it grows wilder, crueller, more absurd – and it gathers pace inexorably. Very old people express astonishment that they have arrived at this age and condition ('I'm eighty-five, you know!') and Hazel is, at times, amused by the vagaries of her memory and the speed with which she has become an elderly lady, so soon after she met a young chap called Syd at the Streatham Locarno. When Syd was dying, he had laughed at the absurd indignities his body was visiting upon him. 'Growing old', wrote Anthony Powell, 'is like being increasingly punished for a crime you did not commit.' Something to look forward to.

I am, in the youthful world of showbiz, pretty much an old-timer now – and I am finally the age I looked when I was ten. In Paris, at the Hotel du Nord, by the Canal St Dennis, on my fiftieth birthday, we all toasted Syd and Hazel. Richard, Nick and I embraced clumsily, like men, in fraternal solidarity. Speeches were delivered. One of them I found especially affecting. It was made not by any of the professional comedians, but by the person I had described in my early autobiography as 'my first friend'. Mary Grimer – Gary – stepped onto the stage:

'My name is Gary Rimmer unless there's anybody here from Streatham tax office . . . I first met Brian when he was sat beside me in Mrs Banfield's class at Kidbrooke Park Junior School. Brian arrived a little late in the term, and by then the top tamale among the boys was a boy named Richard Woolham. Very quickly, a battle commenced between Richard and Brian as to who should rank highest amongst the boys and very soon we all had to decide whose gang we were going to be in.

'And I suppose I want to say that, forty-three years later, I'd like to thank Brian for letting me be in his gang for so long.'

To Gary, and to anyone who has ever been in one of my gangs, may I say that, by and large, it has been a privilege and a pleasure.

CHAPTER 30. LAST FACTS ABOUT MYSELF

I am quite a cheerful boy who tries to take life as it comes. I am usually happy or looking forward to something.

It is more than forty years since I wrote this 'fact about myself' but I am, in spite of the certain pratfalls and batterings of life, still an amiable sort of a bloke, an instigator of conversations and games, a laugh down the pub, however briefly I am there. I'm still getting through and away with it. When Syd wrote to comfort me during the dark interlude of my middle life, he described me as 'happy-go-lucky', which puzzled me then, tortured and desperate as I felt, but is, perhaps, my essential character. People remark on meeting me, 'You're not a grumpy old man at all!' To which I reply, 'I am if you pay me.' I continue to look forward to things, even as I have spent the last eighteen months and hundred thousand words looking back on them.

I think some people hate me within themselves because when I am annoyed I try to hurt them. I am afraid that over the years I have learnt the ways to hurt someone. Over the years I have collected quite a few friends and almost as many enemies.

My advertised cheeriness is sporadically displaced by a combative impulse, a helpful attitude for a stand-up comic. 'Over the years' I have picked fights with critics, journalists or annoying persons of the right; my royal jokes have ensured I will never be commanded to perform by Prince Charles and a verbal exchange in a TV studio made me *persona non grata* on shows presented by

377

Jonathan Ross. Last summer I exhibited a portrait made from a scraggy piece of wood I had found. It was called 'Jimmy Carr's Soul – nothing on thin hardboard'. There are people who dislike me, no doubt, but I can think of only one who might be bothered to hate me – and he hates nearly everyone.

At home I like to wear clean jeans, blue ones. I also like to wear my red shirt (man-made fabric) that is very thick with little or no detail in it. I like to wear white plimsolls, too.

Ah, man-made fabric, the very best. I had a stand-up line in the 1980s: 'Do you remember the days of nylon? You used to have nylon sheets, nylon pyjamas – you'd get into bed at night and you'd be – whoosh! – straight out the other side.'

Every few weeks these days I put on a velvet suit and take a train out of town to perform *An Audience with Arthur Smith* and at any gathering I am pleased, if it gets a laugh, to wear the most ridiculous outfit you can imagine – a garment which, as it happens, I have owned (see photo page fourteen) – but I was scruffy then and I am scruffy now. I shamble around Balham in shorts and faded T-shirt, my glasses hanging from a string around my neck, slouching along, deep lines flowing down away from my big blob of a nose, grimacing in thought and greeting local friends or, occasionally, passers-by who recognise me from TV. It was a family joke that wherever Syd went people seemed to know him and in this, certainly, I emulate my father. Syd could not always identify whoever was waving at him and I too find individuals I hardly recall, recounting shared episodes I cannot remember.

But quite often (usually in bed) I feel the blow of dying. Everyone must die but I cannot think of the world being without me and as I lie in a long slim coffin I will go over my life. Who thought what of me, how did I take life? When thinking of this I once got a deep depression.

There is a panic that lurks on the edge of my vision about the imminence of my death and that of all the people I love, even of the world itself. The big obliteration. Perhaps this is not such a bad thing: 'We do not know where death awaits us so let us wait for it everywhere,' wrote Montaigne, which I take as a call to inhabit moments fully – even if you're doing nothing in them. Most creative endeavour flows from a fear of death. During the writing of this book, in which I have 'gone over my life', I have also declared myself 'the greatest artist of my generation', started a gang ('arturart'), set up a gallery and even won an award for it. Aren't I marvellous?

In some aspects I don't want to grow up but in others I do. I don't want to grow up because I don't want to be too dignified to climb a tree, to always have to eat politely, to be restricted in other things, and to pay extra money for the same things.

My idea of what constitutes adulthood is not as clear to me now as it was then, when I believed all the grown-ups knew what they were meant to be doing, but I have never been too dignified to climb a tree – merely too old. Once, in Johannesburg, at a dinner party for foreign correspondents, I hoisted myself up into the branches of a baobab tree in the garden for a taste of the hot African night, and I felt it was only my nudity that undermined my dignity.

Eating politely is, I suppose, a mark of adulthood; you don't, for example, want to see a banquet for national leaders where, among the suave sophisticates, your boy is slobbering all over his chateaubriand and spitting into the Japanese Premier's soup. Fortunately, for everyone, I will never be in that position; my talents lie elsewhere and, frequently, so does a part of my dinner.

Having substantially more money now than then, I do not

resent paying full fare on buses and the restrictions of age are counterbalanced by all the things I am allowed to do without asking my mother's permission. Growing up has not been so bad. I am still restless to dream schemes, to walk to the next place, to follow trains, to make Beth laugh. Despite my pretensions elsewhere, laughter is the currency I deal in – that peculiar, wondrous noise, which each of us makes slightly differently, a physical expression of an intellectual stimulus. I am a stand-up comic. Give me the cash and I'll set the table on a roar. If I can.

Life is made endurable by the Earth and by all the creatures similar to me who roam it. Everywhere I go I look at us all: we big-brained, hairless bipeds with our infinite dreams and our limited natures. And, with a bit of luck, I laugh.

I've got this idea for a show in Edinburgh next year . . .

EPILOGUE. AND YOU?

And you, where are you when you are reading this? Standing in a W.H. Smith's, perhaps, looking at this last page because it came open there? Or lying on a bed, having read the first chapters and looked to the end to see if there is a big finish, some illuminating revelation. Maybe you are on an aeroplane or a train, or you saw me on stage once, or heard me on the radio, or I slept with your sister in 1986 and you wonder what she might have seen in me. You could have read every page and have come, then, through the conventional route to this point, in which case I hope you are lying on a beach or sitting on a hill overlooking a beautiful city and I hope you enjoyed my little adventures.

But I prefer to think of you in a second-hand bookshop, or its equivalent, fifty or more years after I write these words at the table in our flat in Balham at 3.15 a.m. on 6 September 2008 while Beth sleeps upstairs. You have picked up this book arbitrarily, flicked through it and come to this last page. You have no idea who I was, have never heard of anyone mentioned in the book, except Mrs Thatcher and Bill Clinton. It seems to be a tale, written in old-fashioned English, of a small, disappeared world, inhabited by long forgotten names, antique references and old-fashioned concepts like 'TV', 'second-hand bookshop' and 'the internet'. And it is all unknowing of the cataclysms that have shaped your life. How quaint.

To you I say that I was an entertainer at the turn of the century,

381

one among many. I had no part in the epic sweep of history, but I entertained, cavorted and tried, in my way, to make sense of life and the age in which it fell. Maybe your grandad saw me once. Anyway, thank you for reading this and letting me live again in a tiny way. Now you can put the book down and move on.

ALL THE PEOPLE

If this book were three times longer I would have written about all the people below. I am naming them here to acknowledge their significance in my life and in the blatant hope that they will now buy the book and make me more money. The list is alphabetical, after a fashion.

A. Ainsley Harriet, Allen Scuse, Ali the plumber, Amanda Benson, Andy Smart, Amanda Whiteside, Anne and Stan, Alistair Beaton, Alison Goldie, Alison Campbell, Andy Johnson, Alan Davies, Ava Vidal, Anita Plociniak, Andy Parsons, Alan Nixon, Adrian Oatley, Aldo, Lucy Armitage, Andrew Bailey, Ant.

B. Stella Banks, Brenda Kilcoyne, Barry Bignose, Brian Bowles, Brian at *The Stage*, Bente the Dane, Miss Peterson, Bill Bailey, Briget, Belinda Naylor, Brenda Gilhooly and Pete, Bonesy, Sue and Peter Bloomfield, Brian Spiro, Nica Burns, Bucci, Helen Boaden, Beverly Dean, Bush and his wife from the shop, Billie Johnson, Brian Patten, Bronwyn Cosgrave, Bridget Nichols, Barbara Beckett, Bruce Dessau, Barbara at the Comedy Store, Bartholomew Sausage, Amanda Baker, Bill Paterson, Marcus Brigstock, Ben Moore, Caroline Boris, Barry, Buttercup, Bill at the Store, Brendan and Ted the postmen.

C. Clive Conway, Corrie Cawfield, Cliffhangers, Chiz, Harry Childs, Caroline Raphael, Phil Clarkson, Colin Cattle, Catherine Cooper, Chris the barber, Colin, Calia, Cyndi, Chris Turner, Robin, Maureen, Carol at Rupert's, Charles Spenser, Cyndi Freeman, Dan Coleman, Cath Mahoney, Carla Mendonca, Alex Cox, Charmian Hughs, Jo Coombes, Caryl Beer, Catriona, Cameron, Clare Hardee, Charley Spenser, Clare Norton-Smith, Charley Bunce, Christopher Somerville, Cordelia, Simon Clayton, Richard Curtis, Saint Cuthbert, Cordula, Lee Cornes.

D. Dylan Hearn at Troika, Derek Harris-Taylor, Dex, Diane, Dilly Barlowe, David Davis (not that one), Peter Griffith, Paul and Jennie, Roger Danes, Doreen Evans, Dorothy, Dave Stokely, Pete Brown, Dymphna Flynn, Danny Off the Kerb, Jo Norris, Drena Darrell, John Sparkes, Pete Nichols, Nicole, Sophie Carpenter, all at Double Espresso (esp. Tony, Steve, yes, and you, naughty Lucia), Dave Lamb, Debbie Moser, Doon, Dominic Holland, Dominic Maxwell, Daniel Kitson, Du Cane porters, Dave Long.

E. Eleanor Wroath, Emma Kilcoyne, Emma Freud, Eleanor Garland, Ellie, Ellen Gavin, Elle Heslin, Emma Myant, Emma John, Eamon, Emily Smith, Evie Anderson, Emanuelle Violac, Emma Sutton, Elaine from Bath, Ed, Errol, Paul, Mary and Mark, Eleanour Garland, Ed Day, Emily, Elizabeth Senior, Ernest from Vanunu, Emma Mitchell, Tom Ettling, Miriam Elia.

F. Steve Frost, Flocci, Fred Macaulay, Clive Futter, Francesca Humphreys, Hovis Presley, Lilley Ferrari and Jo, Lesley Primo, Frank from the Empire, Flic, Fanny the Wonderdog, Freddie O'Farrell, Flamo, Fanny of Balham, Freya Gordon.

G. G and Moy, Georgia Garrett, Gerry Macnulty, Georgina, Geoff Webb, Guy Stevens, Annabel Giles, George arturart, Galton and Simpson, Gaby Hinsliffe, Genevieve Wilson, Grub Smith, Gumby, Guy Steven, Gwen and Bob, Guy Stevens, Gary Supple, Geoff Rowe, Graham Ellis, Gavin McKairns, Greg Burn, Gordon Kennedy, Guy Jenkin, green Auntie Mollie, Sheldon Greenburg, Golly.

H. Hattie Hatridge, Henry the dog, Andy Hamilton, Eamon Hardy, Hjordis Radford, Harpie, Howard and Sue, Howard from Middlesbrough, Rob Harley, Helen Atkinson-Wood, Hayley Campbell, Sally-Anne Hayward, Harry Hill, Horatia, Hilary Strong, Hilary Gross, Helen Lees and Doctor Helen, Helen Rose, Heather, Marsha Hunt, Harry Pye, Howard Bird, Hoffman, Harry Smith.

I. Ivan Douglas, Idit, Imogen Stubbs, Imogen Edwards Jones, Ian Cognito, Ian Du Cane, Armando Iannucci.

J. John Kilcoyne, Jan Prince, Janice and Ben Turner, J. R. Hartley, Jayesh and bro, John Connor, Jane Berthoud, Judith Mayne, Jayne Hardee, John Davey, Jackie and John O'Farrell, Jayney Godley, Jeff, Jon King, Joanna Rashid, Josie Lawrence, Jenny Landreth, Jonathan James-Moore, Jimmy Mulville, Judy Ramjeet, Jon Pideon, Jenny-Anne Wyvern, Jennifer Cox, Karen and Jim, Julian Hall, Joy Spink, Jane Tranter, Jenny One Show, Jan Graveson, Jesicca Hines, Jo Romero, John and Tony from Carlon Country, Jackie Smith, Jon King, John Fleming, Jamie Wroath, Julian Young, John Banks, Juliet Wilson, James arturart, Jack Docherty, Joy Carter, Paul Jackson, Julie Reilly, Judith Hanlon.

K. Kevin Day, Rehka Kalia, Kat, Karel Beer, Katherine Smith, Kevin Radio 4, Kevin Eldon, Keef Looney, Karen Cockfield, Kirk from Hay, Kehinde, Karen Dry, Liz Kendall, Kristijana, Ken Livingstone, King Harold Michaels 3rd, Kenton Allen, Khulvinder, Kathie Grant.

L. Laurie Taylor, Lily O'Farrell, Lucy Canning, Linsey Young (and Rupert), Lee Simpson, Laura Denness, Laura Meakin, Lilie and Jo Ferrari, Lesley Retallack, Louise Coates, Louise Boyle, Lorraine, Lem Sissay, Laura Parfitt, Lola arturart, Lee Simpson, Lea, Louise Munden, Les Fallick, Lissa Evans.

M. Maria Mckerlaine, Maureen Turner, Mark Thomas, Marian Fitzpatrick, Mathew Hardy, Marik, Mandy Lynch, Mandy Knight, Mark Glasto, Meryll, Marek, Andrew Maxwell, Morwenna Banks, Maria Symonds, Mags, Melanie Rockcliffe, Maurizio, Deirdre Maher, Mark Watson, (young) Mathew, Mark Borkowski, Marjuka, Mandy Muden, Miles Jupp, Matt the Fireman, Michelle Major, Courtenay Mavity, Marisa Burgess, Michael Morris, Mathew Kelly, Maheesh, Mark Robson, Mundo Jazz, Manos, Mandy Rhodes, Melanie Archer, Malcolm Bailey, Mark at the Store, Mark Beazley, Martin Kelner, Masha Gordon, Paul Mayhew-Archer, Mark Danizer, Mick Clearey, Moray Hunter, Helen Morris, Dave Morley.

N. Neil and Blanche, Naphtali, Nigel Pugh, Nell, Niaill, Natalie Haverstock, Nina Conti, Nick Wilty, Neil Mullarkey, Nicole Tongue, Nora MacGrath, Neil Pearson, Nicola Walker, Nouska, Nikki, Neil Morrisey, Norman Lovatt.

O. Oscar Humphreys, Otiz Cannelloni, Odette, Oli Stones, Oli Horseford.

P. Nikki Pearce, Pete Baikie, Patrick from Bath, Paul Spenser, Pete Nichols, Pat Butcher, Panda, Keith Palmer, Peter Griffith, Pete Brown, Paul and Jennie, Paqui, Prod and Carol, Pretty Boy Williamson, Pirran from Perran, Phillipa Donovan, Panda, John Pearce, Heloise Pilkington.

Q. Quincy, Kathleen Quentin.

R. Rachel Pickup, Rekha Kalia, Peter Rosengard, Robin Turner, Robin Black, Rachel Edwards, Richard Turner, Robert Llewellyn, Rupert, Roma, Regina Cullen, Rubina, Ron Pickup, Roger McGough, Rebecca Shahoud, Rubina, Raquel Cassidy, Richard Tansey, Rosemary, Richard Salmon, Randolph the Remarkable.

S. Sasha Cattle, Sean from Perran, Sigrid Cattle, Sian, Paul Spenser, Sir Ralph, Simon Pearce, Jim Sweeney, Steve Bowditch, Steve Steen, Sara Doctors, Shappi Khorsandi, Suki Webster, Stan the Polish Elvis, Soren, Sarah Mahoney, Sarahs arturart, Charlie Scudamore, Shane Attwoll, Simon Clancey, Steve from Brom, Simon Quigley, Simon Barker, Steve Bennet, Sam and Rosie, Sam Battersea, Sol, Sarah Janes, Sandi Toksvig, Steve Gribbon (and Brian), Steve Wright, Simone Laraway, Suki Smith, Sylvia Ballantyne, Sian Price, Sam, Emily-Rose and Frank, Sir John, Savannah Lamb, Steve with Barry and Ronnie.

Plus The Smiths and Kirks and others of my family.

T. Tamsyn Challenger, Tamsin Hughs and her mum, Sue Terry, Tim Key, Thelma, Torquille Mcleoud, Toothwank, Ted Hayton, Troy, Tim Fitzhigham, Tim Bentink, Tara Saint-GK, Tara Spring, Tim Vine, Tom Nice, Tony at the Empire, Debbie Taylor, Terry Wogan, Tommy Shepard, Toni Arthur, Tripplicakes, Tim Arthur, Tiu, Tim Gordon.

U. Ursula Gibbon, Ully Arnold.

V. Vicci Coren, Jack Vettriano, Vibeke Venema, Vanessa Jones, Vanessa Whiteside, Vaughan Voller, Vicci arturart, Vincent the dentist.

W. Warren Lakin, Wizzo, Will Watts and family, William Cook, Will at Up the Creek, Will at Troika, Edmund White, Bryony Worthington, Luke Wright.

X. Xavier and Xavier Holland.

Y. Yeti.

Z. Zebedee Helm, Benjamin Zephaniah, Zuleika, Muriel Zhaga.

And a whole heap more I should have remembered – probably including you.

And finally heartfelt thanks to the man who waited fifteen years for me to write a book and who edited it with an understated panache that has been a lesson to me, Paul Sidey.

INDEX

Adie, Kate 220, 221
Alas Smith and Jones 165
Albarn, Damon 264, 265
Allen, Keith 147
Allen, Tony 147, 177, 180
Allen, Woody 153
alternative comedy 181–90
An Audience with Arthur Smith 378
An Evening with Gary Lineker 234, 236–8, 245, 263, 267, 268, 311
Anderson, Clive 322
Arthur and Phil Go Off 191, 195, 196
Arthur Cravan Society 265, 266
Arthur Smith Compères Himself 202, 203
Arthur Smith Sings Andy Williams 268, 269, 271, 285, 314
Arthur Smith Sings Leonard Cohen 95, 127, 323–7, 329
Arthur Smith's Last Hangover 354
Arthur Smith's Late Night Alternative Tour of the Royal Mile 195

Bader, Douglas 253
BAFTA 262, 263
Balham 167–8
Ballantyne, Nigel 43, 45, 57
Banana Cabaret 167
Banks, Morwenna 238
Bentink, Tim 103
Bird, Dickie 278
Blackman, Honor 225
Boardman, Stan 164
Bogossian, Eric 175
Borkowski, Mark 212
Bowles, Brian 103
Boycott, Rosie 56
Bradbury, Malcolm 67, 205

Brand, Jo 240, 374
Britten, Noel 274
Broadbent, Jim 114
Brown, Arnold 145
Bussman, Jane 268

Cambridge Footlights Revue 112, 114
Carpenter, Dave 75, 127, 131, 132, 304
Carson, Frank 182
Cartland, Barbara 222–3
Castle, Barbara 286–7
Christie, Julie 220, 221
Churchill, Winston 32, 33
Cinderella 102
ClapalongaCurtaincall 161
Clinton, Bill 330–2
Clore, Vivienne 203, 204
Cohen, Dave 342, 353
Cohen, Leonard 93, 323, 324, 325, 326
Colditz Castle 15, 248–57
Cole, Nigel 290
Cole, Stephanie 307–8
Columbian Cousin, The 205
comedy clubs 174–90
Comedy Store 146, 148, 157, 181, 189, 202, 213, 367
Comic Strip 145, 181, 285
Condell, Pat 184
Connolly, Billy 143, 274
Cook, William 211, 219
Copenhagen 169
Cravan, Arthur 265, 266, 269, 271, 315
Crazy Kristmas Cabaret 169, 172
Cresswell, Addison 203, 219
Cryer, Barry 5, 188

Danes, Roger 103
Dante Alighieri 63, 75, 354
Davidson, Jim 182
Dembina, Ivor 181
Depression 295–7
Desert Island Discs 264, 265
d'Estaing, Giscard 81
Diamond, John 336
Dodd, Ken 164
Dolan, Michael 323
Doonican, Val 225
Dowie, John 156, 157, 192, 289, 316,
    325, 326
Du Cane Court 168
Duncan, Ali 208, 325
Dury, Ian 66, 128

Earth Exchange 174
Éclair, Jenny 184
Edinburgh Fringe Festival 105, 110–16,
    136, 142, 143, 158–62, 192–5, 197,
    268, 272, 327
Edmondson, Ade 145
England, Chris 231, 235, 238, 239, 374
Equity 10, 151
Excess Baggage 320, 352

Fairfax, Daphne 9
Fanshawe, Simon 156, 163
Fascinating Aida 149
Fiasco Job Job 152, 154, 155, 183, 192,
    196
Filthy Rich and Catflap 166
First Exposure 204, 205, 206, 214, 372
Fisk, Robert 278
football 5, 32, 229–30, 231, 236–8, 311
Foster, Andy 374
Fraser, Frankie 302, 303
Fringe Club 114, 115

Gardhouse, Ian 220, 222, 226
Gavin, Rupert 150, 235, 236, 238, 239,
    270, 285, 305
Golden, Ronnie 271, 325, 374
Good Human Guide, The 164, 165
Grade, Michael 199, 200

Grahame, Peter 174
Gray, Muriel 197, 198
Greatest Show on Legs 175, 370
Greenwich 37–8, 98–100
Grumpy Old Men 76, 358–9
Guardian 248, 263, 345, 352

Hale and Pace 166
Hall, Rich 328
Hall, Sara-Jane 276, 277, 279, 283, 288,
    336, 246, 374
HamalongaYorick 136, 137, 307
Hamlet 136, 298, 299–307
Hancock, Nick 230, 231, 235, 236
Hardee, Malcolm 175, 176, 177, 187, 188,
    211, 212, 273, 339, 366–72, 375
Hardy, Jeremy 186
Hawkes, Tony 101, 269, 270, 271, 285,
    374
Hay Literary Festival 329–32
Healey, Denis 27, 278–9
Hegley, John 147, 184, 374
Hemingford Arms 148, 149, 152
Hepple, Peter 242
Hicks, Bill 315, 316
Hislop, Ian 159, 281–2
Hollins, Pierre 149
Howerd, Frankie 163
Humperdinck, Englebert 225
HUNX 271

I'm Still Standing 336
Izzard, Eddie 314

Johns, Milton 240, 241, 242
Jones, Vinnie 229
Jong, Erica 367
Jongleurs 178, 179, 180, 189
Jupitus, Phill 184

Keane, Dilly 342
Kempinska, Maria 178
Kidbrooke 25, 31
Kidbrooke Park Junior School 30, 33
Kilcoyne, Elizabeth Ann 333, 348, 354,
    357, 360, 374

King's Head, The 174
Kinnie, Kim 213
Kirk, Jim 28–9
Kirk, Kitty 28–9
Knott, Alf 40, 44, 240
Konigstein Fortress 248, 249, 255, 256

Landale House 16, 17, 24
Langham, Chris 114
Lapides, Howard 137
Larkin, Philip 71, 290, 363
Lawson, Nigella 336
Letter to A Young Actor 240, 241
Letter to A Young Comedian 240, 241
Letterman, David 156
Lineker, Gary 235, 236, 238
Live Bed Show 53, 206, 208, 210, 212, 291, 357
Live From London 218
Lloyd, John 186
Loose Ends 163, 220, 221, 223–8, 235, 238, 264, 277
Lycée Janson de Sailly 81–94
Lynam, Desmond 312
Lynham, Chris 176

Macpherson, Ian 185
Manning, Bernard 182, 185
Mayall, Rik 145, 166
McDonald, Trevor 182
McEwan, Ian 67
McGrath, Rory 115, 358
McKee, Robert 206, 207
McKee, Vivienne 169, 171
McVicar, John 279
Melly, George 168
Melville, Pauline 145
Memoirs of a Life in Crime 302
Merton Road 117–23, 134, 138, 166
Merton, Paul 184, 187, 218, 238, 320
Miller, Ben 234
Miller, Max 142, 143
Milligan, Spike 144
Mills, Bob 235
Moffat, Alistair 193
Moore, Rebecca 337

Morecombe, Eric 144
Morley, Sheridan 138
Morrissey, Neil 311
Moxom, Paddy 17, 20, 21, 22
Muldoon, Roland and Clare 174, 183
Munnery, Simon 328
My Summer with Des 313, 318, 333

National Revue Company, The 150, 151, 154, 158, 159, 161, 164
Neave, Airey 251
Nether Wallop Festival 274
New York 314–15
News Huddlines, The 140, 165
Nice, Phil 72, 73, 74, 102, 103, 113, 150, 152, 153, 157, 191, 258, 374, 175, 195–7
Noble, Ross 226
Norwich 60
Not the Nine O'clock News 165

Olympic Games 230, 231
Ostwald, Maxine 102, 103, 150, 258, 374
Ovett, Steve 26
Oxford School of English 139

pantomime 170
Paramount City 215–19, 314
Paris 80 96, 365, 373
'Paris Poem' 94–6
Paterson, Don 263
Peter Pan 23, 205
Phillips, Sally 298, 299, 307
Piccalongadillygo 158
Pirate, The 45–8
Pitt, Ingrid 282–3
Planer, Nigel 145
Poetry Society 68
Prebble, Stuart 359
Proops, Greg 180
Pyjamerama 161, 192

Quentin, Caroline 205, 206, 208–10, 230, 234, 237, 238, 299, 320, 354, 374

Raymond Revue Bar 145
Raymond, Paul 215, 216
Red Dwarf 166
Results, The 127–32
Revell, Nick 187, 348
Revue Company, The 142
Richardson, Peter 145, 181
Rimmer, Gary 12, 13, 30, 31, 32, 52, 53,
    99, 100, 117, 259–60, 289, 376
Roan Grammar School 33–6, 37–48,
    49–59
Roan, John 37, 38, 39
Rosengard, Peter 146
Russell, Ken 277

Sadowitz, Jerry 188
Sarler, Carol 126, 127
Satalongamatinee 159
Saturday Live 180, 181, 196
Sayle, Alexei 145, 154
Scargill, Arthur 280–1
Scotsman, The 211
Scott, Ronnie 283–4
Seaview Farm 101, 107
Seinfeld, Jerry 184
Self, Will 359
Sentimental Journey 227, 276–84, 286–8,
    307, 352
Sherrin, Ned 88, 220, 222–8, 242, 292
Slattery, Tony 263
Smith Lectures 374
Smith, Bill 28
Smith, Ethel Adeline 27, 28
Smith, Hazel 4, 6, 28, 29, 50, 92, 107,
    134–5, 245, 246, 256, 344, 354, 360,
    361, 363–4, 375
Smith, Linda 29, 186, 372
Smith, Nick 4, 55, 92, 135, 265, 354
Smith, Richard 4, 16, 19, 33, 51, 54, 55,
    135, 172, 258, 347, 354, 356
Smith, Sydney 4, 6, 15, 27, 33, 42, 49, 61,
    92, 107, 109, 134–6, 168, 233,
    245–57, 294, 344, 354, 360, 361–3,
    376, 378

Soan, Martin 175, 370
Sod 288, 289, 290
Soul, David 227
Southwark Park Primary School 18–24
Stage, The 240, 242
stand-up 141–62
Steel, Mark 186, 187, 265
Suggs 279
Sutton, Babs 64, 68, 74, 113, 119, 150,
    159, 374
Swan Lake 273–4
SwingalongaDante 63, 75, 76, 111

Thatcher, Margaret 157, 158
Thompson, John 185, 272
Time Out Chat Show, The 197, 199–200,
    277
Together Forever 221
Travel Show 285–6
Trench Kiss 232, 234, 235, 237, 312, 314
Tunnel Palladium 175, 176, 177, 189, 367

University of East Anglia 60–76, 101–9
Up The Creek 177

Victor, The 126
voice overs 315–17

Wakeman, Rick 359
Walking Backwards to Brighton 289
Ward, Don 146, 148, 213
Wax, Ruby 199, 200
Weiss, Rachel 311, 333
Whitemoor Prison 242–4
Whose Line Is It Anyway? 262
Wibbley Wobbley 366, 367, 369
Wide, Adam 73, 74, 102, 113, 114, 119,
    150, 163, 170–1, 289, 374
Williams, Andy 270
Williams, Kenneth 163, 164
World War II 15, 122, 247, 252, 253,
    254

Young Ones, The 181